DRIVING TOURS

SPAIN

PRENTICE HALL TRAVEL

New York • London • Toronto • Sydney • Tokyo • Singapore

CONTENTS

Written by Mona King

Copy editor: Helen Douglas-Cooper

Edited, designed, produced and distributed by AA Publishing, Fanum House, Basingstoke, Hampshire RG21 2EA.

© The Automobile Association 1992

Maps © The Automobile Association 1992

Typesetting: Servis Filmsetting Ltd, Manchester

Colour reproduction: Scantrans P.T.E., Singapore

Printed and bound in Italy by Printers S.R.L., Trento

The contents of this publication are believed correct at the time of printing. Nevertheless, the publishers cannot accept responsibility for errors or omissions, or for changes in details given.

Every effort has been made to ensure accuracy in this guide. However, things do change and we would welcome any information to help keep the book up to date.

Published by AA Publishing

Published in the United States by Prentice Hall General Reference.

A division of Simon & Schuster, Inc., 15 Columbus Circle, New York, NY 10023.

PRENTICE HALL and colophon are registered trademarks of Simon & Schuster, Inc.

ISBN 0-13-220419-3

Cataloging-in-Publication Data is available from the Library of Congress

Title page: *Tossa de Mar*

Above: *Ronda, Málaga*

Right: *Floral displays in Córdoba*

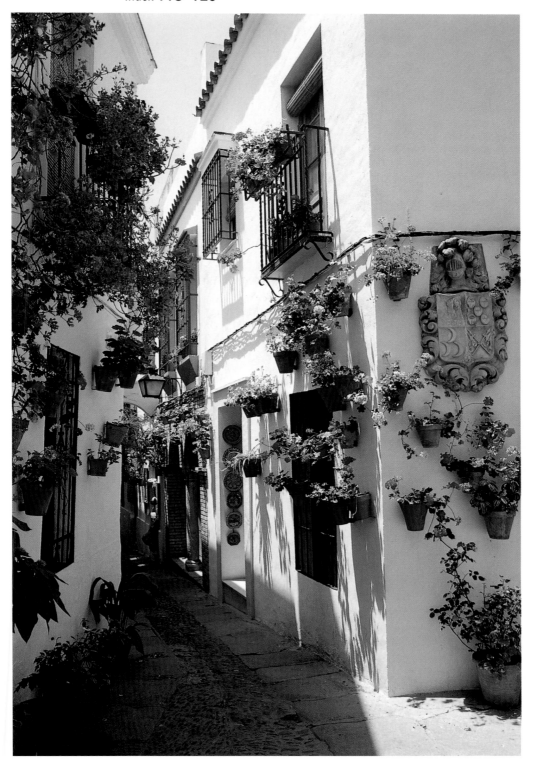

INTRODUCTION

This book is not only a practical guide for the independent traveller, but is also invaluable for those who would like to know more about the country.

It is divided into 5 regions, each containing between 3 and 6 tours. The tours start and finish in major towns and cities which we consider to be the best centres for exploration. Each tour has details of the most interesting places to visit en route. Side panels cater for special interests and requirements and cover a range of categories – for those whose interest is in history, wildlife or walking, and those who have children. There are also panels which highlight scenic stretches of road along the route and which give details of special events, gastronomic specialities, crafts and customs. These are cross-referred back to the main text.

The simple route directions are accompanied by an easy-to-use map of the tour and there are addresses of local tourist information centres in some of the towns en route as well as in the start town.

Simple charts show how far it is from one town to the next in kilometres and miles. These can help you to decide where to take a break and stop overnight, for example. (All distances quoted are approximate.)

Before setting off it is advisable to check with the information centre at the start of the tour for recommendations on where to break your journey and for additional information on what to see and do, and when best to visit.

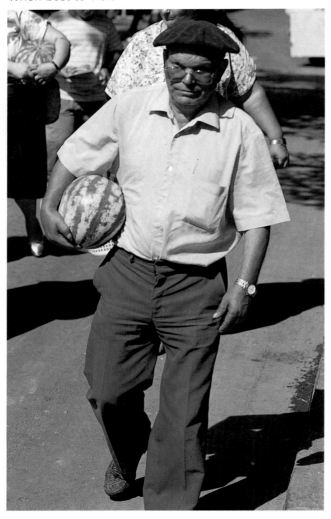

ENTRY REGULATIONS

You require a valid passport to enter Spain. Nationals of European Community countries and some others do not need a visa for stays of up to 90 days. It is always wise to check the current situation with your Spanish tourist office or consulate.

CUSTOMS REGULATIONS

Personal effects can usually be taken into Spain without payment of duty. Small amounts of wine, spirits and tobacco (up to 200 cigarettes or 300 for EC members) are also free of duty. You may have to pay a deposit against duty and taxes on valuable items such as video cassette recorders.

Remember that alcohol in particular is cheaper in Spain than in many other countries.

EMERGENCY TELEPHONE NUMBERS

Policia Nacional 091
Policia Municipal 092

These 24-hour numbers will not necessarily connect you with the nearest station but will get your message relayed. Try to clearly state the nature of *urgencia* (emergency), your location and the services required.
Bomberos (Fire) 080
First Aid 438 24 61
Cruz Roja (Red Cross):
Madrid 533 3900 (urgent – 7777)
Barcelona 205 1414
For emergencies and ambulances check local numbers.

HEALTH

Residents of European Community countries are entitled to medical treatment from the Spanish health service, if they produce form E111 or the relevant form from their country (obtain this before departure). The best advice is to buy a travel insurance policy from a reputable company which provides comprehensive cover in case of accident or illness.

CURRENCY

The peseta is available in the following denominations:
notes – 1,000, 2,000, 5,000, 10,000; coins – 1, 5, 10, 25, 50, 100, 200 and 500.

CREDIT CARDS

The major credit, charge and direct debit cards are widely accepted. Make a note of your credit card numbers and emergency telephone numbers in case of loss, and keep it with your passport. Tell the company immediately if one of your cards is stolen or lost.

BANKS

Savings banks, mostly offering exchange facilities, are called *cajas* (open: Monday to Friday 08.30–14.00 or 14.30 hrs); Saturday (except June to September) 08.30–13.00hrs – note this means banks are generally closed on Saturdays in the summer).

Money exchange facilities are available outside these hours at airports.

Refreshing watermelon is just what is needed in the heat of the day, and the locals are often seen hurrying home with one for the family meal

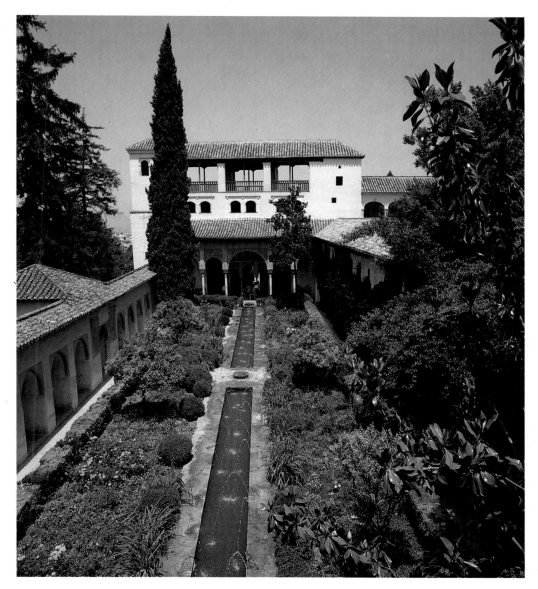

The cool, green water garden of the Generalife, Granada

TIME

Like most of Europe, Spain is two hours ahead of GMT (Greenwich Mean Time) in the summer and one hour ahead in the winter.

POST OFFICES

Post offices are generally open Monday to Saturday 09.00 to 13.00 hrs. Mail can be sent addressed to you at Lista de Correos. Take personal identification when collecting. Post boxes are yellow and some have different sections for different destinations. *Sellos* (stamps) can also be bought at *estancos* (tobacconists).

TELEPHONES

International access codes are as follows: to call Spain from Australia, dial 00 11; Canada 011; New Zealand 00; UK 010; US 011. Country codes are: Australia 61; Canada 1; New Zealand 64; UK 44; US 1. Public phone booths are plentiful. They take 100, 25 and 5 peseta coins and some accept credit cards. Instructions for use are displayed in a number of languages.

MOTORING

Documents

Licences issued by European Community countries are acceptable (for UK and Republic of Ireland driver's licences should be of the pink EC-type). Visitors from other countries should have an international driving licence, which should be obtainable from the motoring organisations in their home countries.

Breakdowns

Special arrangements may be provided by an insurance policy bought from your motoring organisation. In the case of rental vehicles, contact the rental company. Breakdown service is called *gruas*.

Speed limits

Motorways 74mph (120kmph). Outside built-up areas between 56mph (90kmph) and 62mph (100kmph). Built-up areas 37mph (60kmph).

Car hire and fly/drive

The big international firms operate throughout Spain and you can make bookings with them in your home country. Holiday operators have car rental schemes, and airlines offer 'fly-

PUBLIC HOLIDAYS

1 January – Año Nuevo (New Year)
6 January – Día de los Reyes (Epiphany)
Good Friday – Viernes Santo
1 May – Día del Trabajo (May Day)
15 August – Asunción (Assumption)
12 October – Día de la Hispanidad
1 November – Todos los Santos (All Saints' Day)
6 December – Constitucíon
8 December – Immaculada Concepción (Immaculate Conception)
25 December – Navidad (Christmas Day)

ELECTRICITY

220/225 volts AC and 110/ 125 in some bathrooms and older buildings. Plugs have two round pins, so you will need an adaptor.

EMBASSIES

Australia: Paseo de la Castellano 143, 28046 Madrid *tel*: 91 2798504.
Canada: Edificio Goya Calle Nunez de Balboa 35, Madrid *tel*: 91 4314300.
UK: Calle de Fernando El Santo 16, Madrid 4 *tel*: 91 3190200.
US: Serrano 75, 28006 Madrid *tel*: 91 5774000.

TOURIST OFFICES

Spanish National Tourist Offices:
Australia 203 Castlereagh Street, Suite 21a, Sydney NSW 2000.
Canada 102 Bloor Street West, 14th Floor, Toronto.
UK 57–8 St James Street, London SW1A 1LD.
US 665 Fifth Avenue, New York 10022; 8383 Wilshire Bvd, Suite 960, Beverly Hills, California 90211.

Multi-lobed arches and delicate tracery are typical of Hispano-Islamic architecture

drive' deals. Renting from a smaller local firm is usually cheaper.

Accidents

There are no firm rules of procedure after an accident. There is an assistance service for victims of traffic accidents which is run by the Central Traffic Department day and night on every main road in Spain. You are advised to obtain a Bail Bond from your insurer together with your Green Card.

Driving conditions

Driving is on the right.
Tolls are charged on most of the motorways.
The surfaces of the main roads vary, but on the whole are good. Secondary roads are often rough, winding and encumbered by slow horse-drawn traffic.
In the Basque area, local versions of the same place names appear on signposts together with the national version. Most roads across the Pyrenees are frequently closed by winter snowfalls.

Route directions

Throughout the book the following abbreviations are used for Spanish roads:
A – Autostrada
C – Comarcal
N – Nacional

El Escorial, Madrid, the massive monastery-palace built by Philip II in the 16th century

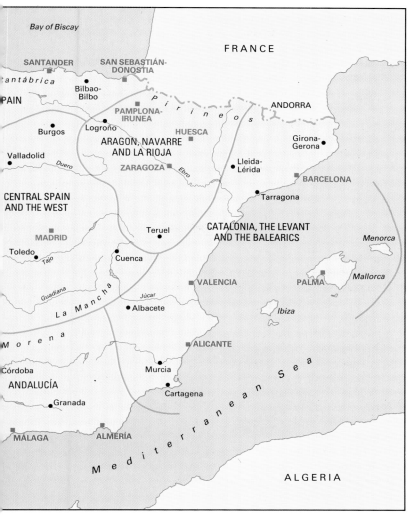

Bay of Biscay

FRANCE

SANTANDER
SAN SEBASTIÁN-DONOSTIA

antábrica

Bilbao-Bilbo

PAIN

Pirineos

ANDORRA

PAMPLONA-IRUNEA

Burgos

Logroño

HUESCA

ARAGON, NAVARRE AND LA RIOJA

Girona-Gerona

Valladolid

Duero

LLeida-Lérida

ZARAGOZA

Ebro

BARCELONA

CENTRAL SPAIN AND THE WEST

Tarragona

CATALONIA, THE LEVANT AND THE BALEARICS

Teruel

Menorca

MADRID

Toledo

Tajo

Cuenca

VALENCIA

PALMA

Mallorca

Guadiana

Júcar

La Mancha

Albacete

Ibiza

Morena

ALICANTE

Córdoba

Murcia

Mediterranean Sea

ANDALUCÍA

Cartagena

Granada

MÁLAGA

ALMERÍA

ALGERIA

USEFUL WORDS

The following words and phrases may be helpful.

English Spanish
hello hola
goodbye adiós
good morning buenos días
good afternoon buenas tardes
good evening and goodnight buenas noches
do you speak English? ¿habla usted inglés?
yes/no sí/no
please por favor
excuse me, I don't understand perdón, no entiendo
could you please speak more slowly? ¿podría hablar más despacio, por favor?
thank you (very much) (muchas) gracias
I am/my name is . . . soy/me llamo
what is your name? ¿como se llama usted?
how are you? ¿como está?
very well muy bien
where is . . . ? ¿donde está . . . ?
open/closed abierto/cerrado
what time is it? ¿qué hora es?
I would like . . . me gustaría . . .
do you have . . . ? ¿tiene . . . ?
how much is . . . ? ¿cuánto es/vale/cuesta . . . ?
1 to 10 uno, dos, tres, cuatro, cinco, seis, siete, ocho, nueve, diez

CATALONIA, THE LEVANT & THE BALEARICS

This region presents a variety of panoramas, although certain features like the long sweep of Mediterranean coastline and common language bind it together. It also includes three of Spain's best-known tourist areas – the Costa Brava, the Costa Blanca and Mallorca.

The capital of Catalonia is Barcelona, a thriving commercial centre. In the north of the region are the eastern Pyrenees, which form a natural border with France and separate the Iberian peninsula from the rest of Europe. This is a sparsely populated area dominated by rugged mountains and green valleys irrigated by the rivers Ter, Llobegrat and Segre, together with tributaries of the Ebro. To the east of these mountains, the wild rugged coastline of the Costa Brava features high cliffs, rocky coves and sandy beaches.

The Levant, which includes the region of Valencia, famous for rice-growing, extends to the lush palm groves south of Alicante. The coastline flattens out into long stretches of golden sandy beaches broken up by rocky promontories. This is the region of the *huertas*, fertile cultivated lands that are irrigated by the Turia and Jacar rivers. The area produces a rich yield of oranges and lemons, olive oil, vegetables and flowers. In the southeastern corner, desolate, lunar-like landscapes are found inland.

Opposite the coast of the Levant region lies Mallorca, the largest of the Balearic Islands. Between the rugged Sierra de Tramuntana in the northwest and the gentler slopes of the Sierra de Levante in the east is a vast plain of orchards, fields and windmills. Known for the beauty of its coastline, pinewoods and olive groves, the island is at its best in spring when the almond blossom is out.

Numerous invasions and occupations have left their mark on the people of the region and shaped their culture. Phoenicians, Greeks, Carthaginians, Romans and Moors have all played their part and left many testimonies to their presence. Catalonia has a rich heritage of churches built in the Catalan Romanesque style that developed in the region, and fine examples of Gothic architecture are also very much in evidence.

The official language is Catalán. Following periods of suppression it is again widely spoken in Catalonia and street names and places are written in Catalán. A similar dialect is spoken in Valencia as a result of it being conquered in the 13th century by King Jaime I of Catalonia. Mallorca has its own version of Catalán, known as Mallorquín.

Tour 1

Scenery is the main emphasis of this itinerary, which takes you into the heartland of the eastern Pyrenees. This provides wonderfully varied landscapes, from mighty mountain ranges to green valleys, rivers and lakes. Along the route are delightful little Pyrenean towns and castles dating back to Roman and medieval times, along with a number of churches built in the typical Catalan Romanesque style of the region. A highlight of the tour is undoubtedly the visit to Spain's most sacred sanctuary in the spectacular setting of the great Montserrat massif.

Tour 2

The once desolate Costa Brava (wild coast) has long since become one of Spain's most popular holiday areas. Parts are still very attractive, however, with picturesque little fishing villages set in sandy coves surrounded by pine-clad hills. The drive offers stretches of stunning beauty, as steep cliffs plunge sharply down to the sea below. The vivid blues and greens of the Mediterranean and purple shades of the mountains, coupled with the fragrance of the pines form a large part of its attraction. Visits to ancient Greek and Roman ruins, inland towns and a beautiful old monastery provide cultural interest.

Tour 3

The first part of the journey takes you down the Costa Dorada (golden coast), aptly named for the splendid sandy beaches that characterise the region. The route passes through attractive scenery, where stretches of twisting hair-pin bends give way to more relaxed driving through a pleasant countryside of rolling hills and valleys. Along the way there are picturesque resorts, old towns and one of Spain's most important Roman cities. Travelling inland along part of the old Cistercian Route, the tour visits three beautiful monasteries in lovely surroundings.

The Spanish galley Neptuno *in Barcelona harbour*

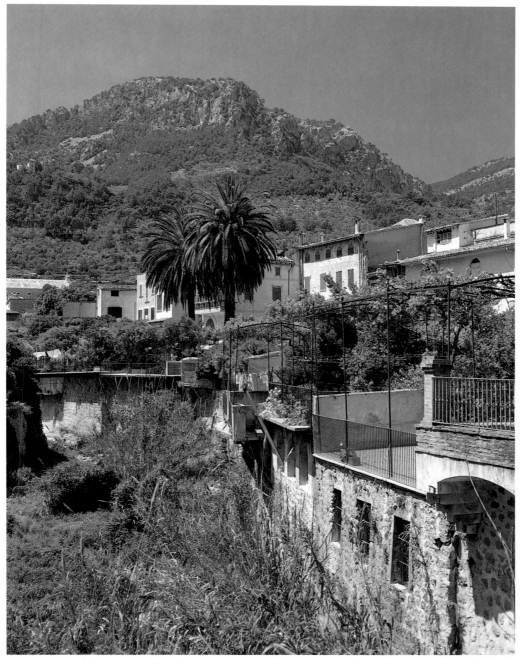

Sóller, Mallorca, in a fertile valley below the Alfabia Sierra

Tour 4

The route begins with Valencia and continues along part of the Costa Blanca (white coast), known for its beaches of fine white sand and mild winter climate. Dramatic rock formations provide impressive landscapes along the route, and there is the chance to visit its best-known resorts. The route then cuts inland, providing a sharp contrast in scenery and interest, with several fascinating old towns to visit in magnificent settings.

Tour 5

A visit to a unique palm forest is followed by a drive down Spain's southeastern coast, where the Costa Blanca leads to the Costa Calida (warm coast). The tour combines wild, rugged mountain scenery inland with beautiful stretches of coastal road. The area of the Mar Menor, with its large saltwater lagoon and new, modern tourist development, is an interesting part of the country. Some prominent port towns combine with several old inland towns to provide a varied and exciting tour.

Tour 6

There are two Mallorcas, the Mallorca of the mass tourism that invades parts of the island in the summer, and the Mallorca of magnificent mountain scenery, almond trees and olive groves. This tour takes in some of its most outstanding features; old monasteries, Roman remains, spectacular caves and picturesque fishing villages. There are beautiful stretches of coastline, with rocky coves and sandy beaches. Together with its blue waters, dense greenery and pine-scented air, they make up the essence of this very Mediterranean island.

2/3 days – 536km (332 miles)

THE CATALONIAN PYRENEES

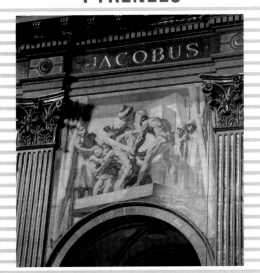

Barcelona ● Montserrat ● Cardona ● Solsona
La Seu d'Urgell ● Puigcerdá ● Ribes de Freser ● Ripoll
Sant Joan de les Abadesses ● Camprodón ● Olot
Vic ● Santa Fé de Montseny ● Barcelona

Barcelona is the capital of Catalonia and Spain's second city, besides being its principal port and a major commercial centre. The old *Barri Gotíc* (Barrio Gótico) or Gothic Quarter, still shows traces of its medieval past. The dark streets and alleys, faded old buildings and antique shops are best explored on foot. Standing on the highest point of the town is the *Catedral*, a majestic Gothic structure (13th to 15th century). Look out for the *Palacio Episcopal* (Bishop's Palace), *Casa Canónica* (Canon's House), the 15th-century *Ayuntamiento* (town hall) and the magnificent 14th-century Catalan Gothic *Iglesia de Santa María del Mar*. The *Plaça Reial* (Royal Square) is an elegant 19th-century Renaissance square, noted for its mellow arcaded palaces and lamp-posts designed by Gaudí. Notable museums in the area include the *Museo Frederic Marés* (Frederic Marés Museum), the *Museo de Historia de la Ciudad* (City History Museum) and the *Museo Picasso* (Picasso Museum).

The Barrio Gótico area of Barcelona is a good place to observe local life as well as exploring its interesting narrow streets

Wall paintings of scenes from the lives of the Apostles and Evangelists in Vic cathedral

ⓘ Gran Via de les Corts Catalanes 658

*From Barcelona, take the **A2** towards Lleida-Lérida. Leave at **junction 22** near Martorell for the **NII**, travelling northwest, and after a few kilometres turn right on to the **C1411** towards Manresa. At Monistrol village follow the road up the mountain to the monastery car park, some 50km (31 miles).*

Montserrat, Barcelona

1 Set among wild rock formations and jagged peaks is the **Monasterio de Montserrat**, which contains Catalonia's most sacred sanctuary. Vast numbers of pilgrims gather each year to venerate the Black Virgin, patron of Catalonia, who is kept here. One of Spain's major tourist attractions, the origins of the monastery centre on the legend of a miracle-working statue of the Virgin, supposedly found in a cave in the vicinity in 880. A **chapel** dedicated to her was erected, and in 976 monks of the Benedictine order founded a monastery that steadily grew in size and importance.

The church was rebuilt by Philip II, who greatly favoured the place. The monastery was fortified by the Catalans during the Peninsular Wars, but in 1812 it was sacked by the French, with the result that most of the present structure is from the 19th century, with some parts completed only after World War II. Before entering the monastery, stop for a moment on the observation platform to have a look at the dramatic surroundings. The most important part of the building is the Basilica, built between 1560 and 1592 in the Renaissance style, and restored in the last century. The interior is a vast dark area lit by a mass of tiny lights. In a glass niche above the high altar is the polychrome statue of the dark-faced Virgin. It can be reached by a staircase and may be touched through a circle cut in the

SCENIC ROUTES

Virtually the whole tour from Manresa up to Puigcerdá and down again is through lovely areas of mountains and valleys, with green forests and sparkling streams. The unique landscapes of bizarre rocks and cliffs to be seen around Montserrat, however, warrant a special mention. The Sierra de Montseny, with a stop at the Santa Fé Sanctuary, also includes spectacular scenery.

glass. The library contains an impressive collection of books, and there are several museums.

A short ride by funicular takes you on a somewhat awe-inspiring journey to the San Juan ridge, where an observation terrace affords spectacular views of the great Montserrat massif.

*Rejoin the **C1411** and continue north to Manresa. Turn left on to the **C1410** and continue northwest for about 52km (32 miles) to Cardona.*

Cardona, Barcelona

2 A final turn in the road reveals the magnificent sight of the old medieval **castle** of Cardona. Rising from a great brown rock cone, it towers over the tiny village below. The castle is made up of a group of buildings that were built between the 10th and 19th centuries, with some reconstruction in the 17th century. It once served to protect the salt mines of the prominent Cardona family. In the castle you can visit the church and crypt, which have been well preserved. The views from here are magnificent.

*Continue on the **C1410** for 20km (12 miles) to Solsona.*

Solsona, Lleida-Lérida

3 Solsona is a picturesque little town with quaint streets, old houses and the remnants of medieval ramparts. There are ruins of a 12th- to 13th-century **castle** at the top of the hill. Near the bridge is the **cathedral**. Erected in the 12th century and rebuilt between the 14th and 15th centuries, it shows a combination of Romanesque and Gothic styles. The **Diocesan Museum** in the **Palacio Episcopal** (Episcopal Palace) has a good collection of paintings, frescos and fine altar-fronts.

The monastery of Montserrat is situated high up in the Montserrat mountains

The **salt museum** is worth a look for its unusual exhibition of objects fashioned out of blocks of salt from Cardona.

*Follow the **C1410** west. At Bassella take the **C1313** north to La Seu d'Urgell (Seo de Urgel), a distance of 76km (47 miles).*

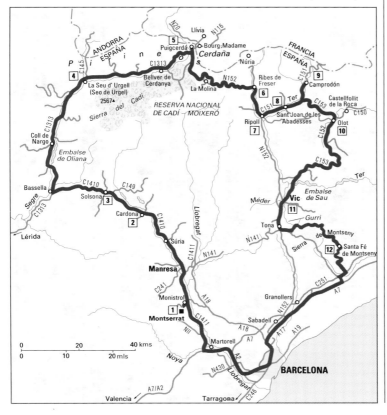

SPECIAL TO . . .

1 *Montserrat, Barcelona* When you visit the Monasterio de Montserrat, make an effort to hear the **Escolanía**. This is one of the oldest boys' choirs in Europe, dating back to the 13th century. The boys are brought up in the monastery and receive religious education. The singing is dedicated to the Virgin of Montserrat. The choir performs at morning mass and later in the day on Sundays, feast days and on special occasions.

FOR HISTORY BUFFS

1 *Montserrat, Barcelona* The legend of the Black Madonna of Montserrat runs very deep in Spain. Her image was supposedly brought from Barcelona in AD50 by St Peter and hidden in a cave. The statue was found later by shepherds, who decided to transport it to Manresa. Upon reaching the site where the monastery now stands, the lady appeared reluctant to proceed further. A chapel was erected in her honour, and this later developed into the monastery. From Montserrat a short trip down the mountain by funicular, followed by a half-hour walk beneath the cliff brings you to the **Santa Cueva** (sacred cave) where the statue is said to have been discovered.

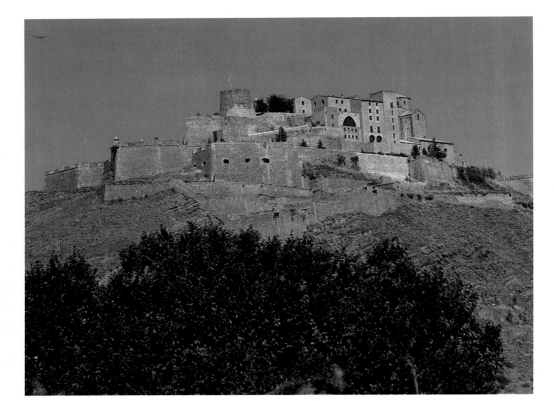

La Seu d'Urgell, Lleida-Lérida

4 Serving as a natural gateway to the
tiny republic of Andorra, La Seu
d'Urgell, known as 'La Seo' for short,
lies in a typical Pyrenean valley, surrounded by high wooded mountains.
It is the seat of a bishop and has a fine
Romanesque **cathedral** dating back to
the 12th century, with later additions.
The **Diocesan Museum** houses an
interesting display of religious art.
Other buildings of note are the 11th-
century Romanesque **Chapel of San
Miguel** and the 15th-century **Casa de
la Ciudad** (town hall), built in the
Gothic style.

ⓘ Paseo de José Antonio

*Continue east for 48km
(30 miles) on the **C1313** to
Puigcerdá.*

Puigcerdá, Girona-Gerona

5 Puigcerdá has a cosmopolitan
atmosphere typical of border
towns. It is attractively situated on a
hilltop overlooking the Cerdaña, a
district that is split between Spain and
France. A bridge connects the town to
Bourg-Madame in France. The main
buildings of interest are the 15th-
century **Ayuntamiento**, the 13th-
century **Iglesia de Santo Domingo**
and the **Iglesia de Santa María**, which
is also 13th-century. The town is a
pleasant place to explore, with its
lively main square, busy little streets
and pretty houses with balconies. The
boating lake to the north is a favourite
resort, both in summer and winter.

You can take a short side trip to
Llívia, about 5km (3 miles) northeast.
This little medieval town is a Spanish
enclave within France and has a small
museum displaying items from its
pharmacy, apparently one of the
earliest in Europe.

*Take the **N152** east for 49km
(30 miles) to Ribes de Freser.*

*The medieval castle of Cardona
perches on top of a rock*

Ribes de Freser, Girona-Gerona

6 This popular resort lies on the River
Freser in an attractive setting of
green forests. It is also a good stop-
over point for a funicular ride up to
Núria. The journey takes about 45
minutes and passes through mountains and pine forests. The **Núria
Sanctuary** is a famous pilgrimage
centre and the place is also a popular
winter sports resort.

*Continue south for 14km
(9 miles) on the **N152** to Ripoll.*

Ripoll, Girona-Gerona

7 Although the town is essentially
industrial, a stop is recommended
to visit the Benedictine **Monasterio de
Santa María** (monastery of St Mary)
which stands on the square. Founded
in the 9th century, it was subsequently destroyed first by an earthquake, then by fire and later restored.
It has a richly carved door in Romanesque style. The cloister has a fine
collection of capitals depicting various religious scenes.

*Take the **C151** northeast for
10km (6 miles) to Sant Joan de
les Abadesses (San Juan de las
Abadesas).*

Sant Joan de les Abadesses, Girona-Gerona

8 As you arrive you will see the lovely
12th-century bridge over the River
Ter. In the centre of the town stands
the magnificent **Abbey of Sant Joan**.
It was founded in the 9th century and
belonged originally to the
Benedictines. During the course of
time it suffered severe damage and
had to be rebuilt several times. The
impressive Romanesque church and
magnificent Gothic cloister are

considered fine examples of the architecture of these periods. In the central apse above the high altar is a beautiful 13th-century carving in wood of the *Descent from the Cross*.

*Take the **C151** north for 14km (9 miles) to Camprodón.*

Camprodón, Girona-Gerona

9 The lovely old town of Camprodón lies in the heart of the Pyrenees, surrounded by mountains and woods. Attractive houses with red-tiled roofs and balconies look down on narrow, winding streets and squares. A familiar sight is the lovely 16th-century arched bridge that spans the river. Buildings of special interest include the Romanesque **Monasterio de Sant Pere** (St Peter's), the **parish church** and the **Ayuntamiento**. Many Spanish families come to Camprodón in the summer to enjoy the healthy mountain air and good walking in beautiful surroundings.

*Return south, join the **C153** and continue southeast to Olot.*

Olot, Girona-Gerona

10 Olot has a long-standing tradition of crafts, and is famed for the painted and carved figures that are used for the Nativity performances. The town is primarily industrial, but has several museums worth visiting. These include the **Museum of Modern Art** (19th- and 20th-century paintings by Catalan artists), the **Museo della Casa Trinxeria** (mainly furniture and interiors of the 17th to 19th centuries), a modest museum with items of religious art from the 18th-century **Iglesia de San Estéban** and the **Museo Garroxta**, which has an interesting display of fossils from the area.

The town is in a volcanic region and evidence of old craters still remain, although they are mostly covered by vegetation. A detour of some 7km (4 miles) east along the C150 will take you to the black basalt village of Castellfollit de la Roca, which is perched on a clifftop over the River Fluvia.

*Take the **C152**, turning right on to the **C153** south for 64km (40 miles) to Vic (Vich).*

Vic, Girona-Gerona

11 The old episcopal town of Vic lies at the confluence of the rivers Méder and Gurri. Its two main attractions are the **Plaza Mayor** (main square) and the **cathedral**, which is situated on the edge of town. Founded in the 11th century and restored in the 18th, it features a handsome Romanesque bell-tower. Inside, look out for the richly ornate 15th-century marble altar and the elegant cloister, which is graced by a splendid monument to Jaime Balmes, counsellor to Pope Pius IX. The adjoining **Museo Episcopal** has an impressive collection of Romanesque art, works from the Gothic period and Roman relics. The heart of the old town is the large and lively Plaza

---

Olives are one of the main crops of the area, as can be seen from the wonderful selection on this market stall in Ripoll

Mayor, which is lined with arcades and handsome buildings. The square is surrounded by an area of narrow streets, winding alleys and little hidden squares. Here is the **Casa Consistorial** (town hall), a fine building of Gothic origin, with more recent additions.

Near by are the remains of a **Roman temple** dating back to the 2nd or 3rd century AD, and medieval walls.

[i] Jardines de las Avenidas

*Take the **N152** south. At Tona take unclassified roads southeast to Santa Fé de Montseny.*

Santa Fé de Montseny

12 The Sierra de Montseny is a magnificent range of mountains largely covered by green forests. There are several routes you could take on your homeward journey; this drive takes you through some exceptionally beautiful scenery to the **Ermita** (Sanctuary) **de Santà Fé de Montseny**, which stands at an altitude of 1,100m (3,610 feet) and offers magnificent views of the area. The tiny village here provides an excellent base for mountaineering in the area.

*Continue southeast and return to Barcelona on the **A7** and **A17**, 59km (37 miles).*

Barcelona – Montserrat **50 (31)**
Montserrat – Cardona **52 (32)**
Cardona – Solsona **20 (12)**
Solsona – La Seu d'Urgell **76 (47)**
La Seu d'Urgell – Puigcerdá **48 (30)**
Puigcerdá – Ribes de Freser **49 (30)**
Ribes de Freser – Ripoll **14 (9)**
Ripoll – Sant Joan de les Abadesses **10 (6)**
Sant Joan de les Abadesses – Camprodón **14 (9)**
Camprodón – Olot **30 (19)**
Olot – Vic **64 (40)**
Vic – Santa Fé de Montseny **44 (27)**
Santa Fé de Montseny – Barcelona **65 (40)**

RECOMMENDED WALKS

1 *Montserrat, Barcelona* Montserrat has several short walks in stunning scenery to places such as Sant Miguel and Sant Joan.

10 *Olot, Girona-Gerona* There is a lovely walk from Olot that takes you through the magnificent **La Fageda d'en Jorda** beech forest to the large crater of the **Volca de Santa Margarida** (Santa Margarita volcano). Another route from Olot follows the River Fluvia down the **Vall d'En Bas**, passing through charming villages.

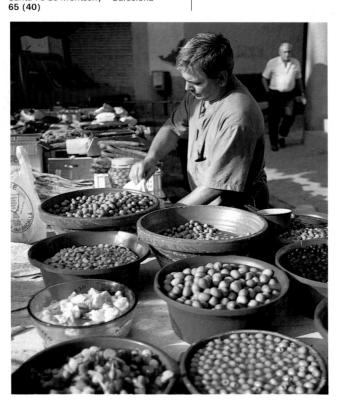

14

2/3 days - 378km (235 miles)

THE COSTA BRAVA

Barcelona ● Arenys de Mar ● Blanes ● Tossa de Mar
Sant Feliú de Guixols ● Palamós ● Palafrugell ● La Bisbal
Girona ● Empúries ● Figueres ● Besalú ● Banyoles
Barcelona

One of Barcelona's greatest pleasures is a stroll down the lovely tree-lined *Ramblas* (a series of avenues), which runs from the *Plaça Portal de la Pau* by the harbour up the eastern side of the *Barri Gotíc* (Gothic Quarter) to the *Plaça de Catalunya* and beyond. By the harbour is the grand Columbus Monument, where an elevator to the top offers a magnificent view of Barcelona. The *Museo Maritim* (Maritime Museum) in the dockyards nearby will appeal to anyone keen on ships. Northwest of the square is the elegant *Passeig de Gràcia* (Paseo de Gràcia) where you will encounter some very unusual architecture. The *Casa Lleo Morera*, embellished with rich floral decorations, is one surprise, but perhaps the most curious are the *Casa Batlló* and *Casa Milá* (or La Pedrera), which were built by Antonio Gaudí at the turn of the century with curving façades resembling waves and ripples.

A stay in Barcelona is not complete without a visit to the unique *Temple of the Sagrada Familia* (Holy Family), Gaudí's best-known work. This massive structure has four lofty bell-towers soaring upwards to the skies and a distinctive façade. Started in 1882, it was never completed due to Gaudí's early death.

i Gran Via de les Corts Catalanes 658

*Leave Barcelona from the Plaza de las Glorias and take the **A19** coast road east. Turn right at Badalona and join the **NII** through Mataró to Arenys de Mar, a distance of 40km (25 miles).*

Arenys de Mar, Girona-Gerona

1 The main attractions in Arenys are its pretty little port and its reputation for excellent seafood. The fishing harbour is fun to explore and is full of activity when the catch comes in. The large marina is now an international regatta centre.

The Iglesia de Santa María (begun in 1584 by the French) is well worth a visit to see the magnificent 18th-cen-

SCENIC ROUTES

The stretch between Tossa de Mar and Sant Feliú is particularly beautiful. Its tortuous bends take you high over mountain tops and down among the pine forests, with magnificent views of cliffs that plunge sharply down to the sea, forming rocky coves and bays.

The stretch between Besalú and Banyoles on the **C150** also offers some splendid mountain scenery.

A member of the fishing fleet at the busy port of Arenys de Mar takes time to relax and mend his nets. The town is famous for its fine seafood

tury retablo by the artist Pablo Costa.

Arenys has a long tradition of white bobbin lace-making and although this is gradually dying out, you may still see some of the local women, known as *puntaires*, sitting out on their doorsteps practising their ancient skills.

*Continue on the **NII** coastal road. At Malgrat branch off northeast to Blanes.*

Blanes, Girona-Gerona

2 Blanes is a popular tourist resort in an attractive setting. After exploring the harbour you can stroll along the promenade to the old town where you can admire a lovely Gothic fountain in the main square. Further up is the Iglesia de Santa María, which looks down on the roof-tops. A climb up to the top of the Sa Palomera southwest of the harbour provides a good view of the sandy bay of Blanes.

i Plaza de Cataluña

Follow the road through Lloret de Mar to Tossa de Mar, 15km (9 miles).

Tossa de Mar, Girona-Gerona

3 Tossa de Mar was called 'The Blue Paradise' by the famous French artist, Marc Chagall, who produced many paintings of the town in the 1930s. Some of his works are exhibited in the Museo Municipal, along with other paintings and an interesting Roman mosaic from the Roman settlement here. This is located in the old town, which is worth a visit, with its narrow streets and medieval houses contained within massive walls, and turrets from the 12th century. There is a splendid view from the lighthouse, which is situated on the highest point of the town.

Continue northeast on the coastal road to Sant Feliú de Guixols.

Sant Feliú de Guixols, Girona-Gerona

4 This large, cheerful town is considered to be the capital of the Costa Brava. Its busy port and lack of a good, sandy beach gives it a different ambience to some of its better-known neighbours. The 11th-century Porta Ferrada (iron gate) and the adjoining church near the promenade, are the remains of a former Benedictine monastery. The Museo Provincial has items from prehistoric, Greek and Roman times.

The Ermita de Sant Elm, on the outskirts of town, offers a splendid view of the coast.

*Take the **C253** for 12km (7 miles) to Palamós.*

Palamós, Girona–Gerona

5 Palamós' main attractions are its beautiful setting in a wide curved bay and its lively port and yacht harbour. A major fishing centre, it is one of the most important towns in the region. Fish auctions take place in

The coastline around the little fishing village of Calella de Palafrugell is pitted with rocky coves and bays where the mountains extend down to the sea

a special hall called the **Lonja** and are colourful occasions.

In the old part of town is the 14th-century Gothic **Iglesia de Santa María** with a Flemish altarpiece, surrounded by the narrow streets of the original fishing village.

i Passeig del Mar 8

Take the **C255** inland for 9km (6 miles) to Palafrugell.

Palafrugell, Girona-Gerona

6 Palafrugell's main functions are commerce and shopping. A few remains of Moorish walls can be seen and a visit to the little Gothic **Iglesia de San Martín** is worthwhile. This is a good spot, however, for a detour to some of the Costa's most delightful resorts. A short drive through pine woods leads to the resort of Tamariu and another road to the fishing resorts of Calella de Palafrugell and Llafranc.

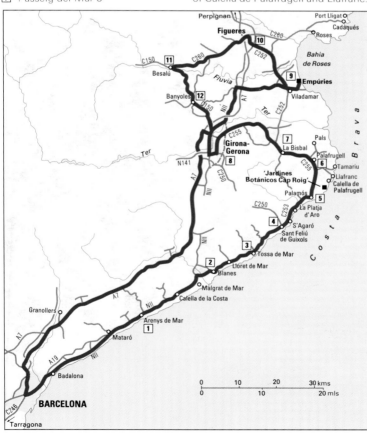

BACK TO NATURE

2 *Blanes, Girona-Gerona* Just beyond the harbour of Blanes is the splendid **Botanical Garden of Marimurta** (sea and myrtle), where you will find hundreds of species of exotic flowers and plants, largely from the Mediterranean area. The garden is beautifully laid out on an original design by the German, Karl Faust, whose bust stands near the entrance.

6 *Palafrugell, Girona-Gerona* To the south of Calella de Palafrugell, a short distance from Palafrugell, lies the lovely **Jardines Botanicos Cap Roig** (Botanical Garden), which features rare plants and Mediterranean shrubs.

FOR CHILDREN

2 *Blanes, Girona-Gerona* Near Malgrat de Mar (follow the road towards Blanes and take a left turn) is the splendid **Marineland**. This large leisure centre offers many amusements, including an aquarium, small zoo, boating pool and children's playground. A major attraction is the sealion and dolphin show.

6 *Palafrugell, Girona-Gerona* Children might also enjoy a visit to the **Museum of Underwater Archaeology**, which is situated in the small medieval village of Pals, north of Palafrugell.

10 *Figueres, Girona-Gerona* The **Toy Museum** in Figueres has a large collection of dolls from different countries and periods of history.

RECOMMENDED WALKS

6 *Palafrugell, Girona-Gerona*
One very attractive walk is along the '**Avenida del Mar**' that links the two pretty little resorts of Calella de Palafrugell and Llafranc (near Palafrugell). The route passes over and round a hill, with beautiful views over each of the bays in turn.

FOR HISTORY BUFFS

8 *Girona, Girona-Gerona* The name of the 'city of a thousand sieges' may be something of an exaggeration, but Girona did spend long periods under siege over the years. The most famous was the siege of 1809, when a large force of Napoleon's troops was kept at bay for some six months by the citizens of the town, including a battalion of women and a few English volunteers. Under the command of Alvarez de Castro, the city finally had to surrender because of lack of food and ammunition. A commemorative monument stands in the Plaça de la Independencia.

There is a stunning view of the bays from the lighthouse below the **Ermita de San Sebastián**, poised on top of the hill.

[i] Avenida Josep Plá, 9

*Continue northwest on the **C255** for 12km (7 miles) to La Bisbal.*

La Bisbal, Girona-Gerona

7 La Bisbal is renowned as a ceramics centre and is the location of the **Escuela de Cerámica** (School of Ceramics). The tradition goes back to the Middle Ages, and contemporary work has been influenced by the ancient designs of the Arabs, French and Italians. The pottery is displayed all over the town and is recognisable by its dominant colours of green, brown and yellow. While here, take a look at the large 14th-century Romanesque **castle**, once the seat of the ruling Bishops of La Bisbal, the parish church and the old bridge.

Continue west on the same road for 24km (15 miles) to Girona.

Girona, Girona-Gerona

8 Founded by the Iberians, Girona was occupied by the Romans, the Moors, and retaken by Charlemagne in 785, later to form part of the kingdom of Catalonia and Aragon. The River Onar separates the new town from the old, which is located on the east bank and best explored on foot. There are good views of the old town from either of the main bridges. Entry into the old town is a step right back into the Middle Ages. You will find yourself among dark, secretive streets, picturesque houses and

hidden squares. The **cathedral** appears unexpectedly, rising majestically from a flight of steps. This impressive monument dates back to the 14th century, with later additions, and is considered one of the finest cathedrals in Catalonia. The huge 12th-century embroidered '*Tapestry of the Creation*' is a unique exhibit among many valuable treasures to be seen in the museum. The adjoining 12th-century cloister is noted for its finely carved capitals.

Other buildings of special interest include the former **Iglesia Colegiata de Sant Feliú** (collegiate church), with its tall tower, the **Art Museum** in the old **Palacio Episcopal** (Episcopal Palace) and the 12th-century **Baños Arabes** (Arab Baths). A short walk from the baths takes you to some pleasant gardens under the ramparts, where you will have a splendid view over the valley of the Ter. Although interesting by day, the old town is fascinating by night, when floodlighting creates a medieval effect.

Among the most pleasant areas in the new town are the central square, the **Plaza de la Independencia**, which is surrounded by attractive arcades, and the **Parque de la Dehesa**, a large park with a tree-lined avenue, fountains and statues.

[i] Ciudadanos 12

*Take the **NII** north and after 21km (13 miles) make a right turn to Empúries (Ampurias), a total of 37km (23 miles).*

The River Onas slices Girona in two. On the right-hand bank is the old town, dominated by the cathedral

Empúries, Girona-Gerona

9 This impressive archaeological site is one of the most important in Spain and has both Greek and Roman ruins. It was originally founded by the Greeks in the 6th century BC and known as 'Emporion', which means market. The place flourished and produced coins which were used in the region. In the 2nd century BC the Romans arrived to wage war against the Carthaginians, and built on to the existing town. Some of the most valuable pieces that have been excavated from the site can be seen in the Archaeological Museum in Barcelona. It became an episcopal seat under the Visigoths, and was then destroyed during conflicts with the Moors. In the lower town is a **museum**, which has an interesting collection of archaeological finds from the area, along with reconstructions of everyday life in Greek and Roman times.

A detour northeast to the coast will take you to the delightful whitewashed village of **Cadaqués** and nearby **Port Lligat**, where the great eccentric Salvador Dalí lived and painted for many years.

*Retrace the route to Viladamar and then take the **C252** northwest to Figueres (Figueras).*

Figueres, Girona-Gerona

10 Figueres is a major town of the Ampurdán region and features a few buildings of historical interest, such as the 14th-century **Iglesia de Sant Pere** (St Peter), noted for its fine Romanesque tower, and the **Castillo de San Fernando**, an impressive 18th-century fortress. The **Museo del Ampurdán** (Museum of Ampurdán), located on the town's pleasant tree-lined Rambla, has a wide variety of exhibits, including items from the ruins of Empúries.

The real interest, however, is undoubtedly the great Salvador Dalí, surrealist artist and eccentric, who was born here in 1904. The **Museo Dalí** (Dalí Museum) is a feature of the town and can be seen from quite a distance, with its distinctive glass domes. Here you can see a vast selection of Dalí's works presented in the most exciting and imaginative way. Whatever your feelings about his work, you should not miss this museum.

*Take the **C260** southwest for 24km (15 miles) to Besalú.*

Besalú, Girona-Gerona

11 A splendid old fortified bridge over the River Fluvia serves as the main entrance to the ancient town of Besalú. Once capital of the Garrotxa region, the town is a medieval treasure, with its narrow streets and old houses. Handsome buildings surround the **Plaza Mayor**, which is lined with attractive doorways. A number of interesting monuments in the town include the massive 12th-century Romanesque **Monasterio de San Pedro** and the churches of **San Vicente** and **Santa María**, also from the 12th century.

*Take the **C150** southeast for 14km (9 miles) to Banyoles (Bañolas).*

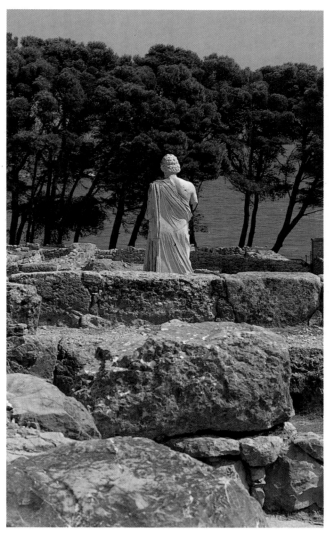

Remains of the Roman town at Empúries, overlooking Roses Bay. The ruins include houses, a forum and an amphitheatre

Banyoles, Girona-Gerona

12 The lakeside town of Banyoles is a popular summer resort. The lake has a good beach, offering facilities for bathing and watersports. On the **Plaza del Fuente** (Fountain Square) is the **Museo Arqueológico** (Archaeological Museum) which displays antiquities from the area. In the **Iglesia de Sant Esteve** (St Stephen), dating back to the 10th century and rebuilt in the classical style, is a 15th-century retablo, the work of the stone mason, Joan Antigo.

*Continue southeast on the **C150**, then join the **A7** back to Barcelona, 118km (73 miles).*

Barcelona – Arenys de Mar **40 (25)**
Arenys de Mar – Blanes **25 (16)**
Blanes – Tossa de Mar **15 (9)**
Tossa de Mar – Sant Feliú de Guixols **23 (14)**
Sant Feliú de Guixols – Palamós **12 (7)**
Palamós – Palafrugell **9 (6)**
Palafrugell – La Bisbal **12 (7)**
La Bisbal – Girona **24 (15)**
Girona – Empúries **37 (23)**
Empúries – Figueres **25 (16)**
Figueres – Besalú **24 (15)**
Besalú – Banyoles **14 (9)**
Banyoles – Barcelona **118 (73)**

SPECIAL TO ...

The **sardana** is an important part of the Catalan folklore. Although the dance's origins are not clear, it is known to have deep roots in the Ampurdán region. It is danced all over Catalonia, at weekends or on festival days. Anyone may take part (although newcomers should try to learn some of the steps before joining in). The participants join hands and dance in a constantly moving circle, following some fairly intricate steps, to the accompaniment of the local *cobla* (band).

2/3 days – 597km (373 miles)

ROMAN RELICS & GOLDEN BEACHES

Barcelona ● Sitges ● Vilanova i la Geltrú ● Calafell
Tarragona ● Cambrils de Mar ● Peñíscola ● Tortosa
Lleida ● Monasterio de Poblet ● Montblanc
Monasterio Santes Creus ● Barcelona

The hills of Montjuic and the Tibidabo offer much in the way of entertainment. Start in the *Parc de la Ciutadella* (Municipal Park) where buildings of interest include the *Arc del Triomf* (Triumphal Arch), built for the exhibition in 1888, the 18th-century *Palau de la Ciutadella*, now the museum of modern art, and the 19th-century concert hall, *Palau de la Musica*. Proceed to the old fishermen's quarters of Barceloneta, known for its fresh seafood, and take the cable-car to Montjuic. The hill of Montjuic is dominated by the 17th-century *Castell de Montjuic*, now a military museum. Other museums include the *Museo d'Art de Catalunya* (Museum of Catalan Art), the *Museo Arqueológico* (Archaeological Museum) and the *Fundación Miró* (Miró Foundation). The *Estadi Olimpic* (Olympic Stadium), built for the 1929 Great Exhibition, has been renovated for the 1992 Olympics. The *Pueblo Espanyol* (Spanish Village), also built for the 1929 Exhibition, is a model of different villages and regions of Spain. On the way to Tibidabo, take a look at the *Parc Güell* (Güell Park), another of Gaudí's amazing creations. Tibidabo's main attractions are its panoramic views and its fun fair.

SPECIAL TO...

Barcelona, Barcelona
Penedés, located southwest of Barcelona, is one of the major wine-producing areas, with production ranging from table and dessert wines to liqueurs. It is also known for its wines of high alcoholic content. On your return to Barcelona you might care to stop off at Vilafranca del Penedés to visit the **Royal Palace** and the wine museum. The **Museo del Vino** presents a whole history of wine through the ages, a definite must for wine-lovers.

ℹ️ Gran Via de les Corts Catalanes 658

*Leave Barcelona from the Plaça de Espana and take the **C246** southwest for 40km (25 miles) to Sitges.*

Sitges, Barcelona

1 Sitges is a traditional resort that lured Spanish families long before it became an international tourist centre. Apart from the obvious attraction of its splendid sandy beach and shallow waters, Sitges is a picturesque little town with great charm. The local church, with its rose-coloured façade, adds to the picture. The **Cap Ferrat Museum** is the former home of the painter, Santiago Rusinol (1861–1931), and houses a collection of his paintings, together with works by El

An athlete holds the Olympic torch aloft at the Barcelona Olympic Stadium

Greco, Picasso, Utrillo and other famous artists. Outside on the pavement is a huge head of Christ by Josep Canas.

ℹ️ Paseo Vilafranca

Take a minor road southwest for 6km (4 miles) to Vilanova i la Geltrú (Vilanueva y Geltrú).

Vilanova i la Geltrú, Barcelona

2 This is an industrial town and a resort, with a fine sandy beach and picturesque fishing harbour. It has three museums of interest: the **Casa Papiol**, or **Museo Romántico**, which presents examples of life in the early 1800s; the **Museo Balaguer**, with its collection of antiquities and paintings, including an *Annunciation* by El Greco; and the restored mansion, **Castillo de la Geltrú**, where you can see religious relics and ceramics from Catalonia.

ℹ️ Parque de la Florida

*Continue down the **C246** coast road for 14km (9 miles) to Calafell.*

Calafell, Barcelona

3 The small fishing village of Calafell is another favourite summer resort with a long, sandy beach. This is a place for a quiet stop and a brief look at the Romanesque parish church and the ruins of the 12th-century castle.

*Continue on the **C246** to El Vendrell and join the **N340** to Tarragona.*

Tarragona, Tarragona

4 The route passes through **El Vendrell**, the birthplace of the famous Spanish cellist, Pablo Casals (1876–1973).

A lovely Roman town, Tarragona was founded by Publius Cornelius Scipio during the Second Punic War of 218BC. There are still many Roman remains in the town worth exploring. A stroll along the attractive tree-lined Rambla Nova leads to the observation platform 'Balcón del Mediterráneo', which offers a sweeping view of the coast. Below is the harbour and the **Parque del Milagro** (Park of Miracles), where you can see the remnants of a 2nd- or 3rd-century BC Roman amphitheatre, once the venue for combats between man and beast. The **Museo Arqueológico** (Archaeological Museum) houses a fine collection of mosaics, ceramics and antiquities from the region. A climb from the centre of town takes you to the **cathedral**, which was built between the 12th and 14th centuries. It shows a harmonious blending of Romanesque and Gothic styles, with a fine façade and lovely rose window in the centre. It is said that St Paul once preached here. The **Paseo Arqueológico** (archaeological walk) is a pleasant shaded walk along the foot of the massive city ramparts, which extend for some 1,000m (1,094 yards) and reach a height of up to 10m (33 feet) in parts.

The **Museo Paleo-Cristiano**, on the outskirts, has a fine display of tombs,

mosaics and jewellery. Adjoining it is an old Christian cemetery dating back to the 3rd century.

i Ayuntamiento, General Primo de Rivera

*Continue on the **N340** south for 18km (11 miles) to Cambrils de Mar.*

Cambrils de Mar, Tarragona

5 Cambrils de Mar is a picturesque little port with a maritime tradition.

The elegant town of Sitges has always lured holiday-makers

The harbour is dominated by an ancient church tower, once used as a Roman defence fortification. It becomes a hive of activity when the catch comes in, and has a reputation for good eating.

*Continue south down the coastal road (**N340**) for 112km (70 miles) to Peñiscola.*

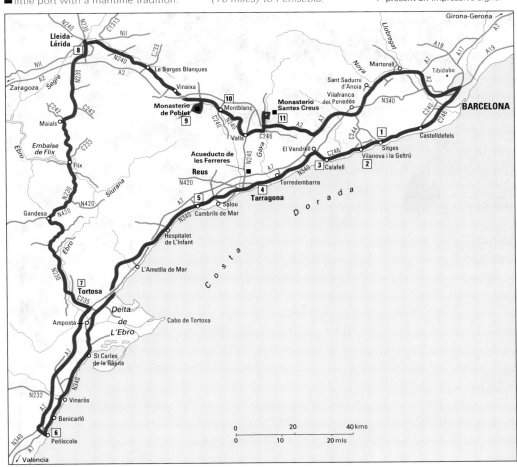

SCENIC ROUTES

The drive from Barcelona down the eastern coast of Spain has some particularly scenic sections. After Castelldefels the **C246** runs along the coast to Sitges, offering splendid sea views. Be prepared for countless curves and bends in the road. There are attractive stretches before Calafell, between Torredembarra and Tarragona; after Salou, on the **N340**; and between Tortosa and Lleida (**N230**).

FOR HISTORY BUFFS

7 *Tortosa, Tarragona* During the Spanish Civil War (1936–9), Tortosa was the scene of an important battle. On 24 July 1938, the Republicans, who were in control of Catalonia at the time, made an attack on Nationalist forces who were advancing to Valencia. They crossed the River Ebro but were unable to advance further and had to remain in trenches until their ultimate defeat, with the loss of thousands of lives. The victory of the Nationalists is commemorated by a monument rising from the river.

BACK TO NATURE

7 *Tortosa, Tarragona* The delta of the River Ebro attracts huge numbers of varying species of birds. Thousands are migrants from northern areas, while many stay permanently. The **Parc Natural del Delta de L'Ebro** (National Park of the Ebro Delta), west of Tortosa, has been created to protect wildlife. Among the many species that can be seen are plovers, avocets, black-winged stilts and red-crested pochards. The Salinas is a favoured breeding area for many species. Here you may see a gathering of flamingos, although their presence and numbers are rather unpredictable. Other inhabitants include otters, the stripeless tree frog and terrapins.

Peñiscola, Castellón

6 This is a veritable jewel of a place, rising like a fortress from a rock peninsula that juts out to sea. The town was taken from the Moors in 1233 by King Jaime I. Its main feature is the **castle**, an impressive structure built by the Templars. Later the deposed antipope, Benedict XIII (Pope Luna), took refuge in the castle and spent his last years here until his death in 1422. The **castle** offers magnificent views of the coastline. Within the surrounding walls is the old town, a labyrinth of tiny winding streets – strictly for pedestrians only.

> *Drive inland to and take the* **A7** *north, turning off after 46km (29 miles) on the* **C235** *to Tortosa.*

Tortosa, Tarragona

7 The episcopal town of Tortosa holds a commanding position over the delta of the River Ebro. The **cathedral** was begun in 1347 and built over a long period of time. The naves are in 14th-century Gothic style, while the façade and the chapel to the **Mare de Deu de la Cinta** (the Virgin), patron saint of the city, are baroque. Other monuments to note are the 14th-century **Palacio del Obispo** (Bishop's Palace) and the **Colegio de Sant Lluis** (St Louis' College), which was founded in 1544 by Emperor Carlos V for converts from the Moorish faith and has an elegant courtyard with some fine decoration. Many splendid old palaces can be seen from the 15th and 16th centuries, as well as remains of the city walls.

ℹ Calle de la Rosa 10

> *Take the* **N230** *north to Gandesa, then turn right on to the* **N420** *before turning left back on to the* **N230** *to Lleida.*

Lleida, Lleida-Lérida

8 Formerly an Iberian settlement, Lleida came under the Romans in the 2nd century BC and was called *Ilerda*. The town was the scene of numerous battles and sieges over the years and suffered many attacks by the French during the conflicts of the 18th and 19th centuries. It was the birthplace of Enrique Granados (1867–1916), famed for his beautiful classical guitar compositions.

Enclosed within the city walls is the **Seo Antigua** (old cathedral), which is dominated by a tall 14th-century octagonal tower. It was built between the 12th and 15th centuries and shows the transition from Romanesque to Gothic. During the 18th century it was converted into a garrison and has been undergoing restoration for some years. It has a fine Gothic cloister, noted for its tall, graceful arches. There are good views over the plains from the bays in the south part of the cloister.

Lleida also has a **Catedral Nueva** (new cathedral), which was built in the 18th century in neo-classical style, and was the first of its kind in Catalonia. A fine collection of 15th- and 16th-century tapestries is displayed in the museum inside. The 13th-century town hall, known as the **Palacio de la Paheria**, is noted for its fine façade and attractive courtyard. Below is a **museum** with Iberian and Roman finds from the area. Other places which merit a visit are the Romanesque-Gothic churches of **Sant Llorenc** (St Lawrence) and **Sant Martín**, (St Martin), the former 15th-century hospital of Santa María which

The cathedral at Tarragona, built over a period of time, shows a mixture of Romanesque and Gothic styles

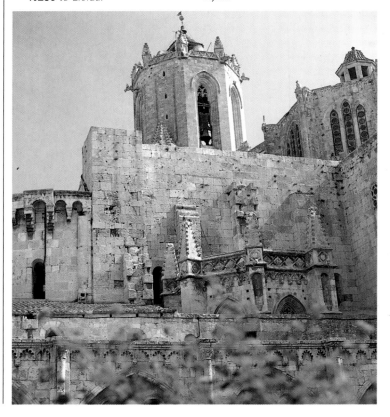

houses an **archaeological museum**, and the **Diocesan Museum** in the **Seminario**.

Lleida makes an excellent centre for any number of excursions in to the Pyrenees.

ⓘ Avenida Blondell 1

*Take the **N240** southeast towards Tarragona. Shortly after going under the **A2** (motorway) turn right to the Monasterio de Poblet (Monastery of Poblet).*

Monasterio de Poblet, Tarragona

9 Tucked away on the lower slopes of the Prades Mountains, among streams and luxuriant forests, is the magnificent **Monastery de Santa María de Poblet**. It was founded in 1149 by Ramón Berenguer IV as a token of thanks to God for regaining Catalonia from the Moors. The following year 12 Cistercian monks, sent from Fontfroide (near Narbonne in France), began building the monastery, which was completed only at the end of the 14th century. It is considered one of the finest examples of Cistercian art in Europe. The monks were able to enjoy living under the patronage of the kings of Aragón, for whom the monastery became a favourite stopping place for royal journeys. Its position was further strengthened when it was selected as the Royal Pantheon.

The monastery is completely encircled by an outer perimeter, built to protect those who worked in the abbey, with the addition of two lower walls. Among the most impressive parts of the monastery are the **Royal Pantheon**, which contains the grand marble tomb of King Jaime I of Aragón, who died in 1276, and the Romanesque **church** with its splendid 16th-century altar retablo. The lovely Gothic cloister and adjoining chapter-house contain a number of abbots' tombstones inlaid in the pavement.

*Rejoin the **N240** and continue for 8km (5 miles) to Montblanc.*

Montblanc, Tarragona

10 Montblanc presents an impressive sight, with its massive medieval ramparts and towers and narrow entrance gates. Overlooking the town is the **Iglesia de Santa María**, first erected in the 14th century and never fully completed. The small main square is charming and a modest municipal museum provides cultural interest.

*Continue on the **N240** southeast to Valls. Turn left on to the **C246**, then left again on a minor road, crossing the **A2** to Santes Creus.*

Monasterio Santes Creus, Tarragona

11 It is well worth making this short detour to visit the Santes Creus monastery, which rises grandly over the forest around it. It is a fine example of the Cistercian style and ranks with Poblet as one of Catalonia's most important monasteries.

The monastery was founded in 1157 and was occupied by Cistercian monks from France. It long enjoyed

Poblet monastery, a fine example of Cistercian art, was the Royal Pantheon of the kings of Aragón

the favour of the Kings of Aragón but, like Poblet, it suffered damage during the wars of the 19th century, and is also under restoration. The Great Cloister was the work of the architect Reinard Fonoll and shows the first traces of the 14th-century Flamboyant style. The church is 12th-century Romanesque and contains the royal tombs of former kings of Catalonia, including that of Pedro III (Peter the Great) and Jaime II. The chapterhouse and royal palace should also be seen.

*Return south to the **A2** and join the **A7** back to Barcelona, 90km (56 miles)*

Barcelona – Sitges **40 (25)**
Sitges – Vilanova i la Geltrú **6 (4)**
Vilanova i la Geltrú – Calafell **14 (9)**
Calafell – Tarragona **31 (19)**
Tarragona – Cambrils de Mar **18 (11)**
Cambrils de Mar – Peñiscola **112 (70)**
Peñiscola – Tortosa **62 (39)**
Tortosa – Lleida **128 (80)**
Lleida – Monasterio de Poblet **53 (33)**
Monasterio de Poblet – Montblanc **8 (5)**
Montblanc – Monasterio Santes Creus **35 (22)**
Monasterio Santes Creus – Barcelona **90 (56)**

2/3 days – 396km (247 miles)

THE COSTA BLANCA

Valencia ● Sagunto ● La Albufera ● Cullera ● Gandía
Denia ● Jávea ● Calpe ● Benidorm ● Guadalest ● Alcoy
Xátiva ● Valencia

Valencia is the capital of its own province and Spain's third-largest city, with a very busy port. In the middle of the town stands the *catedral*, (1262–1482), which shows a mixture of Romanesque, Gothic and baroque styles. A chalice, said to be the Holy Grail, lies in the chapterhouse. The *Iglesia de Santa Catalina*, nearby, has an interesting 18th-century baroque hexagonal belfry. Other monuments of note are *La Lonja*, built in 1483 as the Silk Exchange, the 17th-century *Colegio del Patriarca* (Corpus Christi Collegiate Church), a Renaissance building with an attractive patio, and the impressive *Torres de Serranos*, the 14th-century city gates. The *Museo Provincial de Belles Artes* (Fine Arts Museum) has some excellent works of art by famous masters. Among its many public gardens, the *Jardines del Real*, or Viveros, are known for their beautiful roses.

It is possible to find a quiet spot away from the high-rise blocks that make up the modern resort of Benidorm

i Plaza de País Valencian 1, Ayuntamiento (town hall)

*From Valencia, take the **N340** north for 27km (17 miles) to Sagunto.*

Sagunto, Valencia

1 The original *Saguntum* was founded by the Iberians and later allied to Rome. The town was attacked by the great Carthaginian general, Hannibal, in 218BC. Abandoned by Rome, the citizens resisted for several months until the city finally fell to the enemy, sparking off the commencement of the Second Punic War. Five years later the Romans recaptured the town and rebuilt it. After this, it was under Moorish occupation for a period of time.

On one side of the Plaza Mayor (main square) stands the 14th-century Gothic **Iglesia de Santa María**, which has an 18th-century gilded altar with a fine cross in mother-of-pearl. From the road up the hillside, you can see stone arches over some of the streets, which once framed the old gates leading to various parts of the town. The route will take you by the **Teatro Romano** (Roman theatre). Dating back to the end of the 2nd century AD, it has a diameter of 50m (165 feet), with a capacity for some 6,000 spectators. A small museum alongside completes the visit.

The road winds its way up to the **Castillo de Sagunto** (castle or acropolis of Sagunto), from which there are sweeping views of the coast and the town below. The remains of the old fortress spread over the hillside and show evidence of Iberian, Carthaginian and Roman remains, while the walls are mainly from the Moorish period. The **museum** near the entrance displays material relating to the history of ancient Sagunto.

The fortress at Sagunto spreads across the hillside

2 *La Albufera, Valencia* The large freshwater lagoon of La Albufera is a nature park of great ecological importance, and is a veritable paradise for birdwatchers. Among the species of birds that use this as their breeding grounds are red-crested pochards, purple herons, black-winged stilts and numerous warblers. Little egrets are often seen feeding in the water and, in the autumn, thousands of wildfowl, lapwings and golden plover arrive to spend the winter. From the village of **El Palmar**, on the lagoon, the arrival of these migratory birds can be observed. The flight of ducks is a famous sight in La Albufera.

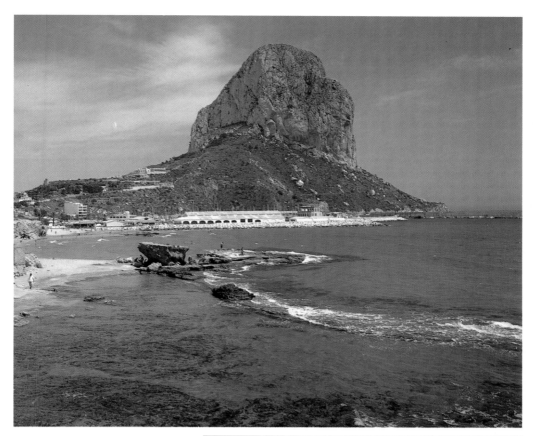

The Peñón de Ifach towers over the resort of Calpe. This extraordinary rock is 1,089 feet (332m) high

*Return south on the **N340** for 6km (4 miles). Join the **A7** heading southwest around Valencia. After 20km (12 miles) turn left off the **A7** and bypass the city on the south and join the coastal road to El Saler and Albufera.*

La Albufera, Valencia

2 A short drive south beyond Valencia's El Saler beach will bring you to La Albufera, Spain's largest lagoon (the name derives from the Arabic for 'small sea'). The lagoon is surrounded by rice fields and separated from the sea by a sand bar known as **La Dehesa**. Three channels carry fresh water into the sea.

Continue on the coastal road for 22km (14 miles) to Cullera.

Cullera, Valencia

3 Like many other places, the effects of tourism have taken their toll on Cullera, once a tiny fishing village and now characterised by high-rise blocks. The place still retains some of its old charm, however, and a walk is recommended up to the **Ermita de Nuestra Senora del Castillo**, which contains a much-venerated image of the Virgen del Castillo, patron saint of the town. Nearby are the ruins of an old castle and a splendid view of the coast and surrounding rice fields.

*Join and take the **N332** south for 27km (17 miles) to Gandía.*

Gandía, Valencia

4 Gandía was formerly the seat of a dukedom given to the Borja family in 1485 by Ferdinand the Catholic.

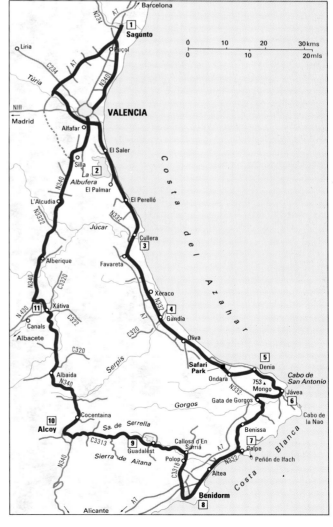

SCENIC ROUTES

The coastal road from Gandía to Denia is very pleasant, with long sandy beaches broken up by dramatic rock formations. There are many areas of lush vegetation with palm forests, orange groves and beautiful oleander and cypress trees. The road south of Jávea to Benidorm, the route to Guadalest, inland on the **C3313**, and the section from Alcoy to Xátiva on the **N340** are particularly scenic.

FOR CHILDREN

5 *Denia, Alicante* East of Denia, near Vergel (just off the **N332** from Gandía) is the splendid **Safari Park**, which has an amusement park and a host of attractions as well as the animals.

8 *Benidorm, Alicante* In Benidorm is a recreation park called 'Aqualung', located in the park north of town, where the children can slide down water chutes and enjoy a range of other amusements.

RECOMMENDED WALKS

7 *Calpe, Alicante* The fit and energetic should enjoy a walk up a good path to the summit of the **Peñón de Ifach** (about 1½ hours), from where there is a panoramic view of the Costa Blanca.

10 *Alcoy, Alicante* Many antiquities displayed in the museum in Alcoy were found in the nearby Sierra Sereta. A steep climb of about half an hour will take you to the top, where there are magnificent views of the surrounding mountainous landscapes.

SPECIAL TO . . .

Valencia, Valencia Those with an interest in musical bands should make a point of visiting **Liria**, a short distance northwest of Valencia. Known as the 'City of Music', it has an international reputation for its bands of musicians. It is said great rivalry exists between the bands, who jealously guard their own territory.

10 *Alcoy, Alicante* The festival of the Moors and Christians is celebrated all over Spain, but is especially colourful in Alcoy, where it takes place between 22 and 24 April, and centres on St George's Day, 23 April. For three days an image of St George (to whom the village had appealed for help in times of need) is carried through the streets and around the walls of a great cardboard castle. Mock battles are fought between the Moors and the Christians, inevitably ending in victory for the Christians. This is all accompanied by bell-ringing, fireworks and jollity.

Of major interest is the **Palacio de los Duques** (Ducal Palace), a handsome Renaissance building notable as the birthplace and residence of Francisco Borja (1510–72), who became the 4th Duke of Gandía. He was superior of the Jesuit Order, and was canonised as Saint Francis Borja in 1671. The building has seen considerable alterations since the 16th century and is now a Jesuit college. The state apartments are richly decorated and the patio is attractively adorned with coats of arms. The flooring is laid out to represent the four elements of the Creation and bordered by lovely ceramic tiles. Close by are the 18th-century **Ayuntamiento** (town hall) and the **Iglesia de Santa María**, which is a good example of the transition from Gothic to Renaissance architecture.

ⓘ Parque de la Estación

*Continue on the **N332** south. At Ondara take a left turn to Denia, 33km (21 miles).*

Denia, Alicante

5 The old Denia is thought to have been colonised by the Greeks before the 8th century BC and known as *Hemeroskopeion*. Under the Romans it was *Dianium*, after the temple of Diana. It began to flourish as a port during the time of the Moors (715–1253), and at one time it controlled the island of Mallorca. Today it is principally a seaside resort and port.

The town is crowned by the remains of the old fortress, which provides a fine view of the surroundings. The area around the fishing port is fun to explore. Take a look at the small 18th-century **Iglesia de Santa María** and the 17th-century **Ayuntamiento**.

The **Sierra del Mongo** towers over the southern end of the town, rising to a height of 753m (2,470 feet). The climb to the top is arduous, but the views from the summit are superb. On a clear day you can see the outline of Ibiza, over 100km (65 miles) away to the east.

ⓘ Patrocinio Ferrandiz

Take the regional road down the coast for 10km (6 miles) to Jávea.

Jávea, Alicante

6 The small fishing port of Jávea spreads along a wide bay between two prominent pine-covered rock masses, which descend sharply to the sea. The attractive setting, combined with a lively yacht marina and fine sandy beaches, make it an appealing little resort. In spring the place is filled with the scent of lemon and orange blossom. It has a late Gothic local **church** and a modern church shaped like a ship's hull. At one end of the resort is the great rock of **Cabo de la Nao**, with some caves dotted about its steep cliff face. Opposite is the tiny island of **Portichol**. There are good views of the coast towards Javeá and Cabo de la Nao from a spot by the lighthouse on **Cabo de San Antonio**.

*Return westwards to the **N332** and continue south for 30km (19 miles) to Calpe.*

Calpe, Alicante

7 Your approach to Calpe will be heralded by the magnificent sight of the **Peñón de Ifach** – a famous landmark of the Costa Blanca – rising majestically from the sea. Nestling beneath this great volcanic mass is Calpe, whose dramatic setting features among its main attractions. It is another in the long line of popular resorts to be found down this coast, with a fine sandy beach and busy fishing harbour. In the old part of town is a small Gothic-Mudejar church and a 16th-century tower, all that remains of the fortified walls.

*Continue along the **N332** for 22km (14 miles) to Benidorm.*

Benidorm, Alicante

8 Benidorm is the Costa Blanca's most famous resort, attracting multitudes of visitors each year. The place has changed beyond recognition since the days when it was a sleepy little fishing village. It is now an international fun city, crammed with bars, shops and nightspots that provide non-stop entertainment, which holds particular appeal for the younger set. Tall apartment blocks dominate the skyline. Whatever your thoughts about Benidorm in season, its setting is dramatic, with its two splendid bays of golden sands and high-rise blocks silhouetted against the high mountains. Steer clear of the tourist area and explore the old fishing quarters, which have narrow streets and a pretty church with a blue dome. A rather elegant look-out terrace, nearby, offers a sweeping view of the bay and the little island of **Plumbaria**. If time allows, take a boat-trip across to the island and enjoy a relaxing swim with refreshments (during the season).

*Take the **C3318** north for 4km (2½ miles) past Polop, then turn left on to the **C3313** to Guadalest.*

Guadalest, Alicante

9 A drive through some spectacular scenery will bring you to the dramatic sight of Guadalest, a tiny village with a Moorish **castle**, perched on top of a lofty mountain crag. The village can only be reached through a tunnel cut through the rock. Most of the village was destroyed by an earthquake, but you can clamber up to the fortress, known as the Costa Blanca's 'eagle's nest' for its impregnable position and superb views over the surrounding landscapes.

*Continue on the **C3313** west for 36km (22 miles) to Alcoy.*

Alcoy, Alicante

10 The town of Alcoy lies in a setting of olive groves and vineyards against a backdrop of the Sierra de Montcabre, presenting an attractive picture as you approach it. Alcoy is famous for its *peladillas*, a very popular sweet in Spain, made of sugar-coated almonds. The town has two fine churches, the **Iglesia de Santa María** and the **Iglesia de Santo Sepulcro**, which has attractive tile decorations. Worth a visit is the **Museo Arqueológico** (Archaeological Museum), which houses an extensive and interesting collection of Iberian clay pottery and Greek tablets found in the vicinity.

ℹ Centro de Iniciativas Turísticas, Avenida Puente San Jorge

*Take the **N340** north to Xátiva (Játiva).*

Xátiva, Valencia

11 The ramparts of Xátiva are apparent from some distance, rising from twin peaks. Set among olive groves and vineyards, Xátiva is an attractive little town of fountains and trim trees, with a number of interesting monuments. Some fine old palaces and fountains can be seen on and around Moncada Street, which is a very picturesque area. The **Colegiata** (Collegiate Church) is a fine example of the 16th-century Renaissance style and the municipal hospital opposite has a fine 16th-century Plateresque façade. Allow

The remains of the Moorish castle at Guadalest, occupying an impregnable position

time for a visit to the **Museo Municipal**, which has an extensive collection of antiquities, including the 'Pila de los Moros', a Moorish basin from the 11th century with unusual decorations of human figures.

There are good views from the cypress-planted **Calvary** and the **Ermita de San Feliú** (hermitage of St Felix). A further climb up the hill takes you to **El Castillo**, a 16th-century castle built on Iberian and Roman foundations, from which there is a magnificent view of the surroundings.

ℹ Alameda Jaime I, 35

*Return to Valencia on the **N340**, 60km (37 miles).*

Valencia – Sagunto **27 (17)**
Sagunto – La Albufera **55 (34)**
La Albufera – Cullera **22 (14)**
Cullera – Gandía **27 (17)**
Gandía – Denia **33 (21)**
Denia – Jávea **10 (6)**
Jávea – Calpe **30 (19)**
Calpe – Benidorm **22 (14)**
Benidorm – Guadalest **25 (16)**
Guadalest – Alcoy **36 (22)**
Alcoy – Xátiva **49 (30)**
Xátiva – Valencia **60 (37)**

FOR HISTORY BUFFS •

11 *Xátiva, Valencia* A short detour of about 8km (5 miles) on a minor road southwest of Xátiva takes you to the small village of **Canals**. The **castle** here is famed as the birthplace of Alonso Borja. The Borja family arrived from Aragón in the 14th century and Alonso was born here in 1378, later to become Pope Calixtus III. He was uncle to Rodrigo Borja (1431–1503), who became Pope Alexander, notorious for his scandalous behaviour, and father of Lucretia and Cesare Borgia.

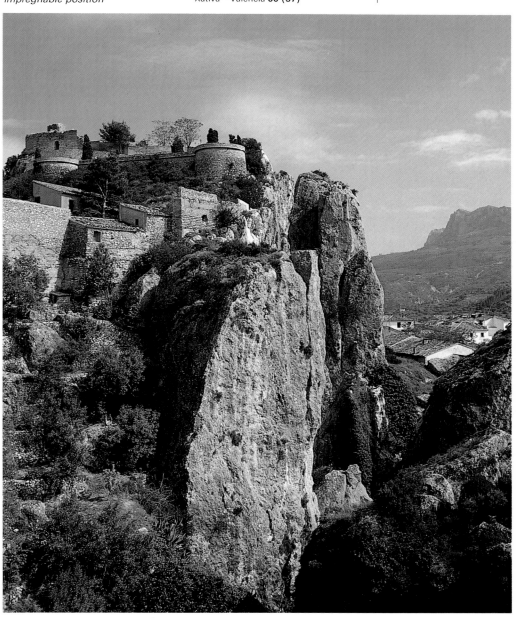

PALM FORESTS & RUGGED PEAKS

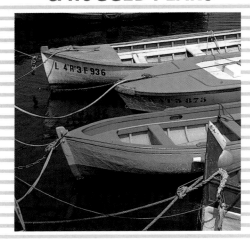

Alicante ● Elx ● Orihuela ● Murcia ● Alhama de Murcia
Aledo ● Totana ● Lorca ● Aguilas ● Mazarrón
Cartagena ● La Unión ● Alicante

Together with Valencia, Alicante serves as an important gateway for the popular Costa Blanca. The main square, *Plaza de Calvo Sotelo*, is the central point of the town. From here Avenida del Dr Gadea takes you down to the harbour and to the *Explanada de España*. This long promenade, shaded by luxuriant palms and paved in multi-coloured mosaics, is one of the most pleasant areas of Alicante in which to take a stroll. Two places of interest in the old town are the *Iglesia de Santa María*, rebuilt several times since the 14th century, with a richly decorated interior, and the *Ayuntamiento* (town hall) which features two impressive square towers and a rich façade. Near by is the 17th-century *Catedral de San Nicolás* (Cathedral of St Nicholas), dedicated to the town's patron saint. Also worth a visit is the *Museo Arqueológico* (Archaeological Museum) with relics from the area, paintings and a collection of coins. There are beautiful views of the town and coast from the *Castillo Santa Barbara*, on top of the hill.

[i] Explanada de España 2

Local boats provide a splash of colour among a host of international pleasure craft in Alicante's busy harbour

*Take the **N340** southwest for 24km (15 miles) to Elx (Elche).*

Elx, Alicante

1 Although the main attraction of this first stop is the unique palm forest, first take a look around the town. It has a rather Moorish look, with its whitewashed houses, flat roofs and luscious palms. There is an excellent view down over the town and palm grove from the tower of the 17th-century baroque **Santa María Basilica**. The **Palacio de Altimira**, nearby, was built in the 1400s as lodgings for the kings of Spain and is listed as a national monument. In the grounds of the **Parque Municipal** (municipal park) is the **Museo Arqueológico**. Among its collection is a copy of the famous *Lady of Elche* sculpture, believed to date back to the 4th and 3rd century BC. The original was found in the vicinity and is displayed in the Archaeological Museum of Madrid. There is also a small **Museo de la Artesanía de la Palma** (Handicraft Museum) in the park.

The **Palmeral de Europe** (Palm Forest of Europe), as it is called, lies to the east of the town. It is recognised as the largest date palm grove in Europe. Guides are on hand to take you around if required. The Moors were responsible for the original plantations. The palms can reach a height of 25m (82 feet), while some grow even taller. In the **Huerto del Cura** (Priest's Orchard) you can see the

The Explanada de España, lined with shady palm trees and with its wavy, multi-coloured pavement, extends along the seafront at Alicante

impressive 'Palmera Imperial' species, which are thought to be at least 150 years old and characterised by seven stems that grow out from the main trunk. Cacti and brilliantly coloured flowers enhance this lovely garden. The dates are cut in the winter months from the female palms. After harvesting some of the male trees are bound up to bleach the fronds. These are then sold all over the country and used for Palm Sunday processions.

ℹ️ Parque Municipal

*Continue on the **N340** for 33km (21 miles) to Orihuela.*

Orihuela, Alicante

2 Orihuela lies on the banks of the River Segura, which provides irrigation for the surrounding orange and lemon groves. The **Cerro de Oro** (Hill of Gold) rises in the background. The name of the town is thought to be a derivation from the Roman *Aurariola*. It suffered severe damage from an earthquake in 1829 and much of the town dates from after that period. Among the old buildings of note, however, are the **El Salvador** cathedral, built in the 14th and 15th centuries, with fine Gothic vaulting; the late-Gothic **Santiago Church**, and the **Santo Domingo College**, former home of the University of Orihuela, founded in the 16th century.

ℹ️ Francisco Diaz 25

*Continue for 24km (15 miles) on the **N340** southwest to Murcia.*

Murcia, Murcia

3 Capital of its province, Murcia spreads along both sides of the Río Segura, in the heart of the *huerta* (a fertile, irrigated region). Murcia is the seat of a bishop and a university town. The **cathedral** is probably the town's most imposing monument. It was originally built in the 14th century,

with later additions in Renaissance and baroque styles. It features an impressive baroque façade and a splendid 18th-century belfry. Inside are lavish Renaissance decorations in the **Capilla de los Junterones** and the rich late-Gothic interior of the Chapel of los Velez. The museum in the cloister houses many valuable treasures. There is a good view of the town and surrounding farmlands from the belfry.

The **Palacio Episcopal** (Episcopal Palace) nearby is noted for its elegant cloister. Be sure to take a look, however, at the grand old **Casino**, one of the most impressive of its kind from the old days, built at the turn of the century. Museums include the **Museo Arqueológico**, the **Museo de Belles Artes** and the **Museo Internacional del Traje Folklórico** (Traditional Costume Museum), which has an interesting collection of costumes from all regions of Spain.

ℹ️ Alejandro Seiquet 4

*Take the **N340** southwest for 32km (20 miles) to Alhama de Murcia.*

Alhama de Murcia, Murcia

4 On the way to Alhama de Murcia, make a brief stop at **Alcantarilla**, 9km (6 miles) out of Murcia, to visit the **Museo de la Huerta** (Huerta Museum) and take a look at the huge old waterwheel called a *noria*, which the Moors used for irrigation. Historical information on the area is furnished by the museum, which is set in orange groves and market gardens.

The tour continues through orange and lemon groves, followed by cornfields to a very large, craggy rock topped by the tower of an old Moorish fort. Below lies the ancient spa town of **Alhama de Murcia**, which is known for its warm, medicinal sulphur springs. Some Roman

SCENIC ROUTES

This itinerary combines mountain scenery with coastal roads. Particularly attractive stretches include the approach to Elx and on to Orihuela through a palm and orange grove; the Leyva Valley, between Alhama de Murcia and Aledo, high up in the wild, rugged mountains of the Sierra de Espuña; Puerto de Mazarrón to Cartagena on the **N332**; and La Unión back to San Javier on the **N332** – this passes to the west of the large saltwater lagoon of the Mar Menor, whose warm, tranquil waters create ideal conditions for yachting and other watersports.

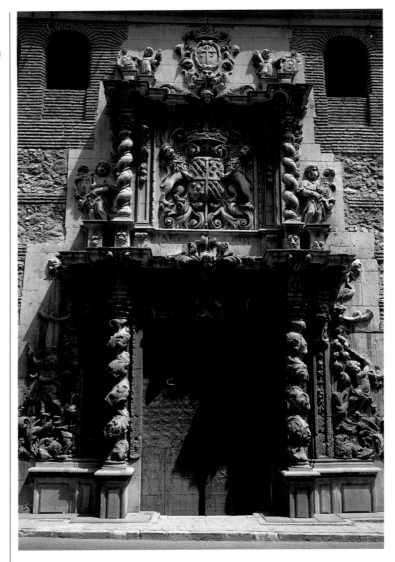

remains are still in evidence and the small churches of **San Lázaro** and **La Concepción** are worth a look.

*Continue along the **N340**. At Totana take a right turn and drive to Aledo, a distance of 21km (13 miles).*

Aledo, Murcia

5 At the southern end of the Sierra de Espuña is the small medieval town of Aledo, famous for its old castle, which was held for a long period by the Knights of the Calavatra (1085–1160) during the Moorish occupation. Take a look at the keep, known as 'La Calahorra', the remains of the old walls and the **Iglesia de Santa María la Real**, which houses a lovely medieval image.

Return on the same road to Totana, 9km (6 miles).

Totana, Murcia

6 Totana was a town of some importance under the Romans. The 16th-century **Iglesia de Santiago** (St James) has a fine 17th-century baroque portal and Mudejar coffered ceiling. The attractive **Fountain** by Juan de Uceta was built in the 17th-century.

Make a detour to visit the **Ermita de Santa Eulalia** (Hermitage of St

The ornate doorway of the Church of San Patricio, Lorca, provides a fine example of baroque carving

Eulalia), the town's patron saint. Situated some 7km (4 miles) away, it is famous for its Mudejar roof and 16th-century murals.

*Take the **N340** south for 20km (12 miles) to Lorca.*

Lorca, Murcia

7 At the entrance to the Valley of El Guadalentín lies the town of Lorca, an important agricultural centre. The town was a bishopric under the Visigoths, called *Ilurco* by the Romans, and *Lurka* by the Moors. Above the town are the remains of the old Moorish **castle**, built between the 13th and 15th centuries, and the medieval churches of **Santa María**, **San Juan** and **San Pedro** (St Mary, St John and St Peter).

Further down the hill is the 16th- to 17th-century **Iglesia de San Patricio** (St Patrick), with a Renaissance tower and baroque doorway. In the same square is the elegant **Ayuntamiento**, built between the 17th and 18th centuries. Other buildings include the **Casa de los Guevara** (House of the Guevara family), the old **Granary** and the **Torre** (Tower)

RECOMMENDED WALKS

5 *Aledo, Murcia* The Sierra de Espuña offers many possibilities for walking in beautiful pine forests and mountain terrain, with fine views at every turn. Park wardens are around to give advice or assistance.

de los García de Alcázar, with an interesting coat of arms.

ⓘ Palacio Guevara, Lopez Gisbert 12

Take the C3211 and the N332 southeast for 39km (24 miles) to Aguilas.

Aguilas, Murcia

8 The town of Aguilas dates back to the 17th century and shows little evidence of change since those times. Its two most impressive buildings are the Mudejar-style **Ayuntamiento** and the **Iglesia de San José**. A climb up to the **Castillo de San Juan de las Aguilas** on the summit of the hill provides a panoramic view of the bay, rocky coves and distant mountains.

Take the N332 northeast for 46km (29 miles) to Mazarrón.

Mazarrón, Murcia

9 The main points of interest in the small inland town of Mazarrón are the **Castillo de los Vélez**, with the remains of an old watch tower, and the **Iglesia de San Andrés** (St Andrew), which has a fine 16th-century Mudejar coffered ceiling.

A short drive of about 6km (4 miles) leads down to **Puerto de Mazarrón**, which lies in a splendid bay and offers good swimming.

Continue for 39km (24 miles) on the N332 northeast to Cartagena.

Cartagena, Murcia

10 Cartagena is Spain's major naval base and a leading commercial port. Founded by the Carthaginian chief Hasdrubal in the 3rd century BC it became the capital of the region under the Romans. It suffered a decline during the Moorish occupation but regained its importance

during the reigns of Philip II and Charles III. Its most interesting buildings include the **Iglesia de Santa María la Vieja** (old St Mary), the Roman **Torre Ciega** (literally, blind tower) and the **Ayuntamiento**. On the main quay of the port stands the first submarine in the world, launched by Isaac Peral in 1888. A flight of steps leads up to the remains of the **Castillo de la Concepción** (Castle of the Conception), which is set in attractive gardens. There is a magnificent view from here of the town and harbour. The **Museo Arqueológico** has a fine collection of Roman relics.

ⓘ Plaza Castillini 5

Take the N332 east for 11km (7 miles) to La Unión.

La Unión, Murcia

11 The old mining town of La Unión goes back about 100 years, when it emerged as an important centre for lead mining. The **Mercado** (market) and the **Casa del Piñon** are two interesting examples of an architectural style from the beginning of the 20th century, making full use of wrought-iron adornments. The market-place is the setting for the famous August festival of the 'Cante de las Minas' (mining songs), when the best performers of Murcia gather and render their own special type of flamenco.

Return to Alicante on the northeast coast road (N332), 98km (61 miles).

Alicante – Elx **24 (15)**
Elx – Orihuela **33 (21)**
Orihuela – Murcia **24 (15)**
Murcia – Alhama de Murcia **32 (20)**
Alhama de Murcia – Aledo **21 (13)**
Aledo – Totana **9 (6)**
Totana – Lorca **20 (12)**
Lorca – Aguilas **39 (24)**
Aguilas – Mazarrón **46 (29)**
Mazarrón – Cartagena **39 (24)**
Cartagena – La Unión **11 (7)**
La Unión – Alicante **98 (61)**

BACK TO NATURE

The natural park of the Sierra de Espuña is Murcia's largest nature reserve with wild, rugged mountains and high peaks. Among its inhabitants are wild sheep (moufflon), wild cats, boar and foxes. Eagles, owls and partridges are some of the birds that can also be seen here, together with rare species of butterflies.

A view across the bay at Aguilas, which is built on a rocky promontory

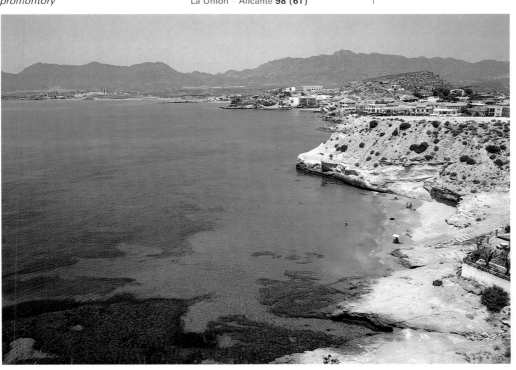

3 days – 358km (223 miles)

THE MAGIC OF MALLORCA

Palma de Mallorca ● Puerto de Andraitx ● Valldemosa
Deià ● Puerto de Sóller ● Monasterio de Lluc ● Pollença
Alcúdia ● Cuevas de Artá ● Manacor ● Porto Cristo
Cuevas del Drac ● Felanitx ● Santanyi
Palma de Mallorca

Although to many it serves merely as a gateway to beach destinations, Palma has charm and is well worth exploring. The tree-lined *Paseo Maritimo*, stretching along the seafront, is a well-known feature of the city. Overlooking the harbour is the *Catedral* (La Seu). Built between the 13th and 17th centuries, it is a landmark with its tall spires and flying buttresses. Nearby is the impressive 15th-century building of *La Lonja* (formerly the Stock Exchange), and behind is the *Paseo del Borne*, Palma's lively main street with shops and bars. Take a look at the impressive 17th-century façade of the *Ayuntamiento* (town hall) and the tree in the square (said to be at least 500 years old). Horse-drawn carriages provide a leisurely way of viewing the town.

A trip to the *Castillo de Bellver* (Bellver Castle), 3km (2 miles) west of Palma, is recommended. Built by Mallorcan kings in the 14th century, it was first a palace and then a prison, and is now converted into a museum. The castle stands in a commanding position on the hilltop, offering fine views of the Bahia de Palma (Palma Bay).

i Avenida Jaime III, 10

From Palma take the C719 southwest for 33km (21 miles) to Puerto de Andraitx (Port d'Andratx).

Puerto de Andraitx, Mallorca
1 From a tiny fishing village, Puerto de Andraitx has become one of Mallorca's most prominent yachting centres, and sailing vessels of all shapes and sizes are moored in the harbour. The town is set in an attractive bay surrounded by hills and has a pleasant seafront promenade lined with bars and restaurants. The yachting set provides an international atmosphere during the season.

Take the C710 and branch off to the right for 43km (27 miles) to Valldemosa (Valldemossa).

Valldemosa, Mallorca
2 To many, the name of Valldemosa conjures up visions of Chopin, music and romance. The Polish composer, Frederick Chopin, spent the

The colourful local pottery is a favourite souvenir among visitors to Majorca, and can be bought all over the island

winter of 1838 to 1839 here with the French authoress Georges Sand. The **Real Cartuja** (Charterhouse) where they stayed is the main feature of the village. After the monks were expelled in 1835 the place served as lodgings for travellers. The apartments, or rather cells, where the couple stayed are furnished in the style of the period, and include the piano on which the great master composed some of his best-known works. In the cloister is a very old **pharmacy**. First established by the monks as early as 1723, it looks much the same as in former times. Take a look, too, at the small museum in the monks' library.

Rejoin the C710 for 10km (6 miles) to Deià (Deyà).

Deià, Mallorca
3 Deià has long been a favourite haunt for writers and artists. Poet and writer, Robert Graves, spent some time here after World War II. The village consists of a cluster of red houses on top of a hill, among almond trees and groves of oranges, lemons and olives. Take a look at the small tile altars in the **parish church**, depicting scenes from Calvary. Behind the church is the cemetery where Graves is buried. There is a wonderful view from here of the surrounding mountains and rocky coves below. A somewhat precipitous climb down the hill leads to the sea.

Continue on the C710. Take a left turn to Puerto de Sóller (Port de Sóller).

Puerto de Sóller, Mallorca
4 The route from Deià passes through the small hamlet of Lluc Alcari, where Pablo Picasso lived for a time.

The picturesque old fishing port of Puerto de Sóller is now a popular tourist spot. It has an attractive harbour, framed by the pine-covered hills of the Sierra de Tramuntana and an excellent sandy beach. The **Santuario de Santa Catalina**, by the old fishing quarter, provides a fine view of the resort. Five kilometres (3 miles) inland is Sóller town, linked to Puerto de Sóller by a narrow-gauge railway or by road, where the **Convento de San Francisco** (St Francis) is worth a visit, along with the handicrafts centre in the local museum.

Rejoin the C710 and branch off left to the Monasterio de Lluc, 37km (23 miles).

Monasterio de Lluc, Mallorca
5 Situated on one of the highest points of the island is Mallorca's principal monastery and pilgrimage centre. The entrance is lined with houses and doorways, which once provided shelter for pilgrims who arrived here to venerate the Virgin of Lluc, patron saint of the island.

The mountain village of Deià, set among almond trees and olive groves, has long been popular with writers and artists

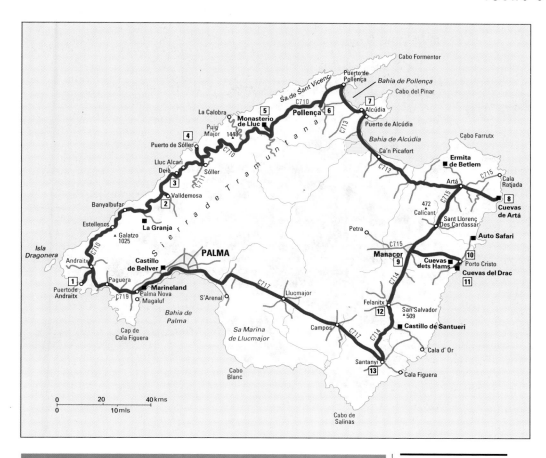

FOR CHILDREN

Palma, Mallorca There are a number of amusement parks in the area. At Costa d'en Blanes, north of Palma Nova, **Marineland** has spectacular shows of performing dolphins, sealions and parrots, an aquarium of sharks, a mini zoo, train rides and much more.

In Magaluf, south of Palma Nova, are two special attractions, **Aquapark** and **El Dorado**, a re-created Wild West town, with gun fights and stage shows.

10 *Porto Cristo, Mallorca* In Porto Cristo, near the Cuevas del Drac, is a water amusement park called **Aquarius**; and on the Porto Cristo/San Severa road is the **AutoSafari Park** where the animals can be viewed from the car.

SCENIC ROUTES

The stretch of road along the magnificent hills of the Sierra de Tramuntana, across the northwest of the island, is outstanding. The corniche from Andraitx to Sóller is one of the most beautiful drives in Mallorca. There are spectacular views of the coast from look-out posts such as the **Mirador R Roca** and **Ses Animes**, and the curious terraced landscapes around **Banyalbufar**.

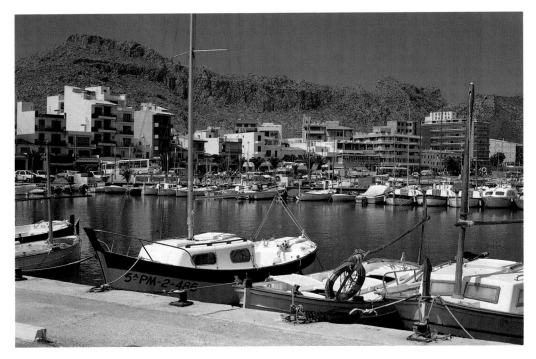

RECOMMENDED WALKS

Mallorca has so many attractive areas for walking that you can more or less make a choice anywhere along the route. The Sierra de Tramuntana in the northwest of the island offers countless hikes in magnificent scenery. Booklets can be obtained from the local tourist office.

6 *Pollença, Mallorca* A pleasant stroll can be taken in Puerto de Pollença along the seafront promenade, which starts from the end of town and follows the sea, well shaded by trees and lined with attractive residential villas and gardens.

BACK TO NATURE

7 *Alcúdia, Mallorca* Birdwatchers should stop at La Albufera, a partly dried-up lagoon in swamp lands southwest of Alcúdia, where you will have the opportunity of observing many bird species. Look for black-winged stilts, stone curlews and little egrets.

In the south of the island **Sa Marina de Llucmayor** is an area of strange rock formations that are of geological interest, with extensive views from the top. The rocks and lagoons are also a natural habitat for sea birds and maritime plants.

Puerto de Pollença, set on a sheltered bay below the San Vicente mountains, is a popular yachting centre

Inside the monastery is a beautiful wooden statue of the Virgin encrusted with jewels. There is also a 17th-century church, a small museum with a collection of paintings, ceramics and religious items. Mass is celebrated each day, when you can hear the stirring singing of the famous boys choir of Lluc.

*Continue on the **C710** for 21km (13 miles) to Pollença (Pollensa).*

Pollença, Mallorca

6 Pollença's crowning glory is **El Calvario** (The Calvary), which stands at the top of an impressive flight of 365 steps lined with cypress trees. Those who make it to the top will find a little white 18th-century **chapel** with an old crucifix and a superb view over the bays of Alcúdia, Pollença and even as far as Cabo (Cape) Formentor. On Good Friday there is a service in the chapel followed by a torchlit procession down the steps.

Back in the town, monuments worth a visit are the Gothic **chapel of Roser Vell**, which has a fine altarpiece, the **church of Montision**, (both 18th-century) and the baroque-style **Convento de Santo Domingo**. There is a Roman bridge just outside town.

Puerto de Pollença, some 6km (4 miles) away, is an attractive little fishing port set in a wide bay framed by the dramatic silhouette of the Sierra de Sant Vincenc (San Vicente mountains). It is a popular yet relatively undeveloped yachting centre and resort.

If time permits you should not miss a side tour to the Formentor peninsula, one of the most scenic parts of the island. A drive to the **lighthouse** at the end of Cabo Formentor (Cape Formentor) offers magnificent views of this superb coastline.

From Puerto de Pollença take the coast road for 15km (9 miles) to Alcúdia.

Alcúdia, Mallorca

7 The little medieval town of Alcúdia is encircled by old ramparts dating back to the 14th century. Inside are small, narrow streets and handsome mansions, mainly from the 16th and 17th centuries. The town once had quite a large Roman population and the local **museum** has exhibits of prehistoric and Roman times. A colourful market takes place on Tuesdays and Sundays just outside the old city walls.

An old Roman **theatre** (about 1.5km (1 mile) south is situated in some fields. The theatre was carved from a rock, and items uncovered here are to be seen in the museum in the **Castillo de Bellver**, Palma.

*Take the **C712** southeast to Artá. Continue southeast on a minor road to the Cuevas de Artá (Caves of Arta), 45km (28 miles).*

Cuevas de Artá, Mallorca

8 On the beach of **Canyamel** are the caves of Artá. The largest known caves on the island, they are said to have provided the inspiration for Jules Verne's famous story, *Journey to the Centre of the Earth.*

The caves are reached by a huge opening in the cliff, standing some 35m (115 feet) high, overlooking the sea. They consist of a vast number of cavities and are noted for the extraordinary, sometimes grotesque shapes of the stalactites and stalagmites.

Artá itself features some attractive mansions, churches and the **Almudain**, an old medieval fortress with a sanctuary inside. The **Ermita de Betlem** (sanctuary of Betlem) is nearby. It stands high on a hill with a fine view of the bay of Alcúdia.

*Take the **C715** southwest for 29km (18 miles) to Manacor.*

A local market in Palma adds colour and provides an alternative to sightseeing

Manacor, Mallorca

9 Manacor has a long tradition of furniture-making dating back to the 17th century, when the place became a centre for wood craftsmen. Its real claim to fame, however, lies in its production of the famous **Majorica pearls**, an important industry in Mallorca and internationally known. You can visit the factory and see the pearls being produced in a simulated process that resembles the natural one. Guided tours are available at specific times of the day. Other places of interest include the Gothic **Iglesia de San Vicente**, the **Museo Arqueológico** and the remains of the old tower, which was once the summer residence of Jaime II, conqueror of Mallorca in the 13th century.

Take the road southeast for 13km (8 miles) to Porto Cristo.

Porto Cristo, Mallorca

10 The attractive little port of Porto Cristo is one of the oldest anchorages on the island, confirmed by the discovery of a sunken Roman ship in the area. The port began to flourish in the Middle Ages when it was used to service the island with materials. As with so many other seaside locations, it has developed over recent years into a very popular holiday destination, which has inevitably changed its old character. Nevertheless it still remains a picturesque little resort with considerable charm.

Near by are the Cuevas del Drac (Caves of Drach).

Cuevas del Drac, Mallorca

11 The caves of Drach are the best-known in Mallorca, and no tourist trip is complete without a visit here. They stretch for some 2km (1½ miles) and the way leads through a superb setting over bridges and past a series of underground pools. **Lago de Martell** (Martell Lake) is the largest underground lake in Europe and its transparent waters reflect the weird and wonderful shapes of the rock formations. In summer, concerts are held aboard a small vessel which floats along the lake.

If you want to see more caves, the **Cuevas dets Hams** (Caves of Hams) nearby are also magnificent, noted for the pure white of the stalactites and lovely underground lakes with names like **Mar de Venezia** (Sea of Venice) and **Lago de las Columnas** (Lake of Columns).

Return to Manacor and take the C714 south for 29km (18 miles) to Felanitx.

Felanitx, Mallorca

12 The old town of Felanitx dates back to the 13th century. Be sure to visit the **Convento de San Augustín** and the parish church, which has a fine Gothic façade. Felanitx is the birthplace of the contemporary artist, Miguel Barceló. He still keeps a studio here.

South of Felanitx is the old convent of **Castillo de Santueri**, perched on top of a huge rock mass.

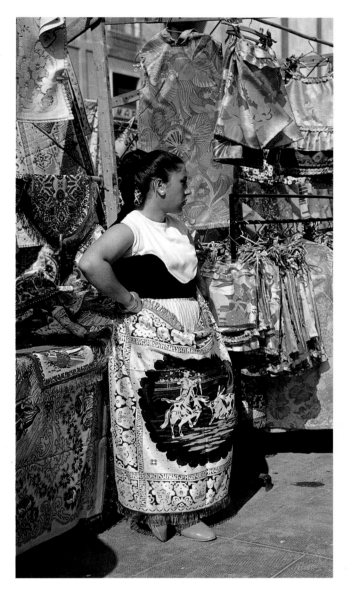

Continue for 16km (10 miles) on the C714 south to Santanyi (Santani).

Santanyi, Mallorca

13 A solid gateway, known as **Porta Murada**, still remains from the town fortifications. This was built as a defence against piracy, which was once a recurring problem in this part of the island. The local **parish church** has an excellent rococo organ, and there is a fine Romanesque-Gothic oratory in the Roser's chapel. Near by are the remains of some prehistoric sites and fortifications.

Take the C717 for 51km (32 miles) back to Palma.

FOR HISTORY BUFFS

9 *Manacor, Mallorca* **Petra** (northwest of Manacor) is the birthplace of the Franciscan, Fray Junípero de la Serra (1713–84), famous for his mission work in California and Mexico. San Francisco, San Diego and Santa Barbara are three of his former missions that grew into large towns. Junípero's former home is now the museum of the **Casa Museo Fray Junípero de la Serra**, and a statue of the evangelist stands in the town.

ANDALUCIA

To many people the image of Spain is the reality of Andalucia, a region which has a tremendous appeal and offers a diversity of attractions. Dazzling white villages perched on mountain tops are silhouetted against brilliant blue skies. Fighting bulls and grazing horses are a familiar part of its landscapes. Sun-soaked beaches and high-rise blocks contrast sharply with the quiet splendour of its Moorish monuments. The region is renowned for its song and dance, from the soul-searching gypsy lament of the flamenco to the twirling rhythms of the typical Andalucian dances known as *sevillanas*. It is also famed for its colourful festivals. Sevilla's Holy Week Processions and Spring Fair are particularly outstanding events.

Andalucia is a vast region occupying a huge chunk of southern Spain. It is made up of the provinces of Huelva, Cádiz, Sevilla, Córdoba, Jaén, Almería, Granada and Málaga, with Sevilla as its capital. It shares its western border with Portugal and has an extensive shoreline to the south which is washed by the Mediterranean and the Atlantic.

To the north is the Sierra Morena, while the south is dominated by the Andalucian Mountains, or Baetic Cordillera, which incorporate the beautiful snow-capped mountains of the Sierra Nevada and include Spain's highest peak, the Mulhacén, 3,482m (11,424 feet).

In the upper regions are the fertile lands of the basin of the River Guadalquivir, where olive groves and cereals create patterns of green and gold. Forests of cork-oak trees flourish here, providing an important commodity. Further south are vast areas of sugar-cane plantations, bananas and cotton fields. There are also important wine-growing regions, mainly around Jerez de la Frontera, Málaga and south of Córdoba.

In the southwestern corner of the region is a great expanse of salt marshes and fenland, called the 'Marismas', which contains one of Spain's most important nature parks. Its long coastline is labelled according to the characteristics of the various sections: the Costa de la Luz (Coast of Light), from Portugal to the Straits of Gibraltar, which boasts white sandy beaches and pinewoods; the Costa del Sol (Sunshine Coast), which stretches eastward and leads in turn to the Costa de Almeria.

Present-day Andalucia is a result of traditions inherited from its past, which has included some 600 years of Roman domination and almost 800 years of Moorish occupation. This brought the region rich cultures and some unique monuments, of which the Alhambra in Granada, the Mosque of Córdoba and the Alcázar in Sevilla are the finest examples. The Moorish past is more evident in Andalucia than in any other part of Spain.

Above: Ronda is built high on a plateau on both sides of the Guadalevín gorge
Opposite: The Great Mosque, Córdoba, is a fine example of Moorish architecture

Tour 7

This tour of eastern Andalucia takes you off the beaten track through a sparsely populated area of rugged mountains, deep valleys and vast plains, suggesting a journey into the unknown. Further north is one of Spain's well-known nature parks in a magnificent setting of high mountain peaks, fresh green forests and rivers. Dotted about the landscapes are interesting little towns with their roots deep in the past. Old cave dwellings also add interest to the journey through this unusual part of Spain.

Tour 8

This tour provides some of the most impressive scenery to be found in southern Andalucia, combining beautiful mountain roads through woods and valleys with a drive along one of the most attractive parts of the coast. The highlight of the trip is a visit to one of Spain's most important

Moorish legacies, which will take you right back into the past. Added to this is the splendid setting of the snow-capped mountains of the Sierra Nevada in the background.

Tour 9

The sun-soaked coastline of Spain's southern coast with its familiar skyline of modern high-rise blocks contrasts sharply with the hinterland, which offers magnificent mountainous landscapes and delightful Andalucian villages. Two special features are the sight of the coastline's famous land-mark, the Rock of Gibraltar, and one of Spain's best known bridges.

Tour 10

This trail through the basin of the River Guadalquivir leads through golden cornfields, and groves of old twisted olive trees with small farm-houses dotted about. There are wine-growing areas among the gentle hills and distant mountains. The delightful villages are Moorish in appearance – dazzling white houses, red-tiled roofs and picturesque old streets. The prize is the visit to Spain's glorious Moorish Mosque, magnificent in all its entir-ety, and a unique attraction worldwide.

Tour 11

The first part of the tour passes through the forested mountains of the Sierra Morena, which give way to olive groves and fig plantations. These, in turn, give way to the shores of the Atlantic, with long stretches of deserted sandy beaches. Down in the southwest, close to the Portuguese border, is the area referred to as the 'cradle of new civilisations'. Many expeditions by Spanish and Portuguese explorers set sail from these shores across the Atlantic in the 15th and 16th centuries.

Tour 12

Some of the most beautiful examples of Andalucia's 'white towns' are included on this route. The names of some are followed by the words 'de la Frontera': from the 200 years of fighting between Moors and Chris-tians, when these towns determined changing frontiers – until Granada, last stronghold of the Moors, fell to the Christians. The tour also explores the coastline of white sandy beaches and pinewoods, and several of Anda-lucia's ports and resorts. A trip into Andalucia's foremost wine-growing region culminates in a visit to its famous sherry-producing area.

2/3 days – 645km (402 miles)

LUNAR LANDSCAPES OF THE SOUTH

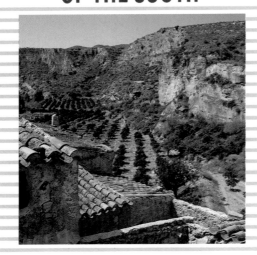

Almería ● Tabernas ● Sorbas ● Mojácar ● Huércal-Overa
Vélez Rubio ● Vélez Blanco ● Baza ● Cazorla ● Úbeda
Guadix ● Almería

Almería, capital of its province, was already a flourishing port under the Romans, who called it *Portus Magnus;* to the Moors it was *Al-Mariyya* – 'mirror of the sea'. The impressive *Alcazába*, or fortress, overlooks the city, and the cathedral, rebuilt between 1524 and 1543 on the site of a former mosque, itself resembles a fortress, due to years of raids by Barbary pirates. Other buildings of interest include the *Iglesia de Santiago el Viejo* (Church of St James the Old), noted for its Romanesque tower; the *Palacio Episcopal* (Bishop's Palace) and the *Ayuntamiento* (town hall). In the 17th-century *Santuario de Santo Domingo* is a statue of the Virgen del Mar (Sea Virgin), found on the beach in 1502. A walk up the hill through the old Gothic Gates to the Alcazába brings you to a magnificent 15th-century *bell-tower* and offers sweeping views. The ramparts run along the hilltop to the ruins of an old castle on the *Cerro de San Cristóbal*.

*Take the **N340** for 30km (19 miles) to Tabernas.*

Sorbas has a wonderful setting. Houses cling to a clifftop and the village has good views all around. Cave dwellings have been found in the surrounding cliffs

Tabernas, Almería

1 The little town of Tabernas has a definite Moorish look about it, but has Roman origins. Tucked away at the foot of a hill, it lies on a vast plain between the Sierra de los Filabres and the Sierra de Alhamilla. There are remains of an old **Moorish castle**, and the **church** has a fine Mudejar coffered ceiling. The wild, desert-like landscapes in this area provided the setting for many spaghetti Westerns during the late 1960s and early 1970s, and some of the scenes for *Lawrence of Arabia* were shot around an area to the northeast, where the dunes provided an excellent location.

*Continue northeast on the **N340** for 27km (17 miles) to Sorbas.*

Sorbas, Almería

2 Sorbas rates as one of the most picturesque towns in the region. A cluster of white houses is perched on top of a high cliff that descends sharply down to the River Aguas and other small streams. The remains of an old **Moorish castle** form part of the skyline. Sorbas is noted for the pottery produced here and some of its workshops can be visited. There are a number of cave dwellings in the area.

*Continue north on the **N340**. Branch off to the right to Mojácar.*

Mojácar, Almería

3 A few kilometres from the sea is the stunning little Moorish town of

The 16th-century Moorish fortress, the Alcazába, dominates the old port of Almería

Mojácar. Its flat white buildings sprawl up a steep hill, and it holds a commanding position over the coast and surrounding plains. Its former name of Meschech-Masstia is one of the oldest known names in Spain. Of Carthaginian origin, the town appears to have been of some importance during Roman times, and strong influences remain from the Moorish occupation.

Steep, winding streets lead to the top of the village, with fine views of the sea and countryside.

Return to the N340 and continue north to Huércal-Overa, making a short detour to see the Cuevas del Almanzora cave dwellings just north of Vera, a total of 48km (30 miles).

Huércal-Overa, Almería

4 Huércal-Overa, situated in the valley of El Almanzora, is an important agricultural centre. Formerly inhabited by the Moors, the town became deserted when they were driven out of Spain. It was gradually repopulated during the 16th century. The most notable buildings in the town are the **Iglesia de Nuestra Señora de la Asunción** (Church of Our Lady of the Assumption), with a fine altar; the **Ayuntamiento** and the **Plaza de Toros** (bullring), which dates back to the beginning of this century. Embroidery features among the traditional crafts practised here.

Take the C321 north and join the N342 west for 43km (27 miles) to Vélez Rubio.

Vélez Rubio, Almería

5 Right in the middle of wild, barren landscapes lies the town of Vélez Rubio, capital of the area since the beginning of the 18th century. It is noted for its monuments of historical and artistic interest. The **Convento de San Francisco** (Convent of St Francis), the **parish church** and the **Iglesia de Nuestra Señora del Carmen** (Church of Our Lady of Carmen) are all fine examples of baroque architecture. The old hospital and the **Ayuntamiento** are also notable buildings, with many elegant private mansions from earlier centuries.

Take the C321 north for 6km (4 miles) to Vélez Blanco.

Vélez Blanco, Almería

6 Built on the slopes of a mountain, Vélez Blanco has a rich heritage, with Roman origins. Buildings of special interest include the **Iglesia de Santiago** (Church of St James), with a fine Mudejar ceiling, and the **Convento de San Luís** (Convent of St Louis), both showing Mudejar and Renaissance styles. Its chief splendour, however, is the magnificent Renaissance **castle** on top of the hill. Built in the 16th century, it overlooks the town and offers panoramic views of the surrounding landscapes. Its courtyard has found its way, strangely enough, to the Metropolitan Museum in New York.

On the outskirts of town are the **Cuevas de los Letreros**, with cave paintings showing examples of neolithic art.

SCENIC ROUTES

Areas of outstanding scenery include the stretch north of Almería through the 'Wild West' mountains around Tabernas to Sorbas (**N340**); the area around Mojácar; Mojácar north up to Vélez Rubio (**N340**, **C321** and **N342**); the approach to the Sierra de Cazorla; from Jódar (south of Úbeda) down to Moreda and beyond (**C325** and **N324**); and Guadix southeast on the **N324** nearly all the way to Almería.

SPECIAL TO ...

6 *Vélez Blanco, Almería* An unusual celebration takes place between Guadix and Baza on 6 September in honour of Nuestra Señora de la Piedad, Patron Saint of Baza. A character from Guadix (known as 'El Cascamorras') has to travel to Baza to take possession of the statue of the Virgin, enduring insults and all sorts of abuses from the people of Baza during the course of the journey.

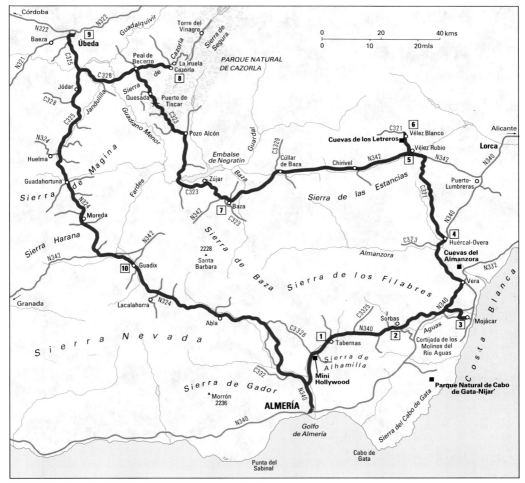

2 *Sorbas, Almería* A road southeast of Sorbas leads to the **Cortijada de los Molinos del Río Aguas**, a good point from which to explore the River Aguas, where you may find tortoises and a wonderful range of colourful flowers typical of this area. Near by are some caves in crystallised gypsum with an inner lagoon. Further along is the **Parque Natural de Cabo de Gata-Nijar**, situated in the volcanic mountain range of the Sierra del Cabo de Gata.

8 *Cazorla, Jaén* The **Parque Natural de Cazorla** (Nature Park of Cazorla) is an area of great natural beauty and of considerable ecological importance. Among its wild rugged mountains, dense forests and rivers is a wealth of wildlife, flora and fauna. The Visitors' Centre at Torredelvinagre has a small museum and presents slide shows.

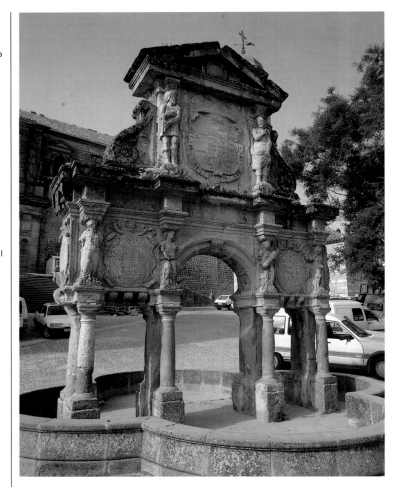

*Rejoin the **N342** and continue on this road west for 73km (45 miles) to Baza.*

Baza, Almería

7 The old Iberian settlement of Baza lies in the valley of Baza, in the heart of a fertile plain surrounded by rather barren mountains. There are some interesting archaeological sites in the area. The discovery of an Iberian stone figure of the **Dama de Baza** (Lady of Baza), excavated here in 1971, was considered a find of some importance. There are a number of buildings and monuments worth visiting. These include the 16th-century **Iglesia Colegiata** (Collegiate Church), built in the Renaissance style; the **Iglesia de Santiago** (Church of St James), also from the 16th century, with elegant Mudejar coffered ceilings; and the **Iglesia de San Juan y Los Dolores** (Church of St John and the Sorrows). Take a look also at the **Palacio de los Enriques** (Palace of the Henrys), the **Caños Dorados** fountain and the ruins of the **Alcazába** (Moorish palace). The **Iglesia de Santo Domingo** (Church of St Domingo) has fine cloisters. In the **Iglesia de la Merced** is the image of Nuestra Señora de la Piedad, the town's patron saint. Of interest, too, are the **Moorish Baths**, which have been preserved as a National Monument.

There are cave dwellings to the north of the town.

*Continue on the **N342** for a short distance before turning right on*

The Santa María Fountain, which takes the form of a triumphal arch decorated with figures, in Baeza, close to Úbeda. The town has many fine old buildings

*to the **C323** north. At Peal de Becerro take the regional road east to Cazorla.*

Cazorla, Jaén

8 Capital of the area, Cazorla is dominated by the mighty mountain ranges of the Sierra de Cazorla and Sierra de Segura. Its two attractive main squares are surrounded by fine mansions. Take a look at the ruins of the **Iglesia de Santa María** (Church of St Mary), showing the Plateresque style, and the two castles, **Castillo de las Cinco Esquinas** (Five Corners) and **La Yedra**. The town is lovely in spring, when the purple blossoms of the Judas tree are out.

Just north of Cazorla is the tiny village of **La Iruela**, perched on a high cliff, with a castle at the top. Just beyond this is the gateway to the Sierra de Cazorla and the Sierra de Segura. The area has been designated a **nature park** and provides excellent walks for serious hikers and a wonderful area for nature-lovers. There are good views of the area from here over the Valley of the Guadalquivir.

*Return to Peal de Becerro and take the **C328** westwards. Where it joins the **C325** turn right on that road to Úbeda, 48km (30 miles).*

1 *Tabernas, Almería* Children will no doubt be fascinated to visit one of the old sets of 'Mini Hollywood', and pick out such familiar sights as the bank and saloon in the reconstructions of the old Wild West towns. If you are lucky you might see a mock gunfight or a stagecoach hold-up.

Úbeda, Jaén

9 Úbeda is noted for its great palatial buildings of artistic and historic value. Considered most noteworthy among its many fine churches is the **Sacra Capilla del Salvador** (Sacred Chapel of St Salvador). Built in an elaborate Renaissance style in the 16th century, it is noted for its sculpture of the *Transfiguration* by Alonso Berruguete. The **Iglesia de Santa María** was begun in the 13th century and not completed until several centuries later. Of note inside are its lovely cloister and splendid grilles. The 13th-century **Iglesia de San Pablo** (Church of St Paul) boasts a fine portal.

The heart of the old town is the **Plaza Vázquez de Molina**, an attractive square surrounded by elegant buildings. The **Ayuntamiento** is in the **Palacio de las Cadenas** (House of Chains), named after the iron chains that were once placed around the courtyard. It is a graceful building, flanked by arcades and with an unusual 16th-century fountain built into the wall. Other buildings worth a mention are the **Montiel Palace**, the **Bishop Canastero's Mansion** (note the coat-of-arms on the outside), the **Tower Mansion**, built in the Plateresque style, and the **Palacio de los Marqueses de Mancera** (Palace of the Marquises of Mancera), formerly the property of the Viceroy of Peru. In the centre of the old **Plaza del Mercado** (market square) is a monument to San Juan de la Cruz (St John of the Cross), famous poet and mystic. He died here in the Oratory, near the Plaza, in 1591. The cell in which he died can be visited, together with a small museum, which contains relics relating to the saint.

Cave dwellings carved out of the rock near Guadix

i Oficina de Información de Turismo, Plaza de los Caídos.

*Take the **C325** south, join the **N324** south and continue on this road east to Guadix, 114km (71 miles).*

Guadix, Jaén

10 The cathedral is the most prominent structure, built in the Renaissance style and featuring a massive tower and a baroque portal. The **churches of Santiago** (St James) and **Santa Ana** (St Anne) have fine Mudejar coffered ceilings. In the upper part of the town is the **Alcazába** (Moorish palace). Other buildings of note are the **Palacio Episcopal** (Episcopal Palace) and the **Palacio Peñaflor**. The main square, **Plaza Mayor**, is a fine example of Renaissance architecture and offers an attractive view of the rooftops and the cathedral tower.

A visit to the cave dwellings, however, is probably the main objective of your visit. These are located in the **Barrio Santiago** (Santiago District) behind the town. These incredible-looking structures are hollowed out from the soft tufa rock. Some open up into further caves within, and a few are designed with two storeys. Conical chimneys protrude from the pathways above, creating an odd spectacle. Nowadays only a few of the caves are inhabited by gypsies.

*Return to Almería on the **N324**, 120km (75 miles).*

Almería – Tabernas	**30 (19)**
Tabernas – Sorbas	**27 (17)**
Sorbas – Mojácar	**34 (21)**
Mojácar – Huércal-Overa	**48 (30)**
Huércal-Overa – Vélez Rubio	**43 (27)**
Vélez Rubio – Vélez Blanco	**6 (4)**
Vélez Blanco – Baza	**73 (45)**
Baza – Cazorla	**102 (63)**
Cazorla – Úbeda	**48 (30)**
Úbeda – Guadix	**114 (71)**
Guadix – Almería	**120 (75)**

RECOMMENDED WALKS

8 *Cazorla, Jaén* The **Sierra de Cazorla** is a superb area for good walking in magnificent surroundings. It offers a wide variety of landscapes. Its rugged peaks will doubtless lure the serious hiker, while its green pine forests, lakes and river offer some gentler strolls. The park also has facilities for horse-riding and canoeing.

FOR HISTORY BUFFS

9 *Úbeda, Jaén* Literary enthusiasts may wish to make the short trip from Úbeda to Baeza (9km, 6 miles west), where the great Spanish poet Antonio Machado (1875–1939) lived from 1913 to 1919. He was known for his philosophical writing, and produced much work during his time here, as well as giving French classes. A monument stands in the large courtyard of the University in his memory.

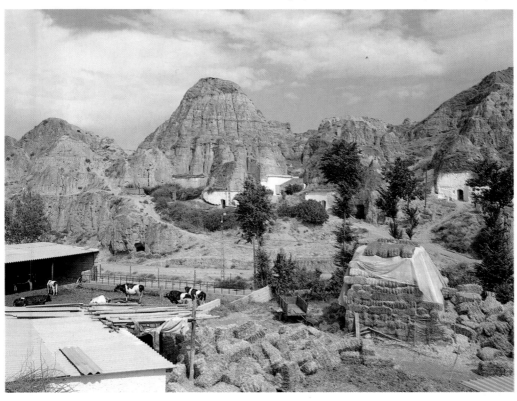

2/3 days – 347km (217 miles)

SPAIN'S MOORISH LEGACY

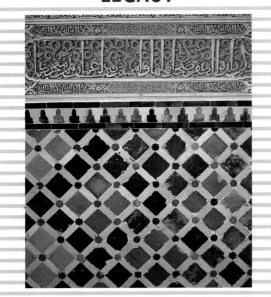

Málaga ● Vélez-Málaga ● Nerja ● Almuñécar ● Motril
Vélez de Benaudalla ● Granada ● Loja ● Antequera
Alora ● Málaga

Málaga is considered by many to be the capital of the Costa del Sol, serving as the main gateway to its famous resorts. The town was founded by the Phoenicians and was later occupied by the Carthaginians, the Romans, and then the Visigoths. In 711 the Moors arrived and stayed until 1487, when they were driven out by the Christians.

The *cathedral* was built between the 16th and 18th centuries, and has a large tower and beautifully carved choir stalls. Near by is the *Museo de Bellas Artes* (Fine Arts Museum), which contains some early works by Pablo Picasso, who was born in Málaga in 1881. The *Alcazába* (Moorish palace), now a museum, is set in attractive gardens, and magnificent views can be had from the 13th-century ramparts of the *Gibralfaro* (lighthouse).

> i Delegación Provincial de Turismo, Avenida de la Aurora.
>
> *From Málaga take the **N340** east. At Torre del Mar turn north on to the **C335** to Vélez-Málaga.*

Intricate plasterwork and glazed tiles decorate the Patio de los Arrayanes in the Alhambra, Granada

Vélez-Málaga, Málaga

1 Lying towards the end of a valley among subtropical vegetation is the little white town of Vélez-Málaga, which is thought to be of Phoenician origin. On top of the hill stands the old Moorish **Alcázar**, or castle. Take a look at the **Iglesia de Santa María la Mayor** (St Mary Major), the **Iglesia de San Juan** (St John) and the **Ayuntamiento**, once the palace of the Marquises of Veniel. Thursday is market day, which is always a colourful event.

> *Return south to and continue on the **N340** for 25km (16 miles) to Nerja.*

Nerja, Málaga

2 Its clifftop setting is one of Nerja's main attractions, with lovely views of the rocky coves below. Near the main square is a terrace with the famous **Balcón de Europa** (Balcony of Europe) lookout point over the Mediterranean, so named by King Alfonso XII when he passed in 1885.

About 2km (1½ miles) away, near the village of Maro, are the **Cuevas de Nerja**. They were discovered in 1959 and contain paintings from Palaeolithic times. The caves are impressive and well worth a visit.

> *Continue on the **N340** for 22km (14 miles) to Almuñécar.*

Almuñécar, Granada

3 This enchanting little town is a cluster of whitewashed houses sprawling up a steep hill, crowned by the remains of an old Moorish **castle**. The ancient **aqueduct** and the **Torre del Monje** (Tower of the Monk) are Roman. Also of interest is the **Cueva de los Siete Palacios** (Cave of Seven Palaces, or Vaults). The nearby beaches of La Herradura and Punta del Mar have contributed to the growth in tourism. The Punta de la Mona, near by, is a wonderful lookout post for views over the Mediterranean.

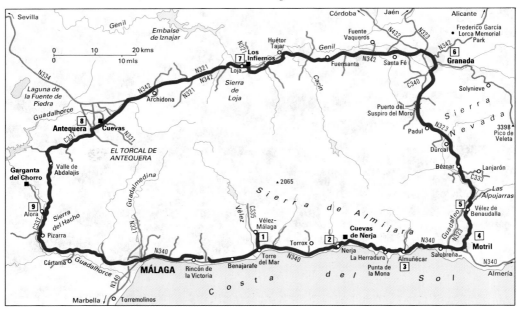

*Continue east for 21km
(13 miles) to Motril.*

Motril, Granada

4 Make a brief stop here before
continuing on the next lap of your
journey. Among its most important
buildings are the **Iglesia Colegiata de
la Encarnación** (Collegiate Church of
the Incarnation) and the **Santuario de
Nuestra Señora de la Cabeza**, said to
have been the home of the mother of
Boabdil, the last of the Moorish kings
of Granada.

*Take the regional road north for
14km (9 miles) to Vélez de
Benaudalla.*

Vélez de Benaudalla, Granada

5 This is a good place for a break
before continuing on the next stage
of the tour, which is quite some drive.
Vélez de Benaudalla is a typical
Andalucian village of sparkling white
houses and red-tiled roofs, with the
silhouette of a large hexagonal tower
and beautiful mountainous scenery
around it.

*Continue north on the regional
road for a short distance, then
turn right on to the **N323** north
for 54km (34 miles) to Granada.*

Granada, Granada

6 The city of Granada is built on three
hills: the Alhambra, the Albaicín
and the Sacromonte, dominated by
the beautiful snow-capped mountains of the Sierra Nevada. The town is
thought to have been founded by the
Iberians. The Romans and the
Visigoths were here later, and in 711 it
was conquered by the Moors. The
town was called Gharnatha and a
fortress was erected on the Alhambra
Hill. During the Reconquest it became
the last stronghold of the Moors until
2 January 1492, when the Moorish
Caliph, Emir Abdallah Mohammad XI,
known to the Spaniards as Boabdil,
the Boy King, was deposed and
handed over the keys of the city to his
Christian victors, and Moorish domination of Spain came to an end.

You can either walk up the hill to
the **Alhambra** or take the longer route
by car. The entrance is through the
Puerta de la Granadas (Gateway of
the Pomegranates), built by the
Hapsburg Emperor Charles V. A short
walk up a pathway lined by elm trees
(planted by the Duke of Wellington)
leads to the **Puerta de la Justicia**
(Gate of Justice). On the west side of
the square stands the oldest structure
of all, the Alcazába. Dating back to the
9th century, only its outer walls
remain.

To the east is the **Palacio de Carlos
V** (Palace of Emperor Charles V).
Begun in 1526 and never completed,
it was built in the classical Renaissance style in sharp contrast to the
style of architecture which character-
ises the Alhambra. Many beautiful
treasures can be seen in the two
museums here, the **Museo Provincial
de Bellas Artes** (Museum of Fine
Arts) and the **Museo de la Alhambra**
(Museum of the Alhambra), noted for
its priceless Alhambra Vase, which
dates back to 1320.

*Terraced gardens in the Alhambra
lead down to the 14th-century Torre
de las Damas, which is elegantly
porticoed*

FOR CHILDREN

1 *Vélez-Málaga, Málaga*
Located in the residential
area of El Tomillar, between
Torre del Mar and Vélez-
Málaga, is **Aqua Velis**, a
splendid new aquapark for
children, which offers 11 sorts
of aquatic delights, including
a large swimming-pool,
waterchutes and fast
kamikazes. There are also
American slopes, a spiral slide
and a children's playground.

RECOMMENDED WALKS

5 *Vélez de Benaudalla,
Granada* A road branching
off northeast from Vélez de
Benaudella leads to the region
of **Las Alpujarras** (which
stems from the Moorish 'Al-
Busherat' meaning the
grassland) and this offers
some excellent walking in
surroundings that are very
agreeable without making too
many demands on your
stamina.

SPECIAL TO...

6 *Granada, Granada* The Renaissance **Palacio de Carlos V** (Palace of Emperor Charles V) provides a beautiful setting for the **Festival of Music and Dance**, which is held here annually at the end of June/beginning of July and is recognised as an important international event. The programme includes daily concerts, ballet, guitar recitals and a number of additional events, with performances by famous artists and orchestras.

FOR HISTORY BUFFS

6 *Granada, Granada* The small town of **Santa Fé** (8km, 5 miles west of Granada) was the scene of two great historical events, the signing of the surrender of Granada in November 1491, and the signing, on 17 April 1492, of the 'Capitulaciones', agreements with Christopher Columbus that paved the way for his first voyage of discovery across the ocean.

A few kilometres away is the village of **Fuente Vaqueros**, where the famous Spanish poet Federico García Lorca was born in 1899 and his former home is now a museum. The **Federico García Lorca Memorial Park**, between Viznar and Alfacar (northeast of Granada) marks the place where he is said to have been shot in 1936.

To the north is the masterpiece itself, the **Alcázar**, or **Casa Real** (Royal Palace). Started in 1334 and completed by the end of 1391, it is a remarkable architectural achievement, characterised by the rich and elaborate decorations. Entrance is through the **Patio del Mexuar** (Mexuar Court), formerly the council chamber and later used as a chapel, which leads to the lovely **Patio de los Arrayanes** (Court of the Myrtle Trees). Adjoining this is the **Sala de los Embajadores** (Hall of the Ambassadors). Originally used as a throne room for the Moorish kings, it is noted for its rich decorations and magnificent domed ceiling. The Mozárabes Gallery leads to the splendid **Patio de los Leones** (Court of Lions), a main feature of the palace and old heart of the harem. Chambers leading off from here include the **Sala de los Abencerrajes** (Abencerrajes Gallery) to the south, with an impressive stalactite ceiling and a marble fountain; and the **Sala de los Reyes** (King's Chamber) to the east, noted for its alcove paintings of historical scenes. The **Sala de las dos Hermanas** (Hall of the Two Sisters), on the north side, features an intricately decorated honeycomb dome. This leads, in turn, to the **Sala de los Ajimeces** (Ajimeces Gallery) and on to the **Mirador de Daraxa**, a charming little lookout balcony. The **Patio de Daraxa** (Daraxa Courtyard) is a lovely inner courtyard with cypresses and orange trees.

More galleries and patios may be visited before you make your way to the Generalife, set in lovely gardens on the Cerro del Sol (Hill of the Sun). The **Palacio del Generalife** was completed in 1319 and served as the summer residence of the Moorish kings. The **Patio de la Acequia** (Canal Court) is planted with roses, laurels and orange trees. The surrounding gardens are laid out in Italian style and exude an air of romance. Allow time to explore the town itself, which is delightful. The heart of the city is a large square called **Plaza de Isabel la Católica**. Here stands a monument to commemorate the Santa Fé Agreement of 1492 made between Isabel la Católica and Columbus. The 19th-century **Ayuntamiento** stands in the smaller Plaza del Carmen. Near by is the 18th-century **Palacio Arzobispal** (Archbishop's Palace). A little further on is the **Catedral de Santa María de la Encarnación** (St Mary of the Incarnation). Begun in 1523 and consecrated in 1561, it stands as a memorial to the victory of Christianity in Spain. It has a richly decorated interior and a fine **Capilla Mayor** (Main Chapel), which is noted for its high dome and beautiful stained glass window. Other buildings of interest include the **Carthusian Monastery**, the **Audiencia** (Law Court), the 16th-century **Iglesia de Santa Ana** and the **Casa de Castríl**, which houses the **Museo Arqueológico** (Archaeological Museum). On the right bank of the Darro ravine is the old Moorish quarter, the **Albaicín**, where a wander around its narrow, cobblestone streets and hidden corners recaptures the past. Behind the Albaicín is the Sacromonte Hill, where the gypsies live in caves and put on flamenco shows.

Beware when the bullfight is on. All streets become one-way, leading right to the bullring, where you might find yourself inadvertently spending the rest of the day!

i Casa de los Tiros, Pavaneras 19

*Take the **N342** west for 52km (32 miles) to Loja.*

Loja, Granada

7 Located in the west of the province of Granada is the small town of Loja, which is dominated by the ruins of an old Moorish castle. Buildings of interest in the town include the 15th-century **Iglesia de la Encarnación** (Church of the Incarnation), the 16th-century **Iglesia de San Gabriel** (St Gabriel) and the **Convento de Santa Clara** (Convent and Church of Santa Clara), which has a fine Mudejar ceiling. Take a look also at the **Ayuntamiento**, the **Granary**, the **Hospital de la Misericordia** and the old **Alcazába** (fortress) that overlooks the town.

In the vicinity enjoy two lovely waterfalls, the **Colas de Caballo** (Horsetail Falls) and **Los Infiernos** (Hell), which cascades into the River Genil.

*Continue on the **N342** west towards Antequera turning off left to the town shortly after passing Archidona.*

Antequera, Málaga

8 The discovery of prehistoric dolmen caves in the area of Antequera gave evidence of this market town's ancient origins. The old **castle** on top of the hill was the first fortress to be taken by the Christians (in 1410) during the reconquest of Spain, although it was later recaptured by the Moors. There is a fine view across the plains from its ramparts, which

Granada is set in the middle of the plain of the Río Genil. The soil here is fertile, but the river is often dry in the summer

have been well preserved. Close to the castle is the 16th-century Renaissance **Colegiata de Santa María la Mayor** (St Mary Major), noted for its Mudejar ceiling. The churches of **San Sebastián** and **St Augustín** feature prominent Mudejar belfries and the churches of **El Carmen** and **los Remedios** have richly decorated baroque interiors. Note too the impressive **Arch of Los Gigantes** (the Giants). If you pay a visit to the **Museo Municipal** (Municipal Museum), look out for the large bronze statue of the Roman boy called Efebo.

The **cuevas** (dolmen caves) are located off the Granada road; take a left turn. These prehistoric caves served as funeral monuments in neolithic times and have great historical significance.

*Take the **C337** southwest for 39km (24 miles) to Alora, which lies slightly off the road.*

Alora, Málaga

9 Alora stands high above the River Guadalhorce in an area of olive, orange and lemon groves. This charming town features the ruins of an old **castle**, a 17th-century **parish church** with an unusual wooden roof and a few fine buildings.

*Go back to the **C337**, turn right and return to Málaga.*

Málaga – Vélez-Málaga **37 (23)**
Vélez-Málaga – Nerja **25 (16)**
Nerja – Almuñécar **22 (14)**
Almuñécar – Motril **21 (13)**
Motril – Vélez de Benaudalla **14 (9)**
Vélez de Benaudalla – Granada **54 (34)**
Granada – Loja **52 (32)**
Loja – Antequera **43 (27)**
Antequera – Alora **39 (24)**
Alora – Málaga **40 (25)**

SCENIC ROUTES

Solynieve is a winter resort in the Sierra Nevada that has been developed recently and offers excellent facilities for winter sports, normally under a brilliant blue sky. The area is reached by a very winding mountainous road southeast of Granada in beautiful scenery. A further drive takes you along one of the highest roads in Europe to the **Pico de Veleta**, second-highest peak in the Sierra Nevada. The area is of particular beauty in spring when the place is a fairyland of pink blossoms.

BACK TO NATURE

8 *Antequera, Málaga* Some 15km (9 miles) south of Antequera is **El Torcal de Antequera**, an area of deep ravines, where great limestone boulders have formed bizarre shapes, suggesting a petrified forest. It is rich in plant life, including the Spanish bluebell, rare species of iris and a number of different types of orchid. Twenty-four kilometres (15 miles) northwest of Antequera, off the **N334**, is the **Laguna de la Fuente de Piedra**, Andalucia's largest lake and an important breeding ground of flamingos. Other species of birds seen here include black-headed gulls, mallards, red-crested pochards and even the occasional white stork.

3 days – 403km (250 miles)

THE SUN COAST & MEDIEVAL VILLAGES

Málaga ● Torremolinos ● Benalmádena-Pueblo ● Mijas
Fuengirola ● Marbella ● Puerto Banús ● Casares
San Roque ● La Línea ● Castellar de la Frontera
Jimena de la Frontera ● Ronda ● Coín ● Málaga

A pleasant feature of Málaga is its lively harbour, and an enjoyable pastime is a stroll along the seafront promenade, or *Paseo Marítimo*. A good place in which to linger over a drink is the *Plaza de la Marina*, and the tree-lined *Paseo del Parque* (Park Walk), which leads away from the square, offers another agreeable stroll. Take a morning walk to the nearby *Mercado* (market hall), which is full of hustle and bustle when the fresh catch of the day comes in. The *old quarter* has narrow, twisting streets and plenty of old bodegas (wine vaults); Málaga is known for its production of sweetish wines from the muscatel grape.

ⓘ Calle Marques de Larios 5

Take the N340 for 13km (8 miles) along the coast to Torremolinos, turning left into the town.

SCENIC ROUTES

Although many stretches of the coast road are dominated by modern high-rise blocks, the sea views and dramatic silhouette of the mountains in the hinterland make up for a lot of shortcomings. The drive to Mijas and back through attractive pine-clad mountain scenery offers lovely views of the coast. The winding mountain road up to Casares is also very attractive. From San Roque the inland road becomes very winding as it approaches Jimena de la Frontera (on the **C3331**), followed by the dramatic landscapes of the Serranía de Ronda, with its wild, eroded rock formations.

Local transport in the colourful village of Mijas provides an entertaining method of sightseeing

Torremolinos, Málaga

1 Like it or hate it, make a stop here just to have a look at the famous Torremolinos, which marks the beginning of the Costa del Sol. It started in the 19th century as a tiny fishing village, with towers (*torres*) and windmills (*molinos*) in the vicinity. Torremolinos was one of the first places to cater for mass tourism, and appeals particularly to youngsters. Its beaches are of fine grit and have facilities for watersports.

One of its more agreeable areas, however, is the **Carihuela** district, which has a lively pedestrian esplanade with many bars, cafés and a reputation for good fish restaurants. On Sundays you will find many Spanish families here, out for a walk with their children.

Continue along the coast road for a short distance to Benalmádena Costa. Turn right for 4km (2½ miles) to Benalmádena-Pueblo, a total of 9km (6 miles).

Benalmádena-Pueblo, Málaga

2 Benalmádena Costa is a popular resort, with beaches, and impressive yacht harbour, a casino and golf club. A short drive inland leads to Benalmádena-Pueblo, a delightful Andalucian village dating back to the Phoenicians, Romans and Moors. At Arroyo de la Miel, near by, you can see the remains of an old **Roman arch**, which was once the entrance to a building known as El Tribunal (Tribune). A local **museum** displays many archaeological finds from the area.

Continue on the regional road west for 8km (5 miles) to Mijas.

Mijas, Málaga

3 The little town of Mijas is so picturesque that it was quickly 'discovered' by tourists, with all the inevitable changes that come about as a result. The village is still appealing, however, with pretty whitewashed

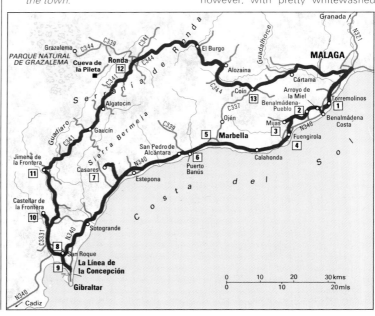

houses, tiny winding streets and brightly coloured flowers everywhere. There are wonderful views down to the coastline far below. Renowned as a **crafts centre**, it specialises in ceramics and basket-weaving.

Take the regional road south for 7km (4 miles) to Fuengirola.

Fuengirola, Málaga

4 Fuengirola has also changed beyond recognition, from a sleepy fishing port to a resort of high-rise blocks. It has extensive beaches, bars, restaurants, lively evening entertainment, and attracts the crowds in the summer. In recent years it has also become a favoured winter retreat for retired people, particularly from more northern climes, with a tendency towards British domination. Culture is minimal here; however, you can always take a look at the ruins of the **Castillo de Sohail**, an old castle first erected in the 10th century.

*Continue on the **N340** for 27km (17 miles) to Marbella.*

Marbella, Málaga

5 Marbella is the centre of the Costa del Sol, although the name is often applied to an area extending for some distance on either side of the town. The description 'playground of the rich' refers to the jetsetters and pop stars who stay in luxurious surroundings and frequent the smart restaurants and nightspots to be found along this part of the coast. The appearance of tall, modern blocks over the years has inevitably changed Marbella's skyline and character. However, it still has some attractive areas, including its busy harbour, where large yachts are moored. It has a pleasant seafront promenade with open-air bars and restaurants.

On a clear day Africa is faintly visible, while at the end of the coastline is the unmistakable outline of the **Rock of Gibraltar**. Its real delight, however, is the old town behind the main street, with its narrow streets, whitewashed houses and flower-decked balconies. These open out on to the **Plaza de los Naranjos** (Square of Oranges), an enchanting square trimmed with orange trees and surrounded by restaurants and elegant boutiques. A walk along the old fortifications overlooks the area, with the old Moorish **castle** way above.

Eight kilometres (5 miles) inland, the pretty little town of **Ojén** is reached by a winding road. It has a pleasant 16th- to 18th-century **church**, a beautifully laid-out Andalucian cemetery, and is well known for its pottery.

ⓘ Avenida Miguel Cano 1, Marbella

Continue for a short distance along the coast road. Branch off to Puerto Banús, 7km (4 miles).

Puerto Banús, Málaga

6 This short stretch between Marbella and Banús, known as the **Golden**

The medieval village of Casares spreads across a hilltop and is overlooked by the ruins of an old Moorish castle

FOR CHILDREN

The **Atlantis Aquapark** in Torremolinos (1) has a variety of attractions, as does the **Aquatic Park** of Mijas, located just outside Fuengirola (4). **Tivoli World Amusement**, in Arroyo de la Miel, Benalmádena-Pueblo (2), caters for all sorts of activities, including a giant roller-coaster, open-air entertainments galore and some water sports. The **zoo** in Fuengirola (4) has a great variety of animals and reptiles.

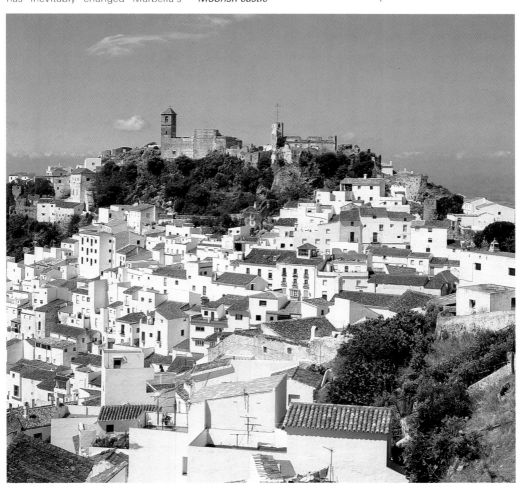

12 *Ronda, Málaga* A few kilometres west of Ronda is the **Parque Natural de Grazalema**, a vast wilderness reputed to be one of the wettest spots in Spain, known for its forest of a rare species of fir (pinsapos). The charming village of Grazalema is a good base from which to make excursions. There is plenty to interest birdwatchers, who may spot owls, eagles, blue rock thrush and chaffinch among many species to be seen here. Botanists can look out for rare species of plants, such as the poppy and yellow-flowered knapwood. Look out, too, for the *'maquis'*, which grows among the scrub forest.

12 *Ronda, Málaga* The **Parque Natural de Grazalema** also offers good walking. Specific routes are laid out for serious hikers, who can obtain information from the park wardens.

If you want the best shots of the famous Puente Nuevo bridge over the gorge, take your camera and steel yourself for a short scramble down the hillside, where you will be rewarded by the famous view that is always associated with Ronda. Take care how you go, however, as it is a steepish climb there and back.

12 *Ronda, Málaga* The bullring in Ronda was built in 1785 and is one of the oldest and most famous in Spain. Modern bullfighting was determined by the rules that were laid down here by Francisco Romero, whose grandson Pedro Romero became one of Spain's best-known bullfighters. The **Bullfighting Museum** beneath the ring has posters of the earliest fights that took place, as well as other memorabilia. Bullfights are normally held in Ronda only during its major festivals in May and September.

12 *Ronda, Málaga* The **Cueva de la Pileta** (Pileta Caves), some 27km (17 miles) southwest of Ronda, are of great interest for their prehistoric paintings of animals in shades of red and black and drawings of huge fish, believed to go back some 25,000 years. The paintings have been found to bear some resemblance to those in the Altamira Caves in northern Spain.

Mile, is one of the most attractive parts of the Costa del Sol, with luxurious properties set in lovely gardens. The area is lush and green, with tropical flowers and vegetation, framed by the dramatic silhouette of the mountains in the background. Puerto Banús was created as a marina for Marbella, resulting in an Andalucian-type village of white houses lining a busy yacht harbour, similar to the concept of Port Grimaud in the south of France. Bars, restaurants and boutiques sprang up and it became a very 'in' resort, with many international yachts moored in the harbour. The place has seen many additions in recent years. One to notice is an incredible Mosque-like structure with gleaming turrets and a marble exterior, looking like something from the *Arabian Nights*, built as apartments.

Continue along the N340 coast road. Just past Estepona take a right turn to Casares, around 20km (12 miles) from the turnoff.

Casares, Málaga

7 This detour takes you inland to the Sierra Bermeja and, although it means returning to the coast by the same route, you will not regret it when you catch your first glimpse of Casares on the hill high above you. This old medieval village is, without a doubt, one of the most attractive in the area. A gentle stroll up the steep, winding streets leads to the ruins of its old Moorish **castle**, which holds a commanding position over the surrounding mountains and valleys below. Take a look at the two main churches, the **parish church** and the **Iglesia de San Sebastián**, both 18th-century. On the way up the hill is the cemetery, beautifully laid out and adorned with flowers in typical Andalucian style.

Return to the N340 and continue for 44km (27 miles) to San Roque.

San Roque, Cádiz

8 The little town of San Roque was founded in the 18th century by Spanish inhabitants of Gibraltar, who left after it was taken by the British in 1704. The town is situated on a low hill, with pleasant views all round. Main buildings of interest include the **Iglesia de Santa María** and the **Palacio de los Gobernadores** (Palace of the Governors).

Take the N351 for 7km (4 miles) to La Línea de la Concepción.

La Línea, Cádiz

9 La Línea de la Concepción stands at the foot of the Rock of Gibraltar and is the border town between Spain and the British colony of Gibraltar. Having been closed for many years, the frontier is now open for travel between the two countries. Whether or not you decide to visit the Rock, it is worth making the drive to get a close look at this gigantic piece of rock silhouetted against the sky, an impressive sight and a famous landmark of the whole coast.

Return to San Roque and take the N340 west for 3km (2 miles)

before turning right on to the C3331 north to Castellar de la Frontera, which lies 7km (4 miles) off this road on an unclassified road.

Castellar de la Frontera, Cádiz

10 Your route now takes you into the hinterland of southern Spain, where you can enjoy some superb mountain scenery, combined with visits to some of Andalucia's famous white towns.

Castellar de la Frontera is one of these lovely old walled cities, crowned by a large Moorish **castle**. Its white houses, red-tiled roofs and surrounding forests all add to its attractions. Ancient walls dating back to the 13th century enclose the old part of town, which has tiny streets and pretty squares.

Return to and continue north on the C3331 for 29km (18 miles) to Jimena de la Frontera.

Jimena de la Frontera, Cádiz

11 The little town of Jimena de la Frontera is also an attractive cluster of whitewashed houses built up a hillside. It was under Moorish occupation for a considerable time and has a well-preserved **castle** from that period, reached through a triple-arched gateway. The town's two main churches are **La Misericordia** (Gothic style) and the baroque church of **La Coronada**, which has a splendid collection of images. You might take a look at the 15th-century Franciscan **convent**.

Take the C341 northeast for 62km (39 miles) to Ronda.

Ronda, Málaga

12 Ronda is well known for its spectacular setting, in particular the dramatic view of the bridge over the gorge of the River Guadalevín, which splits the town in two. It lies on the edge of the Serranía de Ronda, against a backdrop of sheer rock. Its unique situation, together with its attractive old quarter and historic interest, make it a fascinating place to visit. It is one of the oldest towns in Spain and a long-time capital of an independent Moorish kingdom, falling to the Catholics in 1485. In the new part of town is one of the oldest bullrings in Spain. There are magnificent views from here of the deep river valley and rugged splendours of the Serranía de Ronda. Across the famous **Puente Nuevo** bridge is La Ciudad, the old part. The bridge was built between 1775 and 1793 and is an outstanding architectural achievement. The old town is a maze of narrow, twisting streets and houses. It also offers many historic places to visit. The **Colegiata de Santa María la Mayor** (Collegiate Church of St Mary) was originally a Moorish mosque, and now serves as the cathedral of Ronda. The Moorish **Alcazába** was destroyed by the French at the beginning of the 19th century, and the **Puerta de Almocobar** (Moorish gates) were entered by the victorious Ferdinand with his troops in 1485. The **Casa del Rey Moro** (House of the Moorish King) is a beautiful old mansion with lovely terraced gardens. A long flight of steps from here runs

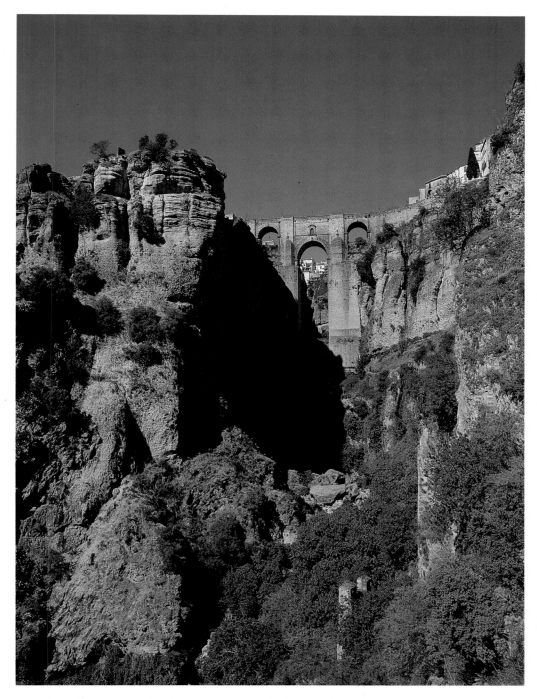

The village of Ronda is perched on top of a plateau, and is divided in two by the gorge of the River Guadalevín

down the rocks to the river far below. The **Casa de Mondragon** (House of Mondragon), taken over by Ferdinand and Isabella after their victory in 1485, has been turned into an exhibition centre.

> *Take the **C344** for 75km (47 miles) to Coín.*

Coín, Málaga

13 Coín is a good place for a break on the last part of the return to Málaga. Situated in the Valley of Orange Blossoms, this is a typical Andalucian market town of white-washed houses and pretty squares, known for its colourful Saturday market.

*Leave by the **C344** and almost immediately branch off left on a minor road which leads northeast towards Cártama. Cross over the Río Guadalhorce and turn right for Málaga, 37km (23 miles).*

Málaga – Torremolinos **15 (9)**
Torremolinos – Benalmádena-Pueblo **9 (6)**
Benalmádena-Pueblo – Mijas **8 (5)**
Mijas – Fuengirola **7 (4)**
Fuengirola – Marbella **27 (17)**
Marbella – Puerto Banus **7 (4)**
Puerto Banus – Casares **49 (30)**
Casares – San Roque **44 (27)**
San Roque – La Línea **7 (4)**
La Línea – Castellar de la Frontera **27 (17)**
Castellar de la Frontera – Jimena de la Frontera **29 (18)**
Jimena de la Frontera – Ronda **62 (39)**
Ronda – Coín **75 (47)**
Coín – Málaga **37 (23)**

2/3 days – 428km (267 miles)

THE GREAT MOSQUE & MOORISH TOWNS

Sevilla ● Carmona ● Écija ● Córdoba ● Baena
Priego de Córdoba ● Cabra ● Lucena ● Estepa
Osuna ● Sevilla

Capital of Andalucia and Spain's fourth-largest city, Sevilla stands on the banks of the River Guadalquivir, with the beautiful *Torre del Oro* (Golden Tower) standing out as a landmark. Believed to have Iberian or Phoenician origins, the town flourished under the Romans, was later ruled by the Visigoths and was taken over by the Moors in 712. In 1248 it fell to Ferdinand III of Castille. The discovery of America brought the city fame, as Columbus returned there from his expedition in 1493. In 1936, Sevilla was a launching pad for Nationalists in the Spanish Civil War.

The *Giralda* stands out as Sevilla's most prominent feature. It was first built in the 12th century as the minaret of the Great Mosque; the large revolving bronze statue of Faith, added later, acts as a weather vane (*giraldillo*), from which its name is derived. The Gothic *cathedral* contains the tombs of Christopher Columbus and St Ferdinand of Spain; and the *Palace of the Alcázar* was built by Pedro the Cruel (1350–69) on the site of a 12th-century Moorish fortress.

[i] Avenida de la Constitución 21

From Sevilla take the NIV east for 32km (20 miles) to Carmona.

A profusion of fruit on an orange tree in a back street of Córdoba. The city is known for its flower-decked streets and patios, whitewashed houses and narrow streets

Carmona, Sevilla

1 The town of Carmona stands on the highest point of a flat plain. It has an old Moorish **fortress**, which holds a commanding position over the town and offers good views of the countryside. Carmona is a delightful little town and has two old entrance gates, known as the Córdoba Gate and Sevilla Gate.

The **Iglesia de Santa María de la Asunción** (Church of St Mary of the Assumption) is 15th-century late Gothic, and you can see the remaining patio of the Great Mosque on whose foundations the church was erected. The 16th-century **Iglesia de San Salvador** is built in the Churrigueresque style; the baroque **Iglesia de Clara** has a magnificently decorated interior, and the **Santuario** (Sanctuary, 1525–51) is notable for the retable adorning the high altar. The **Ayuntamiento** (town hall) is attractively decorated with Roman mosaics.

A Roman **Necropolis** is located west of the town. This network of underground tombs was hewn from the rock and arranged in groups, with a crematorium at the front. Look out for the tomb known as *El Elefante* for its unusual carving of a young elephant.

Continue northeast on the NIV for 55km (34 miles) to Écija.

Écija, Sevilla

2 The ancient town of Écija lies at the end of a small basin on the banks of the River Genil. Thought to date back to Greek times, it was known to the Romans as *Astigi* and excavations and excavations of pottery, mosaics and other items have given some insight into its early history. Its baroque belfries, decorated with colourful tiles, can be seen from quite a distance and are an attractive feature of the town. The **Iglesia de Santiago** (St James) is entered through an attractive 18th-century patio and has interesting Mudejar windows from a former structure. A fine Gothic retable adorns the high altar.

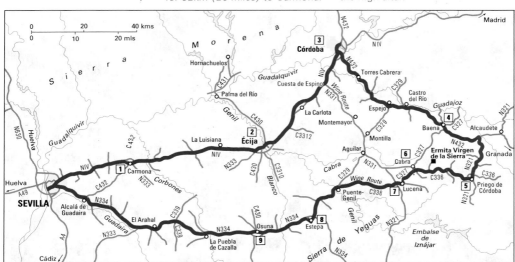

RECOMMENDED WALK

2 *Écija, Sevilla* A detour north of Écija takes you to the village of **Hornachuelos**, which is on the edge of a large game-hunting area. This stretches away to the north of the region and offers some excellent walking.

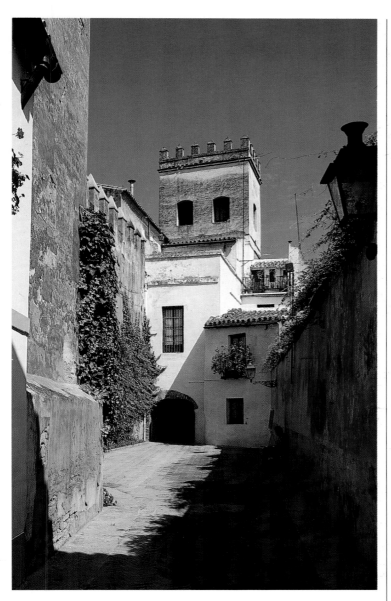

A wander through the cool, quiet streets of the old quarter of Sevilla can provide relief from the bustling pace of the city

Several handsome 18th-century palaces in the town include the **Palacio Benamejí**, with its large gateway in front; the **Palacio Peñaflor**, decorated with paintings on the outside, and the **Palacio Valdehermoso**, which has a fine Renaissance exterior.

*Continue on the **NIV** northeast for 54km (34 miles) to Córdoba.*

Córdoba, Córdoba

3 Córdoba is sited on a plain leading down to the River Guadalquivir. Overlooked by the Sierra de Córdoba, Córdoba suffers from extremes of climate, with very hot summers and cold weather during the winter.

Already quite prominent when the Romans arrived, the town continued to flourish and in 152BC became the capital of Hispana Ulterior. It developed into a prosperous city under the Moors and gained recognition as an important cultural and artistic centre of the western world. The town fell to the Catholic King Ferdinand in 1436, having long been used by various Christian leaders as a centre for plotting the retaking of Granada from the Moors. It was here that Christopher Columbus was granted the commission by Queen Isabella for his first exploratory expedition to the New World.

The great **Mezquita** (mosque) was constructed by the Moors between the 8th and 10th centuries. It is one of the largest mosques in the world and is a remarkable achievement of Moorish architecture in Spain. Its beauty lies in its interior. As you enter you are confronted by hundreds of columns made of onyx, marble and other materials. They are designed to catch the light, forming myriad colours. The columns are topped by capitals and crowned with striking red-and-white-striped arches, typical of Moorish art. An important feature of a mosque is the Mihrab, hollowed out from the wall, where Muslims come to pray. They are always built to face Mecca in the east, although this one points more south than east, due to a miscalculation. From 1436 onwards, when Córdoba was taken by the Christians, the mosque was used as a cathedral.

FOR CHILDREN

3 *Córdoba, Córdoba* Children can enjoy a visit to the **zoo** in Córdoba, which has a wide variety of animals, with an unusual visitor in the form of a beautiful black lion. Another treat for them could be a tour around town in one of the elegant *calendrias* (horse-drawn carriages) that are for hire.

FOR HISTORY BUFFS

3 *Córdoba, Córdoba* On the **N432** between Córdoba and Baena is the small town of **Castro del Río**, where Spain's famous author, Miguel Cervantes, was imprisoned for a time in 1592. You can take a look at his old prison, which is housed in the Ayuntamiento. The town also features the ruins of an ancient **castle** and a **Roman bridge**.

old Moorish battlements. The Gothic **Iglesia de Santa María la Mayor** dates back to the 16th century and is noted for its lateral aisle. The **Convento de la Madre de Dios** (Convent of the Mother of God) was built in the Mudejar style and features an interesting carved retable.

> *Continue southeast on the **N432**. Close to the River Guadajoz turn south on the **N321** to Priego de Córdoba.*

Priego de Córdoba, Córdoba

5 Priego de Córdoba is one of the region's little gems. Its dazzling white houses, flower-decked windows and tiny, winding streets give it a very Moorish look. Elegant 17th- and 18th-century mansions reflect former times when Priego was the centre of thriving silk and textile industries. Several churches are masterpieces of fine baroque architecture. Among them, the churches of **La Asunción** and **La Aurora** are noted for their wonderful baroque interiors. An abundance of springs here has resulted in the construction of the splendid **Fuente del Rey** (Fountain of the King).

Alcalá Zamora, first president of the Second Republic of Spain (1931–6), was born here in 1877. You can visit his former home, which is now a museum (**Museo de Niceto Alcalá Zamora**). A viewpoint from El Adrave, high up on the hill, shows the fertile lands around and distant mountains.

> *Take the **C336** west to Cabra, turning right on to the **C327** for 2km (1 mile) to reach the town.*

Cabra, Córdoba

6 A pleasant park welcomes you as you enter Cabra. The **Parque del Fuente del Río** (Park of the Source of the River) refers to the River Cabra. The town is yet another Andalucian delight, with its white houses, red-tiled roofs and old narrow streets. Buildings of interest include the baroque **Iglesia de la Asunción**, which features a mosque-like interior, and the old **Iglesia de San Juan Bautista**, which dates back to the time of the Visigoths. The old castle is now a college for a religious order.

> *Take the **C327** southwest for 11km (7 miles) to Lucena, which lies just off the road.*

Lucena, Córdoba

7 Lying at the foot of the Sierra de Arcos is the attractive little town of Lucena, regional capital of this southern part of the province. The town is renowned for furniture-making, bronze and copperware. Churches of major interest are the 15th-century Renaissance **Iglesia de San Matéo**, the **Iglesia de Santiago** and the **Convento de San Francisco**. Lucena was the scene of the capture of the boy-king Boabdil, last of the Moorish rulers, by the Count of Cabra in 1483, during an unsuccessful revolt against the Christians.

SCENIC ROUTES

The first part of the journey takes you through the fertile plains of the Guadalquivir valley, with patches of yellow and green fields relieved by olive groves and gently rolling hills, offering pleasant rather than remarkable scenery. There is a very scenic stretch between Priego de Córdoba and Cabra on the **C336**, and some attractive scenery round Lucena.

SPECIAL TO...

6 *Cabra, Córdoba* A turn to the right just before Cabra leads to **El Picacho** and the **Ermita Virgen de la Sierra** (Shrine of the Virgin of the Mountains), which contains the much-venerated image of the Patron Saint of Cabra. Several *romerias* are held over the year.

The province of Córdoba has quite a reputation for wines and enthusiasts can follow the **Ruta del Vino** (Wine Route) by leaving Córdoba on the **NIV** and travelling southwest to Montemayor and ultimately Montilla. You can visit many of the wine cellars, which offer a number of different sherry-type wines.

The **Patio de los Naranjos** (Court of Orange Trees) is particularly attractive in spring when it is filled with the fragrance of orange blossom. Through the **Puerta del Perdón** (Gate of Forgiveness) a flight of steps leads up to the baroque **Campanario** (bell tower). It provides a superb view of the rooftops of Córdoba and the sweep of the River Guadalquivir.

The **Museo Arqueológico** (Archaeological Museum) and the **Museo de Bellas Artes** (Fine Arts Museum) have interesting exhibits of sculptures and Roman antiquities in the first case, and a fine collection of paintings in the latter. Those with an interest in bullfighting should visit the **Museo Taurino** (Museum of Bullfighting). A statue of the famous Spanish bullfighter, Manolete, stands in the Plaza San Marina de las Aguas.

The **Zoco** (from the old Arab *souk*) has displays of handicrafts and occasional flamenco performances.

ℹ️ Plaza de Juda Levi 3

> *Take the **N432** southeast for 61km (38 miles) to Baena.*

Baena, Córdoba

4 The route continues through some of Andalucia's delightful *pueblos blancos*, or white towns. While sharing many common characteristics, each has its own character and style.

Baena is an oil-producing town and is typically Andalucian. A cluster of whitewashed houses climbs up a slope, dominated by the remains of

About 2km (1 mile) west of the town take the **C338** for 45km (28 miles) to Estepa.

Estepa, Córdoba

8 Estepa is known throughout Spain for its excellent confectionery, especially its typical Christmas cakes known as *mantecados* and *polvorones*. The town lies among farmlands and has the typical Andalucian look. Monuments include the churches of **Santa María la Mayor**, **La Asunción** and **Los Remedios**. The 18th-century **Palacio de los Marqueses de Cerverales** (Palace of the Marquises of Cerverales) is worth a look, along with the Gothic interior of the old castle keep and the splendid **Torre de la Victoria** (Tower of Victory), which is all that remains of a former convent. There is a good view of the area from a nearby lookout-point called **El Balcón de Andalucía**.

Take the **N334** west for 24km (15 miles) to Osuna.

Osuna, Córdoba

9 Osuna's history dates back to the time of the Iberians. Occupation by the Romans was followed by the

---

The interior of the mosque at Córdoba, one of the largest mosques in the world

Moors until 1239, when the town was captured by Ferdinand III. Of the many fine monuments to be seen here, special mention must be made of the **Colegiata** (Collegiate Church), an elegant Renaissance building from the 16th century, that houses some valuable works of art. **La Universidad** (University) is another noteworthy building from the same period, with two circular towers built like minarets. The main churches of interest are those of **San Agustín**, **La Merced** (17th-century) and **La Victoria**. The **Casa de los Cepeda**, the **Palacio del Cabildo Colegial** and the **Palacio de la Antigua Audiencia** are noted for their elegant façades and stand out among the many fine mansions and palaces to be seen here. The **Museo Arqueológico** (Archaeological Museum) is housed in the old Torre de Agua (Water Tower).

Return to Sevilla west on the **N334**, 90km (56 miles).

Sevilla – Carmona **32 (20)**
Carmona – Écija **55 (34)**
Écija – Córdoba **54 (34)**
Córdoba – Baena **61 (38)**
Baena – Priego de Córdoba **29 (18)**
Priego de Córdoba – Cabra **27 (17)**
Cabra – Lucena **11 (7)**
Lucena – Estepa **45 (28)**
Estepa – Osuna **24 (15)**
Osuna – Sevilla **90 (56)**

BACK TO NATURE

6 *Cabra, Córdoba* Located around Aguilar de la Frontera, northwest of Cabra, is a series of salt-water lakes, **Lagunas de Córdoba**, which are inhabited by many different species of waterfowl in the winter. An attractive and rare visitor is the white-headed duck, with its lovely blue bill. Other species include the mallard, tufted duck, red-crested pochard and marsh harrier. Some of the lakes shrink or dry up during the long hot summers, but fill up again with water after the rains and attract many birds. Flamingos and shelduck inhabit the Laguna del Salobral, the largest of the lakes.

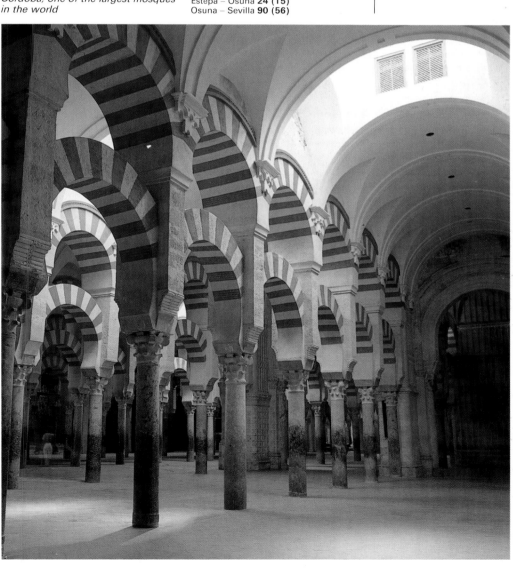

3 days – 353km (218 miles)

THE TRAIL OF THE NEW WORLD EXPLORERS

Sevilla ● Santiponce ● Itálica ● Aracena ● Cortegana
Zalamea la Real ● Valverde del Camino ● Gibraleón
Huelva ● Monasterio de la Rábida ● Moguer ● Niebla
La Palma del Condado ● Sevilla

Sevilla's two major art museums are the *Museo del Bellas Artes* (Fine Arts Museum) and the *Museo de Arte Contemporaneo* (Museum of Contemporary Arts). The former is set in the old Merced Monastery and has an outstanding collection of Spanish works. The latter is housed in the former chapel of the Cathedral Chapter of Sevilla. Two further museums of importance are located in the large *Parque de María Luisa* (Maria Luisa Park). Housed in the *Palacio del Renacimiento* (Renaissance Palace), which was erected for the Exhibition of 1929–30, is the *Museo Arqueológico* (Archaeological Museum); and opposite is the *Museo de Artes y Costumbres Populares* (Museum of Folklore).

Sevilla's parks and gardens show varying influences; the beautiful gardens of the *Alcázar* have sections from Moorish to Renaissance times; and the *María Luisa*, originally laid out in British style, was redesigned by the French architect Forestier, who gave it a more Spanish flavour.

The town of Aracena is built in tiers up a hillside, among plantations of olives, figs and almonds. It is a popular health resort

[i] Avenida de la Constitución 21

From Sevilla take the motorway west over the river. Turn right on to the N630 for 8km (5 miles) to Santiponce.

Santiponce, Sevilla

1 A major feature of Santiponce is the former **Monasterio de San Isidro del Campo** (St Isidore in the Fields), which was founded in 1298 by Alfonso Guzmán as a Cistercian house. Guzmán, known as 'El Bueno' (The Good One) was renowned for the heroic role he played in defending the castle in Tarifa against the Moors. The church contains a remarkable 17th-century retable by the artist Martínez Montañés, noted for the figure of St Jerome. Montañés also carved the effigies on the tombs of Guzmán (died 1609) and his wife. A second church marks the first resting place of the body of Cortés, conqueror of Mexico, before it was taken to Mexico.

Take an unclassified road northwest for about 1km ($\frac{1}{2}$ mile) to Itálica, on the left.

Itálica, Sevilla

2 The Roman ruins of Itálica are considered of major significance. Originally founded in 206BC by Scipio Africanus as a place of retirement for his veteran soldiers, the city flourished and by the 2nd century AD had become one of the most important Roman cities in Spain. Two great Roman emperors – Trajan (AD52–117) and Hadrian (AD76–138) – were born here. The most important building is the large **Amphitheatre**, which was one of the largest of its kind in the Roman Empire, with a capacity of up to 40,000 spectators. Still faintly visible traces can be seen of a forum,

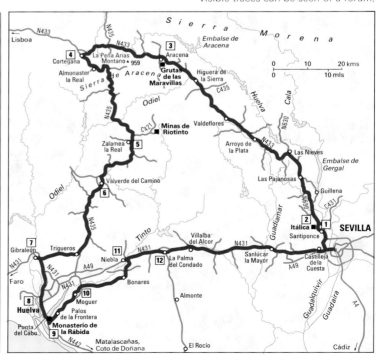

SCENIC ROUTES

Parts of this journey offer some very attractive scenery. After you have joined the **N435** from Cortegana the route becomes very scenic through to Zalamea la Real and on to Valverde del Camino, with a twisting mountain road through the Sierra de Aracena to Zalamea. There is also appealing scenery around Moguer. The route from Huelva to Matalascañas, should you decide to visit Coto Doñana, offers a beautiful coastal drive along miles of deserted beaches.

city streets, the foundations of villas, mosaic floors and other evidence of the old city. The most valuable treasures found here are displayed in Sevilla's Museum of Archaeology.

Keep on this unclassified road to rejoin the N630. Turn left to travel north on the N630, then after 25km (15 miles) turn left on to the N433 which leads northwest to Aracena.

Aracena, Huelva

3 The Convento de Santa Catalina (Convent of St Catalina) has a notable doorway. On top of the **Cerro del Castillo** (Castle Hill) are the remains of an old **castle**, which was built in the 13th century by the Knights Templar. Of mixed Gothic and Mudejar styles, it features an old tower, originally a minaret and decorated in similar style to the Giralda of Sevilla.

One of Aracena's main attractions is the nearby **Grutas de las Maravillas** (Grotto of Marvels). These vast caves extend to over 1,000m (1,094 yards) in length. Noted for their variety of shapes and unusual colours, the stalactites and stalagmites are reflected in the clear waters of the underground pools and rivers.

Continue northwest on the N433 to Cortegana, which lies just south of this road.

Cortegana, Huelva

4 The small town of Cortegana was originally a Roman settlement known as *Corticata*. Its main assets

The Roman ruins at Itálica, a large Roman town. It is possible to identify features such as streets and houses

are its beautiful setting, an interesting little **parish church** and old **castle**.

Take the regional road southeast. On joining the N435 turn right to Zalamea la Real, 49km (30 miles).

Zalamea la Real, Huelva

5 The town's most notable building is the Iglesia de la Asunción (Assumption), an elegant neoclassical monument from the 17th century. There are several interesting old hermitages.

The impressive **Minas de Ríotinto** (Rio Tinto Copper Mines) are about 6km ($4\frac{1}{2}$ miles) east of town. Already in use during Iberian and Roman times, the mines were abandoned when the Visigoths came, and regenerated in the last century. For a long time they were a British concern, reverting to Spanish ownership in 1954. There are still English-style houses, and a small **museum** in an old engine shed.

Continue on the same road south towards Valverde del Camino. Turn left where signposted into the town, 20km (12 miles).

Valverde del Camino, Huelva

6 The town of Valverde del Camino is noted for its production of wood, metal and leather goods, including

RECOMMENDED WALKS

3 *Aracena, Huelva* Aracena is a good base for many splendid walks in the surrounding countryside of the Sierra de Aracena, where you will find orange and lemon groves, great oak forests and tiny isolated villages. There is a superb view of the area from the top of La Peña Arias Montano.

BACK TO NATURE

8 *Huelva, Huelva* The **Coto Doñana** is one of Spain's largest and most important nature parks. This vast expanse of flat salt marshes (*marismas*), dunes and pine forests lies in the delta of the River Guadalquivir, covering an area of some 50,625 hectares (125,000 acres). The area is the habitat of thousands of migratory birds, and large colonies of birds nest in the cork-oak trees. It is also the home of many varieties of animals, and has many rare species of flower and plant life. **Matalascañas**, located down the coast southeast of Huelva, is the usual starting point for visiting the reserve. It can only normally be visited as part of a guided tour or with special permission.

FOR HISTORY BUFFS

8 *Huelva, Huelva* **Palos de la Frontera**, 13km (8 miles) southeast of Huelva is the place from which Christopher Columbus set sail on 3 August 1492 in the *Santa Maria* on his first voyage of discovery. Columbus first sighted land on 12 October and set foot on Cuba and Haiti, where he left some of his men behind to establish a colony before returning to Palos on 15 March 1493.

In May 1528, Hernán Cortés landed in the port after he had overthrown the mighty Aztec Empire and conquered Mexico.

FOR CHILDREN

8 *Huelva, Huelva* There are splendid beaches in Huelva province. Just south of Huelva is **Punta Umbria**, the main resort on this coast, with the nearby beach of **La Bota** and the lagoon of **El Portil**, which provides a delightful place to stop for a swim.

leather wine bottles. Buildings of special note include the attractive **Ermita de la Trinidad** (Hermitage of the Trinity) and the **Iglesia de Nuestra Señora del Reposo** (Church of Our Lady of Rest).

*Rejoin and take the **N435** south. At Trigueros turn right on an unclassified minor road to Gibraleón, 39km (24 miles).*

Gibraleón, Huelva

7 Gibraleón is a town with ancient roots. Some of the people have negroid features and are often referred to locally as negroes; they may be descendants of the slaves brought here by the Spaniards in the 15th century. Among the most interesting buildings in the town are the **Iglesia de Santiago** (St James), the **Iglesia de San Juan** (St John) and the **Chapel of El Carmen**. The **Convento del Vado** (16th-century) still preserves the remnants of its old walls.

*Take the **N431** south. Continue straight on to Huelva when the **N431** branches off east.*

Huelva, Huelva

8 The region played an important role in the events leading to the Voyages of Discovery across the ocean. Christopher Columbus came to Huelva with his son in 1485 and stayed in the nearby Monasterio de la Rábida. The first expedition set sail from the area in 1492, to reach land

two months later. At the end of the **Paseo del Conquero** is the modest white shrine of **Nuestra Señora de la Cinta**, with a Mudejar roof and a wall painting of the Virgin, Patron Saint of the city. A tile painting by the artist Zuloaga commemorates a visit made here by Columbus on his return from one of his voyages.

Huelva was severely damaged by an earthquake in 1755 and only a handful of buildings remain from the past. The 17th-century **Iglesia de la Merced** (now a cathedral) has an elegant doorway of mixed styles and houses an image of the Virgen de la Cinta (Patron Saint of Huelva). The 16th-century **Iglesia de San Pedro** (St Peter) features a tower with attractive tile decorations. The **Iglesia de la Concepción**, also 16th-century, is noted for its paintings by the Spanish artist Zurbarán.

The **Museo Provincial Arqueológico** (Provincial Museum of Archaeology) has an interesting collection of antiquities from the region, including some beautiful Roman amphorae (vessels). Its fine arts section features works from the Flemish school of painting and includes paintings by local artists.

ℹ️ Plus Ultra 10

Kite-flying is a popular activity on top of the hill outside Aracena, with the ruins of an old Knights Templar castle in the background

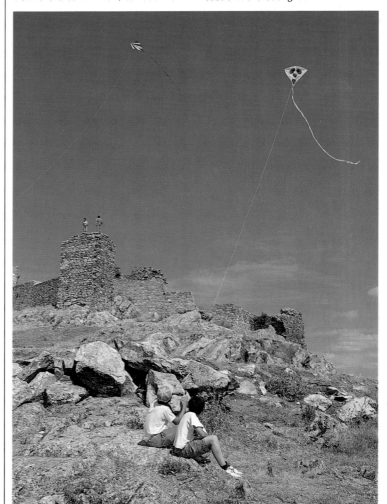

*Take the **N442** and cross over the Río Tinto. Shortly after, take a left turn to the Monasterio de la Rábida, 9km (6 miles).*

Monasterio de la Rábida, Huelva

9 This old Franciscan monastery lies in beautiful surroundings at the mouth of the Río Tinto. It is the place where Columbus received the necessary stimulus to persevere with his plans to sail across the ocean in search of the Indies. Columbus came to the monastery in 1485 with his son. He was well received by the monks, and Father Antonio Marchena, in particular, was instrumental in bringing influence to bear with Queen Isabella. After lengthy negotiations, the agreement was finally signed and Columbus was able to fulfil his dreams. The **Lecture Cell** is where Columbus held many meetings with the monks; the **Chapter-house** displays relics of the explorer, and the **Gallery** has models of the three caravels that undertook the first voyage. The church and courtyard date back to the early 15th century and are very attractive. Note the 14th-century statue of the Virgen de los Milagros, to whom Columbus offered his prayers before setting sail. In the beautifully laid out garden is the **Latin-American University**, a centre for American studies, and a monument to the Discoverers of America.

Continue on the same road northeast for 10km (6 miles) to Moguer.

Moguer, Huelva

10 Moguer is renowned as the birthplace and home town of the great Spanish poet, Juan Ramón Jiménez (1881–1958), Nobel prizewinner for literature in 1956 and author of the delightful Spanish classic *Platero y Yo*, about a boy and his donkey. His former home is now a **museum** with relics from the poet.

The 14th-century Gothic-Mudejar **Convento de Santa Clara** contains the tombs of the convent's founders and has been declared a National Monument. The **parish church** is noted for its tall, impressive tower, and the **Ayuntamiento** is 18th-century.

*Continue on the regional road east, along the south bank of the Río Tinto, bearing north at Bonares. Join the **N431**. Turn left to Niebla, 24km (15 miles).*

Niebla, Huelva

11 The ancient town of Niebla (mist) lies on the bank of the Río Tinto. It was the last town in the valley of the Guadalquivir to fall to the Christians during the Reconquest of Spain, and is noted as being the first place in Spain where gunpowder was used. Its most historical monuments are the Roman bridge over the river and four splendid Moorish entrance gates, known as the Puertas of Sevilla, Socorro, del Buey and del Agua. Of particular charm is the little church of **Nuestra Señora de Granada** (Our Lady of Granada). The **Iglesia de San Martín** and the 12th-century **Castillo de Los Guzmanes** also warrant a visit.

*Continue on the **N431** to La Palma del Condado.*

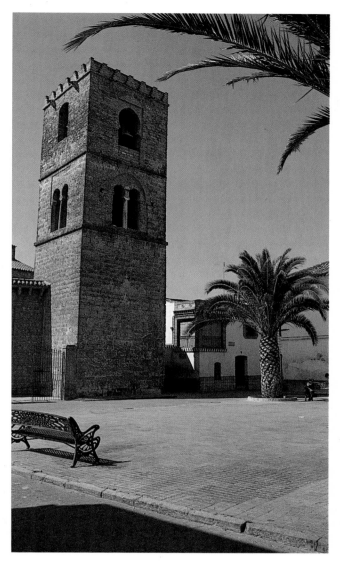

One of Niebla's fine old churches looks on to an attractive square and provides some shady corners for a rest

La Palma del Condado, Huelva

12 La Palma del Condado has long been the centre of a wine-producing area and is known for its pleasant white table wine. One of its main attractions is the 16th-century baroque **Iglesia de San Juan Bautista**, a beautiful white monument with an attractively decorated steeple. The **Ermita del Valle** (Hermitage of the Valley), built in the 1400s, is a fine example of the Mudejar style.

*Return to Sevilla east on the **N431**, 53km (33 miles).*

SPECIAL TO...

10 *Moguer, Huelva* South of Almonte in the village church of El Rocío is the Shrine of El Rocío, scene of Spain's most famous *romería* (pilgrimages to an isolated church or shrine, involving large crowds). This takes place at Whitsuntide. Thousands of people from all over the region take part in a procession to El Rocío on foot, horseback or in gaily decorated horse-drawn wagons, dressed in traditional costumes. Upon arrival in the village they celebrate with music, dancing and drinking until the climax of the festival, when the statue of the Virgin is brought out from the church at dawn and paraded among the crowds by members of the Brotherhoods. Church bells peal forth, fireworks explode and there is much exuberant celebration all round.

3 days – 399km (249 miles)

THE WHITE TOWNS
OF ANDALUCIA

Sevilla ● Utrera ● Arcos de la Frontera ● Medina Sidonia
Vejer de la Frontera ● Chiclana de la Frontera ● Cádiz
El Puerto de Santa María ● Rota ● Chipiona
Sanlúcar de Barrameda ● Jerez de la Frontera ● Sevilla

Sevilla's festivals are world-famous, the best-known being the Holy Week Celebrations and the Spring Fair. Holy Week has been celebrated here since the 16th century. There are evening processions every day and one at dawn on Good Friday. These consist of *pasos*, which are carried by barefoot members of the Penitent Brotherhoods, called *costaleros*. The *pasos*, or platforms, represent scenes of the Passion of Christ, and are followed by the penitents, or *Nazareños*, in their long tunics and pointed hoods with eye-slits, each carrying a long, lighted candle.

The *Feria de Sevilla* (Seville Fair) takes place for six days in April, with magnificent horseback parades, the men in elegant Cordovan hats and the women in beautiful traditional costumes. Song and dance is an important feature of the city's life: the joyous dances known as *sevillanas* are the very essence of Spain.

A wall painting in Chipiona dedicated to Santa María de la Regla, who is venerated by seamen

[i] Avenida de la Constitución 21

*From Sevilla take the **NIV** south. Turn left to Dos Hermanas. Travel a few kilometres northeast towards Alcala de Guadaira, then turn right on to the **C432** and continue south to Utrera, 38km (24 miles).*

Utrera, Sevilla

1 The old town of Utrera features an impressive **Alcázar** with a square tower, a few fine Gothic churches and an attractive little main square. The **Convento de Nuestra Señora de la Consolación** (Our Lady of the Consolation) on the outskirts of the town contains an image of a much venerated Virgin, who is believed to have miracle-working powers and is the object of an important annual pilgrimage in September.

*Join the **N333** south. On joining the **NIV**, turn left and after a short distance turn left again and continue on the **C343** south to Arcos de la Frontera, 62km (39 miles).*

Arcos de la Frontera, Cádiz

2 The first stop in the province of Cádiz is Arcos de la Frontera, one of the most attractive towns in the region. It is perched on top of a high rock, surrounded by steep ravines that descend to the River Guadalete. The town is a mass of white and stone-coloured houses, silhouetted by a castle and two churches. Tiny narrow streets and alleys wind their way up the steep slopes, offering splendid views. The **Hospital de San Juan de Dios** has a white baroque façade and

Arcos de la Frontera perches on a cliff overlooking the River Guadalete. The bell tower of the massive church of San Pedro overlooks the town

a notable 16th-century crucifix in the temple. Other outstanding churches are those of **Santa María**, noted for its Plateresque west façade and **San Pedro**, a Gothic structure of massive proportions that has some significant religious paintings and a huge baroque bell tower, that stands out as a landmark for miles around.

*Continue south on the **C343** for 39km (24 miles) to Medina Sidonia.*

Medina Sidonia, Cádiz

3 This is a historic little town whose origins can be traced back over 1,000 years, and its name is derived from a combination of Phoenician and Moorish. The **Iglesia de Santa María Coronada** was built in the Gothic style at the time of Granada's recapture by the Christians. Some important religious paintings may be seen in the church. The **Arch of 'La Pastora'** (the Shepherdess) is set in the old Moorish walls in a horseshoe shape. Built in the 18th-century, the **Ayuntamiento** (town hall) features an elegant, tiled staircase and the churches of **San Agustín** and **Santiago** are also worth a visit.

Some 7km (4½ miles) away are caves known as the **Tajo de las Figuras**.

*Continue south on the **C343** for 29km (18 miles) to Vejer de la Frontera.*

Vejer de la Frontera, Cádiz

4 The medieval town of Vejer de la Frontera is situated on the banks of the River Barbate high above Cabo de Trafalgar (Cape Trafalgar). The place is Moorish in appearance – in the dazzling white houses and tiny twisting streets, and also in its womenfolk, some of whom dress in black from head to toe, Arab-style, and are known as *Las Cobijadas* (the covered ones). The town features little hidden squares and flower-filled patios, with streets so precipitous that handrails have been added for safety. Its most important building is the **Iglesia de El Divino Salvador**. Built in the 13th century, soon after the town was taken from the Moors, it shows a combination of Romanesque, Gothic and Mudejar styles and contains some fine 17th-century paintings.

Having come this far, you should make a detour to Tarifa, southeast on the N340. When you stand on the **Punta Marroquí**, also known as Punta de Tarifa, you will have your feet on the most southerly tip of Europe, with the coast of the African continent only 14km (8 miles) away. This is the meeting point of the Mediterranean and the Atlantic. Tarifa has a Moorish look and some Roman remains.

*Take the **N340** northwest for 29km (18 miles) to Chiclana de la Frontera.*

Chiclana de la Frontera, Cádiz

5 Chiclana has neat white houses rising up the hillside and a Mosque-like parish church. A few kilometres away to the west is the splendid sandy beach of La Barrosa, bordered by fresh green pinewoods and a popular summer resort.

*Continue on the **N340** northwest for a short distance and join the **NIV** for 23km (14 miles) to Cádiz.*

Cádiz, Cádiz

6 The old port of Cádiz is noted for its lovely setting. It is built on a rock platform jutting out into the Atlantic Ocean and is connected to the mainland by a bridge. The town is encircled by massive ramparts, which serve as a protection against the force of the waves. It is characterised by tall white houses, many of which have *miradors* (lookout towers) and *azoteas* (roof terraces).

Cádiz is thought to be one of the oldest towns on the Iberian peninsula. It was founded by the Phoenicians in 1100BC under the name of Gadir and was used as a trading port. It was later controlled by the Carthaginians, then the Romans, under whose rule it rose in importance.

Cádiz was used as a base for Spanish treasure fleets, which resulted in great prosperity. In 1587 Sir Francis Drake burned the ships of the Spanish Armada that had been destined for England by Philip II. In 1805 Lord Nelson set sail from Cádiz to embark upon the Battle of Trafalgar. Here, in 1812, the Spanish

FOR HISTORY BUFFS

4 *Vejer de la Frontera, Cádiz* Fourteen km (7 miles) southwest of Vejer de la Frontera is **Cabo de Trafalgar** (Cape Trafalgar). It was off this coast that the famous battle of Trafalgar took place in 1805, resulting in victory for the British over the French and Spanish fleets and the establishing of British domination of the seas. The battle also resulted in the death of Lord Nelson.

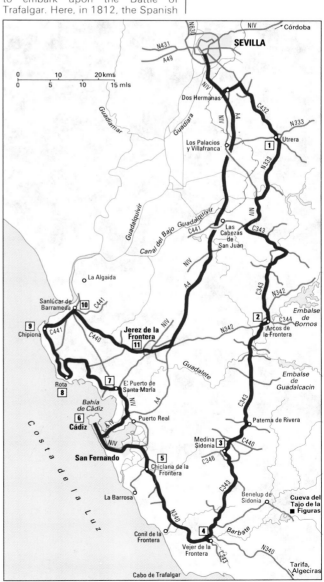

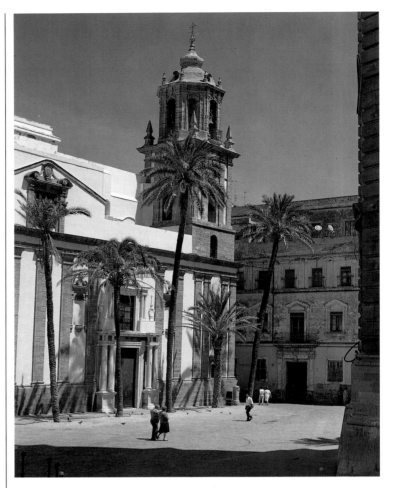

Parliament met to establish the first liberal constitution.

One of the town's most pleasing aspects is its lovely parks, among which those of **Genovés**, **Alameda Marqués de Comillas** and **Alameda de Apodaca** rate as the most attractive. The **cathedral** features a golden dome and a baroque façade. It was built in the 18th and 19th centuries, during the town's most affluent period, and hoards of gold and silver treasures and precious gems may be seen in the museum. Its most priceless piece is a processional cross by Enrique de Arfe, which is brought out for the Corpus Christi processions. In the crypt is the tomb of the famous Spanish composer, Manuel de Falla (1876–1946), who was born in Cádiz and drew much of his inspiration from the folklore of Andalucia.

The **Museo de Bellas Artes** (Fine Arts Museum) features some great canvasses by Zurbarán and works by Murillo. The **Museo Arqueológico e Arte** (Museum of Archaeology and Art) contains a sarcophagus of the Greco-Phoenician style, dating back to the 5th century BC. An interesting item in the **Museo Historico Municipal** (Municipal Museum) is a 19th-century mural that portrays the drawing up of the 1812 constitution. Its masterpiece, however, is a fascinating model of the town as it was in the 18th century, beautifully worked in ivory and mahogany and showing all the little streets and houses in minute detail. Spain's first constitution was declared in 1812 in the **Oratorio de San Felipe de Neri** (Ora-

The elegant façade of one of Cádiz's churches overlooks a quiet, peaceful square

tory of St Philip). Over the altar hangs a painting of the Immaculate Conception by the Sevillian artist, Murillo.

The old town is a labyrinth of narrow streets opening out on to pleasant squares. Its central point is the attractive **Plaza de Miña**, shaded by palms and surrounded by elegant buildings.

i Calderon de la Barca 1

> *Leave by the toll bridge and join the **NIV** north to El Puerto de Santa María, 13km (8 miles).*

El Puerto de Santa María, Cádiz

7 The small fishing port of El Puerto de Santa María is noted for its sherry and brandy *bodegas* (cellars) and tours of these famous cellars are available (and recommended). It lies at the mouth of the River Guadalete and features a busy port, lively streets and miles of sandy beaches. The most prominent monument is the old Moorish **Castillo de San Marcos** (St Mark's Castle), a watchtower over the river, where you can enjoy a lovely view of the coast.

> *Take the regional road for 27km (17 miles) northwest to Rota.*

Rota, Cádiz

8 The Spanish-American naval base is the major feature of Rota and has brought a cosmopolitan atmosphere to the town, with the advent of lively bars, shops and evening entertainment. The town has several pleasant beaches, which include those of La Costilla, La Almadraba and Punta Candor. Take a look at the old walls and the **Luna Castle** by the fishermen's quarters. The 16th-century **parish church** is decorated with glazed tiles. Apart from its importance as a maritime town, Rota is also an agricultural centre, noted for its tomatoes and watermelons.

Continue north on minor roads to Chipiona for 16km (10 miles).

Chipiona, Cádiz

9 The **lighthouse** of Chipiona is a famous landmark for navigators and can be seen from a great distance. This is a popular holiday resort with splendid beaches of fine white sand and good fishing in some areas. The little town is charming, with whitewashed houses, quaint streets and a profusion of flowers. Muscatel wine is in evidence here. A visit to the **Iglesia de Santa María de la Regla** will reveal a shrine to the virgin, who is much venerated by the seamen.

*Take the **C441** east for 9km (6 miles) to Sanlúcar de Barrameda.*

Sanlúcar de Barrameda, Cádiz

10 Lying in an attractive setting at the mouth of the River Guadalquivir is the little port of Sanlúcar de Barrameda, whose origins go back to the Romans. Its old port was the point of departure for Christopher Columbus's third voyage to the New World in 1498, and that of the Portuguese Magellan, who sailed from here in 1519 on his first voyage around the world.

The 16th-century **Iglesia de Nuestra Señora de la O** is noted for its fine Mudejar doorway. A visit to the lively fish auction in the afternoon can be most entertaining. This is also the home of the famous Manzanilla wine, which serves as an excellent accom-paniment to the delicious fresh seafood found here.

*Take the **C440** southeast for 24km (15 miles) to Jerez de la Frontera.*

Jerez de la Frontera, Cádiz

11 Lying among extensive vineyards is the town of Jerez, home of sherry, to which it has given its name. The *bodegas*, some of which are very grand, are the great attraction of the town, and no visitor should fail to take a tour of one.

The town exudes a somewhat aristocratic air, with broad avenues and large squares. The **Colegiata** (Collegiate Church), built in the 17th and 18th centuries in Gothic style, contains paintings by Zurbarán. There are good views of the surroundings from the tower. The **Alcázar** is an impressive 11th-century building featuring a Gothic church and Arab baths. The **Museo Arqueológico** (Archaeological Museum) has a varied collection of interesting items and a library.

ℹ️ Alameda Cristina

*Return to Sevilla north on the **A4**, 90km (56 miles).*

Sevilla – Utrera 38 (24)
Utrera – Arcos de la Frontera 62 (39)
Arcos de la Frontera – Medina Sidonia 39 (24)
Medina Sidonia – Vejer de la Frontera 29 (18)
Vejer de la Frontera – Chiclana de la Frontera 29 (18)
Chiclana de la Frontera – Cádiz 23 (14)
Cádiz – El Puerto de Santa María 13 (8)
El Puerto de Santa María – Rota 27 (17)
Rota – Chipiona 16 (10)
Chipiona – Sanlúcar de Barrameda 9 (6)
Sanlúcar de Barrameda – Jerez de la Frontera 24 (15)
Jerez de la Frontera – Sevilla 90 (56)

Chipiona's sandy beach is overlooked by a fine church. The lighthouse is in the distance

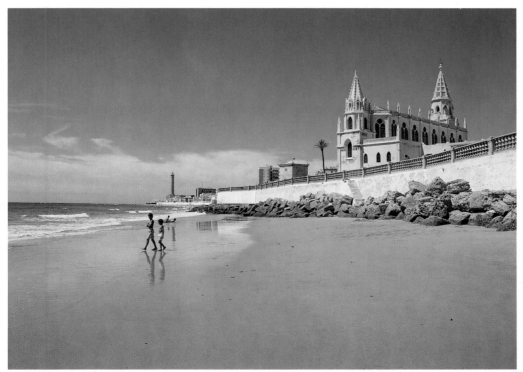

ARAGON, NAVARRE & LA RIOJA

The area of Aragon, Navarre and La Rioja lies to the north and south of the basin of the River Ebro, which runs from the Cantabrian Mountains in the northwest through the Catalonian Mountains and down to the Mediterranean. Along the banks of the Ebro are the green irrigated lands known in Spain as *huertas*. The capital of Aragon, Zaragoza (Saragossa), lies in the Ebro depression on the right bank of the river and is a major agricultural centre for this fertile region, which produces almonds, figs, olives and vines.

Southern Aragon is an area of arid plains and the bleak windswept plateaux that form part of the Montes Universales mountain range. The region suffers from extreme temperatures.

To the northwest is the small province of La Rioja, one of Spain's most important wine-growing regions, known particularly for its popular red wines, which have an unmistakable flavour. The Upper Rioja is mountainous and humid, while the Lower Rioja consists of irrigated flatlands and enjoys a mild climate.

Upper Aragon and the northern part of Navarre lie within the great Pyrenees chain known as the Central, or Aragonese, Pyrenees and the Navarre Pyrenees to the west. High mountain peaks, lush green valleys and waterfalls, and rough stone houses with steep slate roofs are typical. To the west, the countryside gradually divides into small fields.

Navarre has links with the Basques and was once the home of the 'Vascons', who were their ancestors. At the end of the 8th century the area was wrested from the Moors by Charlemagne. During the 11th century Navarre was annexed for some time by the kingdom of Aragon. It was ruled by the kings of France between 1234 and 1512, when it was gained for King Ferdinand by the Duke of Alba and integrated with Castile. In the 11th and 12th centuries Navarre became very important to the pilgrims along here on the first stages of their pilgrimages to the shrine at Santiago de Compostela. As a result there was a great flowering of Romanesque art, of which fine examples can be observed all along the 'Way of St James'.

Folklore forms an integral part of the people's lives, especially in the mountain areas and many traditions in Navarre have their roots in the Basque culture. The lively *jota* is danced in Navarre and Aragon, with differences, and one of Spain's most famous celebrations is Pamplona's riotous festival of '*Sanfermines*'.

Tour 13

Southern Aragon is an area of arid plains, windswept plateaux and wild rugged mountains. While it may not appear to be the most hospitable of regions at first glance, there is some magnificent scenery. A visit to an oasis surrounding an old monastery, however, does provide a change. Stops are included at several interesting little towns and villages, built from the stone of the region and barely distinguishable from the surrounding landscape. The area is rich in Mudejar art (work of the Moorish people under Christian rule), and many fine examples of this intricate style of decoration can be seen along the route. South of Zaragoza is the most important wine-growing region of the province, labelled the 'wine route'.

Tour 14

Leaving the plains of Huesca, the route turns north and follows the course of the rivers to one of the important staging points of the Pilgrim's Way to Santiago. The landscapes change continuously with great panoramas of mountain peaks, eroded gorges and wooded valleys, fresh green forests and clear sparkling streams. All along the route are delightful little Pyrenean villages, walled towns and castles, which bear traces of their medieval past. Many consist of a cluster of semi-detached houses rising up a steep hill to form a protective enclave. Here you will find much evidence of the Mozarabic-Romanesque style that is characteristic of the region. A visit to an old fortress – ancient stronghold of King Sancho Ramirez of Aragon – is also included. Another attraction is a visit to one of Spain's most impressive national parks, which offers spectacular scenery and interesting wildlife.

A resident of Agreda works on his vegetable patch. The town is perched on a rocky crag on the frontiers of Aragon and Castile

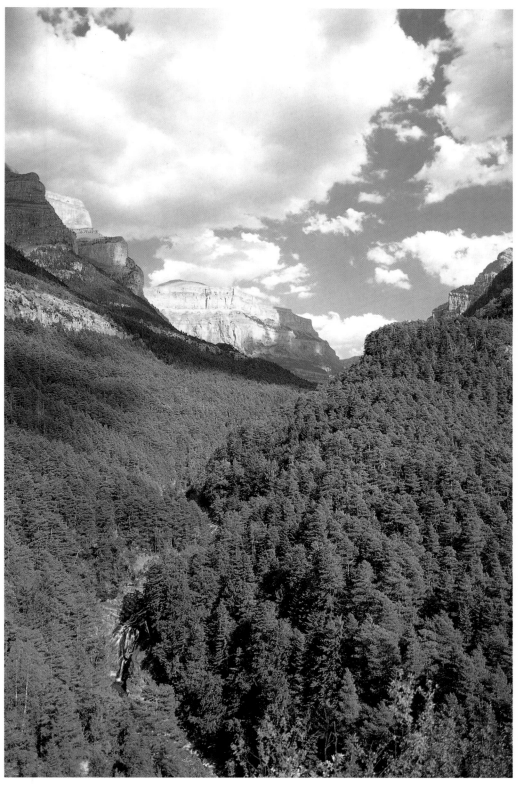

The grand and beautiful scenery of the Ordesa National Park

Tour 15

On this tour you will be treated to a variety of landscapes, ranging from the desolate plains of the south, characterised by the rich reddish-brown colour of the terrain, to the fertile regions and mountains of La Rioja. This little rectangular piece of land lying on the western side of the Ebro Valley is one of Spain's most important wine-growing regions. The route passes through many fascinating old medieval walled towns and castles. A number of these were built in strategic positions on hilltops overlooking the neighbouring provinces of Aragon and Castile, which were separate kingdoms at the time. You will find many fine examples of Moorish, Romanesque and Gothic art in the churches and buildings, with some special historic interest provided by one of the old staging points along the 'Way to Santiago'.

2/3 days – 635km (394 miles)

THE ANCIENT KINGDOM OF ARAGON

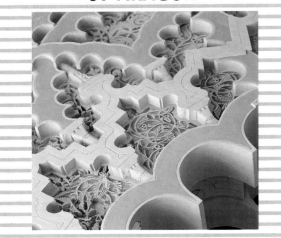

Zaragoza ● Calatayud ● Monasterio de Piedra ● Daroca
Calamocha ● Orihuela del Tremedal ● Albarracín
Teruel ● Alcañiz ● Zaragoza

Zaragoza is a busy commercial town, placed midway between Madrid and Barcelona. The *Seo* (Old Cathedral) was started in 1119 and completed only in 1520, with an impressive belfry added in the 17th century. Fine examples of Mudejar art are evident in the choir area and 'Parroquieta' (Gothic Chapel). The graceful towers and domes of the *Iglesia de Nuestra Señora del Pilar* (Our Lady of the Pillar), of the mid-1600s, rise from the banks of the River Ebro. In the *Capilla de Nuestra Señora del Pilar* (Lady Chapel) is the much venerated small statue of the Virgin, the object of important pilgrimages. Frescos by Goya decorate the ceiling of the chapel and dome.

La Lonja (Exchange), built in 1551 in Renaissance style, and the 11th-century *Aljafería*, built by the Moors and used as a residence by the Kings of Aragon after the Reconquest, are other grand buildings. There are also several museums, including the *Museo del Cabildo* (Chapter-house), with a priceless collection of Brussels tapestries.

Decorative plasterwork in the Aljafería, Zaragoza. This particular style of decoration is typical of Moorish and subsequent Spanish art

$\boxed{i}$ Plaza de Sas 7

*Take the **NII** southwest for 87km (54 miles) to Calatayud.*

Calatayud, Zaragoza

1 The history of Calatayud goes back to the time of the Moors and its name is derived from Kalat-Ayub, who founded the old **castle** in the 8th century, now in ruins. The town is on a hillside, merging with its surroundings.

The **Iglesia de Santa María la Mayor** (St Mary the Elder) has an elegant 16th-century Renaissance doorway and the **Iglesia de San Sepulcro** (12th–17th century) was once the centre of the Knights Templars of Spain. A number of other churches in the town show attractive examples of the Mudejar style of art.

$\boxed{i}$ Puerta Alcántara

*Take the **C202** southwest for 28km (17 miles) to the Monasterio de Piedra (Monastery of Stone).*

Monasterio de Piedra, Zaragoza

2 The beautiful oasis that surrounds the Monasterio de Piedra makes a welcome change from the surrounding arid land, and a tour of the gardens will probably be as much of an attraction as a visit to the monastery itself. The area has been turned into a lovely parkland of grottoes, pools and cascades sloping down to the banks of the River Piedra. There are pathways and observation platforms offering good views. Look out for the **Cola de Caballo waterfall**, which tumbles down from a consider-

FOR HISTORY BUFFS

Zaragoza, Zaragoza Those with a special interest in art may enjoy a visit to the birthplace of the great Spanish painter, Francisco Goya. This is the small village of **Fuendetodos**, (about 24km (15 miles) east of Cariñena, which is on the **N330** between Zaragoza and Daroca). You can see the modest house where he was born in 1746 and visit the small museum which contains relics and a collection of transparencies of his works.

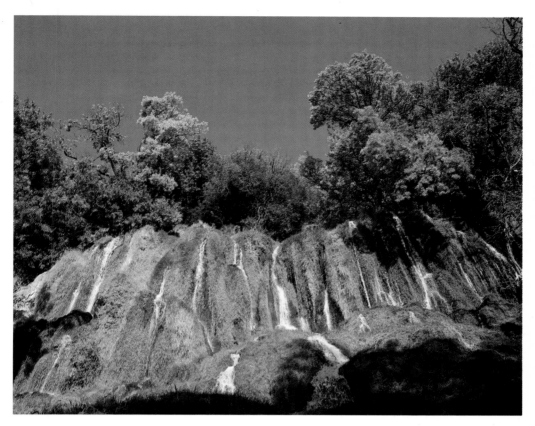

able height and is most impressive. You can look down on it from a 'mirador' (look-out point), while a splendid view is had from the **Iris Grotto**. On the way to the monastery you will see two beautiful little lakes known as the **Baño de Diana** (Diana's Bath) and the **Lago del Espejo** (Mirror Lake) lying between two tall rocks.

The monastery was founded as a Cistercian house in 1194 and features a keep, a chapter-house and a refectory. The attractive cloister is 13th century, and the elegant staircase with an impressive vault dates from the 14th and 15th centuries.

*Take the **C202** back to Calatayud and join the **N234** (direction Teruel) to Daroca.*

Daroca, Zaragoza

3 Daroca is a true medieval delight. It lies tucked away in a gorge on the River Jiloca, surrounded by hills. The walls date back to the 13th century and extend for some 3km (2 miles), with over 100 towers still remaining from the past.

The **Colegiata de Santa María** (St Mary's Collegiate) was built between the 13th and 15th centuries and contains an item of particular significance in the Chapel of the Holy Relics. In the shrine are holy altar-cloths said to have been used to wrap the consecrated hosts during an attack by the Moors in the course of morning mass in 1239. The cloths were later found stained with blood and proclaimed sacred relics. The church **museum** has an interesting collection of ecclesiastical art, including some notable retables. It also has an interesting display of Mexican robes dating back to the 17th century.

*Continue on the **N234** for 26km (16 miles) to Calamocha.*

One of the waterfalls, in the parkland around the Monasterio de Piedra, provides a refreshing and welcoming sight

Calamocha, Zaragoza

4 Calamocha is a picturesque little village with old, narrow streets, squares and some fine, well-preserved mansions. It features an old Moorish bridge and tower, and has an attractive **parish church** built in the baroque style.

Continue south on the same road. Turn right to Santa Eulalia then continue west to Orihuela del Tremedal.

Orihuela del Tremedal, Teruel

5 The tour continues through some lovely mountain scenery to the small town of Orihuela del Tremedal, set among the pine-clad slopes of the Sierra de Albarracín. The **parish church** is an impressive example of baroque architecture, and the **Ayuntamiento** (town hall) is a fine 16th-century building.

Take a winding regional road southeast to Albarracín, 40km (25 miles).

Albarracín, Teruel

6 Cave paintings discovered in the area show that the mountains of Albarracín were inhabited in prehistoric times, and it would seem there was a very early settlement on the site of the present town of Albarracín.

Designated a National Monument, the town is very picturesque, with steep winding streets, old archways and timbered houses. Many have overhanging storeys, with wooden balconies and lovely wrought-iron grilles. The **cathedral**, rebuilt in the

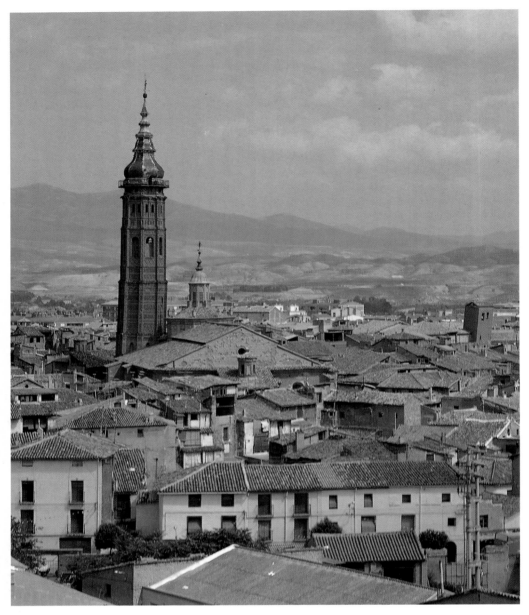

RECOMMENDED WALKS

7 *Teruel, Teruel* The Montes Universales to the south also has a **National Game Reserve** and offers splendid walks among its wild landscapes of barren rocks and mountains with strange rock formations.

SPECIAL TO . . .

7 *Teruel, Teruel* The **Lovers of Teruel** is a famous legend dating back to the early 13th century, when a love affair between Diego de Marcilla and Isabel de Segura, two young people from Teruel, ended tragically with their deaths. The bodies of the young couple lie interred in a splendid mausoleum in a chapel adjoining the church of San Pedro. This romantic story is popular all over Spain, and has been the subject of many poems and dramas.

The red-brown roofs of the Moorish town of Calatayud blend in with its arid surroundings. It has examples of Mudejar art

16th century, features a large square belfry topped by a lantern. The chapter-house contains a collection of valuable 16th-century tapestries from Brussels and some notable retables.

Important prehistoric rock paintings can be seen in the caves of **El Callejón de Plou** and **El Navazco**, located a short distance to the south.

*Take the regional road southeast to join the **N234**. Turn right to Teruel, about 47km (29 miles) in total.*

Teruel, Teruel

7 Teruel, capital of its own province, stands high on a plateau surrounded by a deep moat, through which the River Turia flows. The original town of Turba was Iberian. In 218BC it was sacked by the Romans. It was then under Moorish domination for several centuries before being retaken by the Christians. A large number of Moors remained here, however, and were known as Moriscos. Renowned for their skills in masonry and ceramics, they applied their art in Teruel.

The town has five **Torres Mudejares** (Mudejar towers) built between the 12th and 16th centuries. They have square belfries on top adorned with ceramic tiles, and are excellent examples of the Mudejar style. The base of each structure has an arched opening, which gives access to the street, and the façade is richly decorated with brickwork and tiles. The ornate towers of the churches of **San Martín** (St Martin) and **El Salvador** (the Saviour) are considered among the finest examples of their kind. Built in the 12th century, almost side by side, the 'twin towers' are a handsome landmark of Teruel.

The original structure of the **cathedral** dates back to the 12th century and was recognised as a cathedral only in the 16th century, after some additions had been made. It is noted for its tall, slender tower and cupola, which was built in 1538 and is covered with colourful tile decorations. Note the intricate artwork of the ceiling. The choir has a fine Gothic wrought-iron grille (late 15th-century) and the retable at the high altar is by the French sculptor, Gabriel Joli, who produced this in the 16th century in the Plateresque style. The 13th-century **Iglesia de San Pedro** (St Peter's) was renovated in the 18th century, but examples of Mudejar art can still be seen, principally in the tower, which has a similar shape and decoration to that of the cathedral.

Remains of the old fortifications are still in evidence. The solid tower, **Torre Lombardara**, was once part of the ancient city walls, and the gates of La Traición and La Andaquilla also belonged to the old battlements. A prominent feature of Teruel is the **Acueducto de los Arcos** (Aqueduct of the Arches), which was constructed in 1558 by the French architect Pierre Vedel along the lines of a Roman model.

ⓘ Tomas Nogues 1

*Take the **N420** northeast. At Montalbán take the **N211** east to Alcañiz, 158km (98 miles).*

Alcañiz, Teruel

8 The ancient town of Alcañiz is built up a hillside, surrounded by orchards and olive groves. This is a fertile area, noted for the production of high-quality olive oil. It is also known for *almendrados*, a sweet paste made from almonds.

The town is crowned by the impressive 12th-century **Castillo de los Calatravos** (Castle of the Calatravos), which was once the seat of the military Order of Calatrava in Aragon. Parts are Romanesque in style, from the 12th century, and paintings from this period can be seen in the chapel. Other sections show examples of Gothic style. The castle is now a parador, but can be visited.

One of Alcañiz's most impressive buildings is the **Colegiata de Santa María la Mayor**. Built in 1736, it is a very tall building with a magnificent portico, giving the appearance of a cathedral. Among the town's most delightful features, however, is the **Plaza de España**. This large square is the focal point of the town. One corner of the square is overlooked by the attractive Gothic building **La Lonja** (the Exchange), whose tall, elegant portals were once the meeting place of the market. Adjoining is the 16th-century **Ayuntamiento**, noted for its handsome, Renaissance-style front.

At **Valdealgorfa**, about 12km (7½ miles) away, is the **Cueva del Charco del Agua** (Cave of the Pool of Bitter Water), where you can see some fascinating prehistoric rock paintings, considered of great significance to Lower Aragon.

ⓘ Plaza de España 1, Alcañiz

*Return to Zaragoza on the **N232**, 101km (63 miles).*

Zaragoza – Calatayud **87 (54)**
Calatayud – Monasterio de Piedra **28 (17)**
Monasterio de Piedra – Daroca **68 (42)**
Daroca – Calamocha **26 (16)**
Calamocha – Orihuela del Tremedal **80 (50)**
Orihuela del Tremedal – Albarracín **47 (29)**
Albarracín – Teruel **47 (29)**
Teruel – Alcañiz **158 (98)**
Alcañiz – Zaragoza **101 (63)**

Goats surrounding a water hole in the barren landscape of the Aragon region

2/3 days – 408km (253 miles)

PYRENEAN LANDSCAPES OF UPPER ARAGON

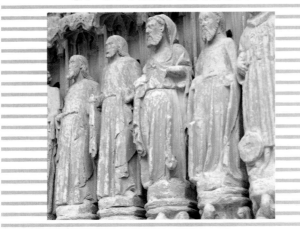

Huesca ● Castillo de Loarre ● Ayerbe ● Berdún
San Juan de la Peña ● Jaca ● Sabiñanigo ● Biescas
Torla ● Parque Nacional de Ordesa ● Ainsa ● Barbastro
Alquézar ● Huesca

Huesca is a typical Pyrenean town, built on the slopes of a hill that rises above the River Isuela. The Gothic *cathedral*, with its beautiful doorway, stands high above the town. It was first built at the end of the 13th century and completed in about 1500. The almost square interior has three naves, a transept and five chapels, as well as a notable alabaster altarpiece. Opposite is the *Ayuntamiento* (town hall), a graceful 16th-century Renaissance building.

San Pedro el Viejo (St Peter the Old) is a Romanesque former monastery from the 11th century. The town's two museums are the *Museo Arqueológico Provincial* and, adjoining the cathedral, the *Museo Episcopal* with a display of Romanesque-Gothic murals and notable Gothic altarpieces.

Weathered stone carvings on the beautiful ornate façade of the Gothic cathedral in Huesca. The figures surround the 14th-century main doorway

ⓘ Coso Alto 23

Take the C132 northwest. At Esquedas turn right and take the regional road to Loarre, about 28km (17 miles) from Huesca. Branch off right before the village to Castillo de Loarre.

Castillo de Loarre, Huesca

1 The last part of this journey takes you through some stunning scenery to the impressive Castillo de Loarre (Loarre Castle), which towers majestically over the Ebro Valley beneath the Sierra de Loarre. It was originally built as a fortress, and was established as a monastery in the 12th century, even though the area was under Moorish domination at the time.

The building is encircled by massive walls with cylindrical towers and two entrance gates, from which there are magnificent views of the surrounding landscape. The **church** was completed in the 12th century and features a tall nave and a cupola in pure Romanesque style. The capitals are decorated with fine geometric and floral motifs. Below lies the crypt, which is noted for its rectangular shape with a semicircular apse and a cylindrical vault.

Return to the regional road and turn right through the village of Loarre to Ayerbe, 8km (5 miles).

Ayerbe, Huesca

2 Make a brief stop here, where two monuments are worth a visit. The

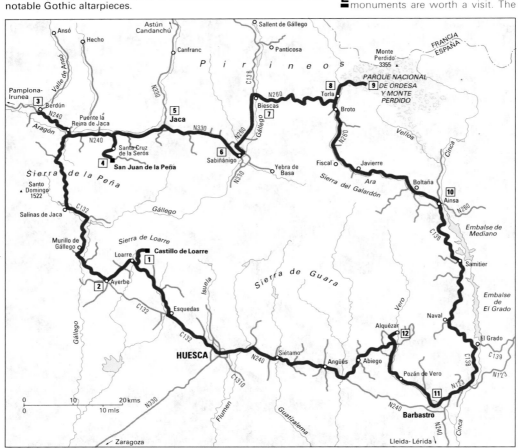

Ayuntamiento (town hall), housed in the old **Palacio del Marqués de Ayerbe** (Palace of the Marquis of Ayerbe) is a fine old building from the 15th century. The **Torre de San Pedro** (St Peter's Tower) dates back to the 12th century.

> Take the **C132** north to join the **N240** for 54km (34 miles) to Berdún.

Berdún, Huesca

3 Berdún is a cluster of houses huddled together up the hillside. Towns and villages in the region were built in this way during the Middle Ages as a form of protection. This is a good place to explore and forms an excellent base for excursions north into the Valle de Ansó, which offers some spectacular scenery of deep gorges and green valleys, together with some charming little villages.

> Return to and continue along the **N240**, then turn left on to the **C134**. Turn right on to a regional road to San Juan de la Peña, 29km (18 miles).

San Juan de la Peña, Huesca

4 Tucked away under a great rock is the ancient **Monasterio de San Juan de la Peña** (St John of the Crag). It has a magnificent setting overlooking a desolate Pyrenean valley with a beautiful view of the snow-capped mountains to the north.

The original monastery was founded in the 9th century by a monk called Juan, who is said to have decided to end his wanderings on this spot. Later additions were made to the former structure, which was built from the rock, and the Benedictine monastery of San Juan de la Peña was then formally founded by Sancho Ramírez, son of King Ramiro I. The monastery is associated with the legend of the elusive Holy Grail, claimed to have been passed on to the monks here for safekeeping by King Ramiro.

The cloister was built in the 12th century and is a superb example of pure Romanesque art, with beautifully carved capitals showing scenes from the bible. Tombs of the noblemen are to be seen in the Pantheon of Nobility and the Pantheon of the Kings. Don't miss the delightful Gothic-style **Capilla de San Vicente** (Chapel of St Vincent).

> Rejoin the **N240** and continue east to Jaca, 21km (13 miles).

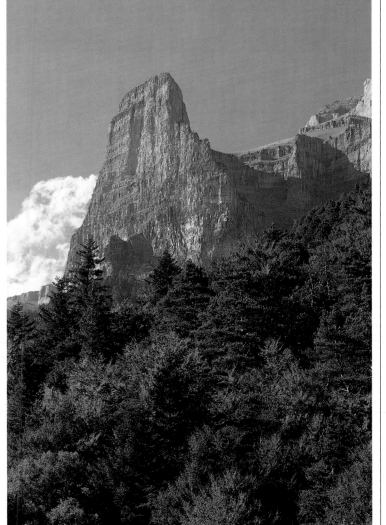

A spectacular limestone rockface towers over magnificent Ordesa National Park

FOR CHILDREN

There are a number of colourful festivals that would appeal to children if dates permit. On the first Friday in May a pilgrimage takes place in Jaca to commemorate the Christian victory over the Moors. This is a colourful festival, with mock fights between the warring forces, music and dancing. On 25 June is the feast of Santa Oroisa, which is celebrated with processions and traditional dances performed by dancers from Yebra de Basa.

SPECIAL TO ...

Aragon has a rich folklore and a very attractive traditional dance called the *jota*, which dates back to the 18th century. This is a very lively, joyous dance involving great bounding steps, to the accompaniment of stringed instruments, which may be guitars or a small version of the guitar known as the *bandurrias*. The dance is performed all over the region at festival times, when the male participants dress in the traditional costume of black velvet jacket over a blouse with slashed sleeves, black knee breeches, a colourful cummerbund and a bright handkerchief on the head.

FOR HISTORY BUFFS

3 *Berdún, Huesca* From Berdún a road leads north through some magnificent scenery to the small, traditional town of Ansó. Its **Museum of Costume** has another, very poignant feature. Inscribed on one of its walls is a list of names of all those who were killed in the Spanish Civil War (1936–9). Heading the list is José Primo de Rivera. Son of General Primo de Rivera, who had served as prime minister under the former monarch and was the founder of the Falangists, he was shot in prison in Alicante in 1936, shortly after the outbreak of the war.

SCENIC ROUTES

5 *Jaca, Huesca* An interesting detour can be made by taking the **N330** north through a beautiful mountainous route to **Canfranc**, a frontier town with France. Built high up on a hill overlooked by a **castle**, this old town has changed little with the passage of time. The international railway station is a relic of the past and worth a look. Near by are the popular winter resorts of **Astún** and **Candanchú**.

BACK TO NATURE

4 *San Juan de la Peña, Huesca* The solitude of San Juan de la Peña and its surroundings provides ideal conditions for birdwatching. Look out for such species as griffon vultures who come to roost in the high cliffs that surround the monastery. Kestrels, golden eagles and rock thrushes may also be spotted here.

9 *Parque Nacional de Ordesa, Huesca* The Ordesa National Park is an area of startling landscapes and great geological interest. You might catch a glimpse of mammals such as ibex, chamois, mountain goat, polecat, badger or wild boar. The park is also home to a great number of different species of birds, including some rare ones. The golden eagle and bearded vulture are among the many varieties to look out for.

A woman selling linen in Jaca, one of the major stages on the pilgrimage route to Santiago

Jaca, Huesca

5 Jaca is one of the major stages on the Way to Santiago, the pilgrimage route to Santiago de Compostela in Galicia that was established after the supposed tomb of the Apostle James the Great was discovered there in the 9th century. The greatest days of the pilgrimages were in the 11th and 12th centuries and pilgrims came from all over central Europe.

The **cathedral** of Jaca is an outstanding example of Spanish Romanesque art. This style of architecture, which was developed between the Pyrenees and Galicia, became known as the Romanesque style of the Pilgrim's Way. Of special interest are the chapels of **San Miguel** (St Michael), noted for its Plateresque retable, the 16th-century **Trinidad** (Trinity), where the Romanesque grille should be observed, and the **Capillo de San Jerónimo** (St Jeronimus), which shows a fine example of baroque art. In the church is the **Museo Episcopal**, which displays items of Romanesque art and Gothic paintings.

The **Benedictine monastery** is another notable building in Jaca, containing the sarcophagus of the Infanta Sancha. The **Ayuntamiento** (town hall), built between 1544 and 1546, is noted for its lovely wrought-iron grilles and is a good example of the Aragonese-Plateresque style. The **Ciudadela** (Citadel) has an impressive moat and dates back to the time of Philip II. In contrast, take a look at the modern style of architecture of the **Palacio de Congresos** (Congress Palace) and the **Palacio de Hielo** (Ice Palace).

i Paseo Calvo Sotelo

*Continue southeast on the **N330** for 18km (11 miles) to Sabiñanigo*

Sabiñanigo, Huesca

6 The main attractions of this small mountain town are its beautiful surroundings and the interesting **Museo Etnológico de Artes Populares** (Ethnological Museum of Popular Arts), which features items of regional interest. In the vicinity are several little churches of Moorish-Romanesque style, including those of Larrede, Oros Bajo, Satue, Lasieso and San Juan de Busa.

*Take the **N260** north for 15km (9 miles) to Biescas.*

Biescas, Huesca

7 Biescas is a pretty little summer resort with neat white houses and red-tiled roofs. The **parish church** was erected by the Knights Templar. Look out for the **Ermita de Santa Elena** (Hermitage of St Helen) on the outskirts of town, perched on top of a steep rock.

If time permits, take a side trip up to the picturesque little villages of **Panticosa** (with a nearby spa and lake) and **Sallent de Gallego**, a good fishing and mountaineering centre (reached north on the **C136**).

*Take the **N260** east for 24km (15 miles) to Torla.*

Torla, Huesca

8 The drive continues through typical Pyrenean scenery to the picturesque little mountain village of Torla, with narrow, winding streets and hidden corners. Torla serves as the entrance to the Parque Nacional de Ordesa.

Take the road for a short distance into the Parque Nacional de Ordesa y Monte Perdido (Ordesa National Park and Monte Perdido).

Parque Nacional de Ordesa, Huesca

9 This is an area of exceptional beauty, covering a vast expanse of mountains, valleys and forests. It has been designated a National Park since 1918 as a means of protecting its rich flora and fauna and its natural surroundings. The park has been increased in size over the years. A deep canyon through ridges of limestone has created gigantic rock formations, in magnificent shades of grey, red and ochre, caused by the effects of the soil. Weather conditions are normally suitable for access by car between May and September. The park has been laid out with many pathways, which take you to caves, pools and waterfalls, with a number of lookout points offering magnificent views. Among the numerous beauty spots, look out for the **Tamborrotera Waterfall**, which can be viewed from a look-out point near the park's entrance.

*Return to Torla and take the **N260** south to Ainsa, 49km (30 miles).*

Ainsa, Huesca

10 The old walled town of Ainsa is built on a promontory overlooking

the junction of the rivers Cinca and Ara. Way back in the 11th century it was the capital of a small kingdom formed by García Jiménez after his victorious battles against the Moors. The town is picturesque, with old, grey-coloured stone houses and a pretty main square, the Plaza Mayor, which is bordered by attractive arcades. The Romanesque **parish church** features an interesting bell-tower and an elegant cloister.

*Take the **C138** south and join the **N123** for 68km (42 miles) to Barbastro.*

Barbastro, Huesca

11 Barbastro is a city with ancient roots. The original town was devastated by Pompey and received the name of Brutina, after Decius Brutus. After occupation by the Moors it was retaken by the Christians in 1064. The **cathedral** is a fine monument, built in the 16th century in the late Gothic style. It has an elegant interior, with lovely stellar vaults. Of particular interest are the 16th-century altarpieces by Damian Forment and his pupils. The **Museo Episcopal** merits a visit. The **Ayuntamiento** is housed in the old Palacio de los Argensolas, built in the late 15th century.

Take the regional road northeast for 23km (14 miles) to Alquézar.

Alquézar, Huesca

12 A drive through rugged terrain takes you to this fascinating little village straggling up the slopes of a

Torla is a typical mountain village with narrow streets and secret corners, backed by the characteristically dramatic cliffs of the mighty Pyrenees .

rock, overshadowed by a large castle. The town has a Moorish appearance, with reddish-brown buildings that merge in with the natural colours of the surroundings. The best plan is to leave your car in a parking area at the entrance to the village and proceed on foot. You will find old narrow streets lined with large arcades, eaves and galleries. A walk up the hill leads to the old **castle**, which was originally built as a fortress in the 12th century. The **Colegiata** (Collegiate Church) inside the castle has the remains of an elegant Romanesque cloister and a small museum, which contains a beautiful Gothic statue of Christ.

*Take the regional road southwest and join the **N240** back to Huesca, 61km (38 miles).*

Huesca – Castillo de Loarre **30 (19)**
Castillo de Loarre – Ayerbe **8 (5)**
Ayerbe – Berdún **54 (34)**
Berdún – San Juan de la Peña **29 (18)**
San Juan de la Peña – Jaca **21 (13)**
Jaca – Sabiñanigo **18 (11)**
Sabiñanigo – Biescas **15 (9)**
Biescas – Torla **24 (15)**
Torla – Parque Nacional de Ordesa **8 (5)**
Parque Nacional de Ordesa – Ainsa **49 (30)**
Ainsa – Barbastro **68 (42)**
Barbastro – Alquézar **23 (14)**
Alquézar – Huesca **61 (38)**

RECOMMENDED WALKS

9 *Parque Nacional de Ordesa, Huesca* The whole tour offers endless possibilities for walking in the mountains and valleys of the Aragonese Pyrenees. Torla is a good base for a number of walks into the **Ordesa National Park**, offering superb scenery of mountains and forests. Trails are marked and there is an information office.

12 *Alquézar, Huesca* From Alquézar there is an interesting walk to the **Grotto of Villacantal** which is believed to date back to prehistoric times. Near by is another cave where animal paintings can be seen from the outside, thought to be some 4,000 years old.

2 days – 425km (263 miles)

NAVARRE & WINE COUNTRY

Pamplona ● Artajona ● Tafalla ● Ujué ● Olite ● Tudela
Tarazona ● Agreda ● Soria ● Logroño ● Estella
Pamplona

Pamplona (Irunea) is famous for its celebrated festival of *Sanfermines*, or the running of the bulls, which is held between 6 and 14 July. Originally a Roman town, *Pompaelo* (City of Pompey), it was occupied by the Moors briefly in the 8th century, and between the 10th and early 16th centuries was capital of the kingdom of Navarra. Today Pamplona is capital of Navarra.

A maze of old narrow streets surrounds the massive *cathedral* with its 14th-century cloister which is regarded as one of the finest examples of medieval architecture in Europe. The town's focal point is the large *Plaza del Castillo*, partly encircled by old ramparts. Also worth a look are the *Museo de Navarra*, the *Ayuntamiento* (town hall) with its ornate baroque façade, and the nearby church of *San Saturnino*, Pamplona's oldest church.

[i] Duque de Ahumada 3

> *Take the **N121** south. Branch off right and take the regional road southwest to Artajona, 32km (19 miles).*

La Rioja is famous for its wines and is one of Spain's most important wine-growing regions

Artajona, Navarra

1 From quite a distance you can spot the great mass of fortifications that surround the medieval town of Artajona. Known as El Cerco de Artajona, this conclave of solid ramparts and square towers is a very impressive sight. On the summit stands the imposing fortified **Iglesia de San Saturnino**. Dating back to the middle of the 13th century, it is noted for its finely sculpted front and a 15th-century retable.

> *Take the regional road southeast for 11km (7 miles) to Tafalla.*

Tafalla, Navarra

2 The ancient town of Tafalla lies on the banks of the River Cidacos, overlooked by the old 14th-century fortress of Santa Lucia. The old part of town is around the main **church** and here you will come across the attractive **Plaza de los Fueros**, together with a network of fascinating little streets and handsome mansions with elegant façades. The Romanesque **Iglesia de Santa María** is noted for the large 16th-century Renaissance altarpiece by the Basque sculptor, Juan de Ancheta. Of interest, too, is the 16th-century retable from La Oliva by the Flemish artist, Roland de Moys, in the **Convento de la Concepción** (Convent of the Conception).

> *Take the **C132** east and branch off southeast to Ujué, just after San Martín de Unx.*

Ujué, Navarra

3 A last bend in the road reveals the sight of this quaint hilltop village, dominated by a huge **fortified church**.

The main square, Pamplona, home of the encierra

A walk through its tiny winding streets and alleys and up narrow steps is a journey back into the Middle Ages. The Romanesque **Iglesia de Santa María** dates back mostly to the late 11th century, with 14th-century additions. In the central chapel is a statue of Santa María la Blanca, made of silver plate on wood. The church is surrounded by the massive towers of the old fortifications. These hold a commanding position over the area and offer sweeping views of the Pyrenees.

Return to San Martín de Unx and take the regional road southwest to Olite, 19km (12 miles).

Olite, Navarra

4 The medieval **castle** of Olite gives the appearance of a whole city in itself. It was once the seat of the Court of Navarra and has been excellently preserved. The castle was built in the 13th and 15th centuries and restored in 1940. It is an imposing structure of massive walls and tall square towers, part of which has now been turned into a parador. Below lies the little town of Olite. The **Iglesia de Santa María la Real** is noted for its 14th-century Gothic portal. The **Iglesia de San Pedro** (St Peter) and the convents of San Francisco and Santa Clara all date from the Middle Ages.

*Take the **N121** south for 53km (33 miles) to Tudela.*

Tudela, Navarra

5 Tudela is the second city in Navarra and an old episcopal town. It lies on the banks of the River Ebro and is the centre of a rich agricultural area. It was taken from the Moors in 1119, but retained Moorish influences for several centuries. This is evident in the old Moorish quarter and the Mudejar-style architecture of many of the houses, which were built of brick.

The **cathedral** is an imposing monument, built between the 12th and 13th centuries. An outstanding feature is the Gothic entrance, known as the **Puerta del Judicio** (Doorway of the Last Judgement). A wide archway over the door is decorated with a large number of sculpted figures portraying the Last Judgement. Inside, the church has many notable works of art from the Gothic period. The 18th-century Capilla de Santa Ana is noted for its rich interior and fine baroque altarpiece. The Romanesque cloister, with finely carved capitals, contains the tomb of Don Fernando, son of King Sancho El Fuerte (The Strong One). In the nearby **Iglesia de San Nicolás** (St Nicholas) is the tomb of Sancho El Fuerte, who died in 1234 and lay there until he was reburied in Roncesvalles.

Other buildings of interest include the **Ayuntamiento** (town hall), with notable archives, the Renaissance **Casa del Almirante** (House of the Admiral) and the **Iglesia de la Magdalena**, which has a Romanesque tower and finely sculpted door. The **Plaza Nueva** (New Square) was designed in the 18th century.

i Plaza de los Fueros

*Continue on the **N121** southwest for 23km (14 miles) to Tarazona.*

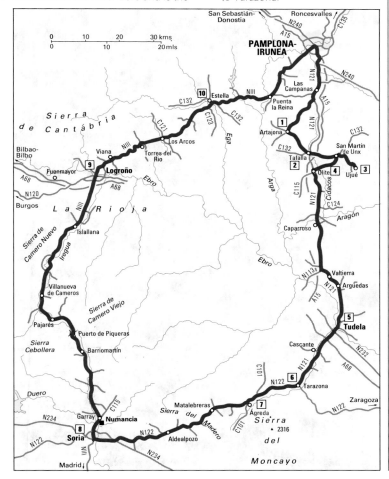

☐ Ayuntamiento, Plaza Navarra 7

Take the N122 southwest for 20km (12 miles) to Agreda.

Agreda, Soria

7 Perched high on top of a rock is the old town of Agreda, once an important frontier town overlooking the one-time kingdoms of Aragon and Castile. Dominating the town is the **Castillo de la Muela**, which still has a few remnants of old Moorish ramparts. Buildings of particular interest include the **Iglesia de San Miguel**, which features a notable Renaissance painting; the **Iglesia de Nuestra Señora de la Peña**, with panel paintings from the Gothic period; and the **Convento de la Concepción** (Convent of the Conception), which contains the tomb of Sister María de Agreda (1602–65), mystic and religious advisor for many years to Philip IV of Spain.

Agreda is a good base for trips into the **Sierra del Moncayo**, which can be explored by car or on horseback.

Continue southwest on the N122 for 50km (31 miles) to Soria.

Soria, Soria

8 Soria has inspired many Spanish poets. One of the most famous was the Sevillian poet, Antonio Machado (1875–1939), who lived here for a time and expounded the town's many virtues.

Outstanding among its many fine monuments is **San Juan de Duero**, a 12th-century monastery just outside the centre, on the left bank of the river. It was once a house of the Templars and features a beautiful cloister. The **Palacio de los Condes de Gómara** (Palace of the Counts of Gómara) is a majestic building, built in the 16th century in the Renaissance style and dominated by an impressive tower. The **Catedral de San Pedro** (12th–16th century) is noted for its elegant Plateresque doorway and Romanesque cloister. The 12th-century **Iglesia de Santo Domingo** has a richly decorated Romanesque façade, and the **Iglesia de San Juan de Rabanera** is noted for its colonnades, which have been preserved from the original cloister and have an unusual Romanesque-Oriental design. The **Museo Numantino** (Numancia Museum) contains antiquities from nearby Numancia. There are good views of the surrounding plains from the top of the hill, which bears traces of the old castle.

About 8km (5 miles) north of the town are the remains of **Numancia**, an old Celtiberian fort renowned for its resistance to a siege by the Romans, until it fell in 133 BC. The Romans built over the old city and many objects of significance were discovered after excavations started at the beginning of the 20th century.

☐ Plaza Ramon y Cajal

Take the NIII north for 107km (66 miles) to Logroño.

Logroño, La Rioja

9 Logroño, capital of the region of La Rioja, stands on the banks of the Ebro between Upper and Lower Rioja. Its tower and the outline of its

---

RECOMMENDED WALKS

One of the most pleasant areas for walking on this itinerary is around **Roncesvalles**, which offers beautiful surroundings of meadows, woods and valleys, with little villages dotted about the countryside. If you enjoy walking in woods, try the **forest of Garralda**, which is in the vicinity and famous for its magnificent oaks.

BACK TO NATURE

Centred around Monte Adi, located to the west of Roncesvalles, and just south of the French border, is the nature reserve **Coto Nacional de Quinto Real**, which covers a large area of high mountain peaks and forested slopes. The black woodpecker features among the many different species of birdlife that live and nest here. This bird is very striking since it is the size of a crow and has a very loud call.

A local inhabitant watches the world go by in Soria, an old-world town with many fine buildings

Tarazona, Zaragoza

6 The present town of Tarazona was built on the site of the Celtiberian city of Turiaso. It was occupied first by the Romans, then the Moors, and was recaptured in 1118 by the Christian King Alfonso I of Aragon. It continued as a royal residence until the 15th century. The town is noted for the number of Mudejar-style buildings and is often referred to as the 'Aragonese Toledo'.

The **cathedral** was begun in the 12th century and shows a combination of styles, mainly Mudejar and Gothic, with influences of baroque and Plateresque art. The **Iglesia de la Magdalena** has an impressive Mudejar tower, and the **Guildhall** has an interesting façade with reliefs of scenes from the legends of Hercules. The 14th- to 15th-century **Palacio Episcopal** (Bishop's Palace) was once the residence of the Kings of Aragon. The 16th-century **Ayuntamiento** has a frieze around the building with scenes depicting the capture of Granada.

buildings form a graceful silhouette, which centres around the **Iglesia de Santa María de la Redonda** (St Mary the Circular One) with its impressive baroque towers and finely carved altars. The Imperial Church of **Santa María de Palacio** was founded in the 11th century and has a lofty pyramid-shaped tower built in the 13th century. The 15th-century **cathedral** has a fine baroque façade built in the 18th century, and the **Iglesia de San Bartolmé** (13th century) is noted for its fine Romanesque-Gothic doorway. Over the River Ebro is an historic stone bridge used by the pilgrims in ancient times on their expeditions to the shrine of Santiago de Compostela.

*Take the **NIII** north for 48km (30 miles) to Estella.*

Estella, Navarra

10 The old town of Estella lies on the banks of the River Ega. During the Middle Ages it was the residence of

Terraced gardens in the little town of Agreda. It was once a stronghold on the frontiers of Castile and Aragon

the Kings of Navarre and also a staging point for the pilgrims on their way to Santiago de Compostela, who called the town 'Estella la Bella' (Estella the Beautiful). The 12th-century **Iglesia de San Pedro de la Rua** has a fine façade and Romanesque cloister. The **Iglesia de Santo Sepulcro** (Holy Sepulchre) stands on the pilgrim route. The **Palacio Real** (Royal Palace), **Palacio de los Reyes de Navarra** (Palace of the Kings of Navarre) and the **Palacio del Duque de Granada** (Palace of the Duke of Granada) feature among its many fine palaces and old mansions.

i Bajos del Ayuntamiento

*Return to Pamplona northeast on the **NIII**, a distance of 43km (27 miles).*

Pamplona – Artajona **32 (19)**
Artajona – Tafalla **11 (7)**
Tafalla – Ujué **19 (12)**
Ujué – Olite **19 (12)**
Olite – Tudela **53 (33)**
Tudela – Tarazona **23 (14)**
Tarazona – Agreda **20 (12)**
Agreda – Soria **50 (31)**
Soria – Logroño **107 (66)**
Logroño – Estella **48 (30)**
Estella – Pamplona **43 (27)**

FOR CHILDREN

9 *Logroño, La Rioja* Children would very much enjoy a festival that takes place in Anguiano (southwest of Logroño) on 21 and 22 July in honour of Mary Magdalene. The celebrations centre around the **Danza de los Zancos**, or Stilt Dance, when a troupe of dancers descend the steps of the church on stilts and then proceed down the hill at great speed. They are attired in colourful traditional costumes and present a fascinating and unusual demonstration of folklore.

CENTRAL SPAIN & THE WEST

A vast area of Spain is formed by the great central plain known as the Meseta, or tableland, an inland region ringed by a series of hills and bordering Portugal to the west. In the centre lies Madrid, capital of Spain and the highest capital in Europe, standing at an altitude of 646m (2,120 feet).

Within north Meseta is the region of Castile-Leon, while south Meseta contains Madrid and Castile-La Mancha. In the southwestern section is Extremadura, which also forms part of the Meseta. The great mountain chain of the Central Cordillera sweeps down the Castilian plain from the northwest to the southwest, divided into the Sierra de Guadarrama, Sierra de Gredos and the Peña de Francia. The dry, barren Toledo mountains dominate the landscape south of Madrid, while to the east are the wild, Serranía de Cuenca.

The Duero, Tajo, Guadiana and Guadalimar are four important rivers that rise in the heartlands of the region and flow down to the Atlantic, with the addition of many tributaries, producing areas of fertile, irrigated lands. Dramatic changes of scenery and climatic differences are contained within the region, where wild eroded landscapes contrast with fresh green forested slopes and valleys and the dry flatlands of the south.

Castile is derived from the word *castillo*, meaning castle in Spanish. This was once a land of castles and fortresses that were built in the 12th century to defend its borders during the conflicts between the Moors and Christians. Later, further lines of fortification were erected to protect the frontiers between the kingdoms of Castile and Aragon, with some of the principal fortresses belonging to the great feudal families of Spain. The marriage of Isabella of Castile and Ferdinand II of Aragon in 1469 joined these two important kingdoms and led to the unification of Spain.

La Mancha is a vast region of fields and plains, where windmills and castles serve as a reminder that this is Don Quixote land. Its fields are cultivated with cereals, olive groves and saffron, and it is also Spain's largest wine-growing region.

Extremadura has played a very important role in history as the birthplace of many of the great explorers and conquerors of the New World. Life can be tough in Extremadura, which presents a panorama of dry, rocky moorlands. There are irrigated areas around the rivers Alagón and Tajo that produce a number of crops, including cotton, tobacco and wheat.

Among the most important crafts still practised in Castile are the traditional blue-and-yellow ceramics from Talavera and pottery in La Mancha.

The 15th-century castle at Manzanares el Real has elaborately decorated turrets

Tour 16

Art is the essence of this tour. Admirers of El Greco can see his greatest masterpieces in the best possible setting – Toledo. This jewel of a town is one of Spain's major attractions, renowned for its spectacular setting as well as for the wealth of treasures to be seen here. Another highlight is a visit to one of the famous Royal Palaces, with their lavishly decorated rooms and elegant gardens. A long drive south through the plains of south Meseta is rewarded by a glimpse of La Mancha country.

Tour 17

This eastern section of Castile-La Mancha offers an unusual itinerary with terrific scenery. The route takes in some of the splendid old fortified towns that once protected the borders between warring kingdoms. A total contrast is provided by a visit to the fascinating 'hanging houses', and a drive through some spectacular scenery to an area of extraordinary rock formations. Old Roman ruins provide more cultural interest. The journey picks up the trail of the legendary Don Quixote, which leads

down to the great plains and wind-mills of La Mancha.

Tour 18

The first part of this tour travels west through the Central Cordillera, with magnificent scenery provided by the Guadarrama Mountains to the north and the southern peaks of the Sierra de Gredos. In the midst of the mountains are two special monuments: a great monastery and a commemoration to the fallen of the Civil War. Great architectural achievements have produced these two totally contrasting structures, close in proximity but centuries apart. An old mystical walled city in a dramatic setting and an ancient monastery of historical interest combine with visits to some fine churches and an important crafts centre.

Tour 19

Royal palaces and ancient castles form the basis of this tour, with the focus on a beautiful golden city, where the famous Alcázar and Aqueduct rate highly among Spain's many attractions. A number of palaces in this area were originally built as hunting lodges and favoured by the Royals, who came to hunt in the surrounding parklands. The route makes a circular tour northwest of

Madrid, passing through the magnificent forests, lush green valleys and clear sparkling rivers to be found in the area around the Guadarrama Mountains.

Tour 20

This tour explores a lesser known area of Spain. Extremadura is a sparsely populated region situated in the extreme west of the country, sharing an extensive border with Portugal. The fascination of the area lies in its very remoteness and the desolation of its forgotten landscapes, some of which are magnificent. The area is steeped in history and was the birthplace of Cortés and Pizarro, among many other great explorers and discoverers of the New World.

Tour 21

This tour covers an area northwest of Madrid and will appeal to those with an interest in cities and cathedrals of historical interest. The region has close associations with Spain's great hero, El Cid, valiant conqueror of the Moors, and many traces of his life and exploits can be followed up. A dominant feature of the tour is one of the country's most famous cathedrals, which is known for its impressive interior, where you can see the tomb of El Cid.

2 days – 293km (181 miles)

ART TREASURES OF CASTILLA-LA MANCHA

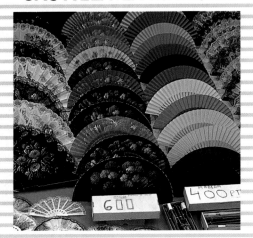

Madrid ● Illescas ● Toledo ● Consuegra ● Aranjuez
Chinchón ● Ciempozuelos ● Valdemoro ● Pinto ● Getafe
Madrid

Madrid, capital of Spain, is a modern city with a fast pace of life. However, old Madrid still preserves traces of its long history. The medieval city extends on either side of the *Calle Mayor*, leading from the *Puerta del Sol*, Madrid's busy focal point. A stroll here will reveal narrow streets, interesting old buildings and elegant façades.

To the north of the Calle Mayor is the small 12th-century *Iglesia de San Nicolás de los Servitas*, noted for its fine Mudejar tower, the oldest in Madrid. A collection of valuable maps and documents relating to the old city is kept in a recess inside the church and may be viewed through a grille. Other places of interest include the *Iglesia de San Pedro* with another splendid Mudejar tower; the 15th-century house of the Lujanes family on Plaza de la Villa; the Mudejar entrance to the *museum*; and the square of the Marquis of Comillas.

ⓘ Plaza Mayor 3

From Madrid take the **N401** *southwest for 36km (22 miles) to Illescas.*

The richly carved altarpiece in Toledo Cathedral

SPECIAL TO...

La Mancha is an important wine-growing region, with several large vineyards in the area. Among the best known are the light red and white table wines from Valdepeñas in the south. A wine festival is held here early in September to celebrate the grape harvest.

2 *Toledo, Toledo* There is a long tradition of Arab-originated craftwork in Toledo, which is known for its damascene articles, metalwork and steel ornaments inlaid with gold or silver. Knives, jewellery and all sorts of adornments for the home make attractive, if somewhat overdone, souvenirs.

FOR CHILDREN

2 *Toledo, Toledo* During your visit to the **Alcázar** in Toledo, be sure that the children see the fascinating collection of toy soldiers, which is displayed in some of the rooms on the first floor.

A colourful selection of fans, a traditional accessory, on display at a stall in Madrid

Illescas, Toledo

1 Those with a special interest in art will want to stop here to look at paintings by El Greco. A collection of five works by the great master himself are to be seen in the church of the **Hospital de la Caridad**, featuring paintings from 1600 to 1604. While here, take a look at the 13th-century **parish church of Santa María**, which dates back to the 16th century and has a fine Mudejar tower.

Continue on the **N401** *for 34km (21 miles) to Toledo.*

Toledo, Toledo

2 Toledo is undisputedly one of Spain's finest jewels. It is rich in art and treasures, combined with a great deal of historical interest. Once the capital of an Iberian tribe, it was taken over by the Romans in 192BC and called *Toletum*. In 1085 the city was captured from the occupying Moors by King Alfonso VI of Castile and after that became the residence of the kings of Castile, continuing to flourish as a centre of art and learning. It reached the height of its splendour towards the end of the 15th and first half of the 16th centuries. When King Philip II transferred the capital to Madrid in 1561, however, Toledo lost all its political status.

The **Cathedral** stands majestically on the Plaza Mayor (main square). Built between 1227 and 1493 on the site of the Great Mosque, it is widely regarded as the finest Gothic cathedral in Spain after Burgos, with influences of the Mudejar style to be seen in some parts. Its elegant tower looks over the city. The **Sanctuary** is the most richly decorated area of the interior. Expanded in the 16th century, it is noted for the retable depicting the *Life of Christ*. The **Chapterhouse** is distinguished by its fine Mudejar ceiling and stucco doorways.

One of the famous windmills on the flat La Mancha plain. They were immortalised by Cervantes in his novel Don Quixote

The **Sacristy** has an excellent collection of paintings by El Greco, Goya, Van Dyck and other famous artists. The **Treasury Room** boasts an elegant Plateresque door by Covarrubias and a fine Mudejar ceiling. Of particular interest, however, is the splendid 16th-century gold- and silver-gilt monstrance by Enrique de Arfe. It stands 3m (10 feet) high and weighs about 200kg (440 pounds) and is carried through the streets during the Corpus Christi processions.

Toledo has been an inspiration for many writers and poets. Mention Toledo, however, and most people think of El Greco. Domenikos Theotokopoulos (known by the rather more pronounceable name of El Greco) came from Crete to Toledo around 1577. Here he remained and painted, producing many masterpieces. The **Iglesia de Santo Tomé** contains *The Burial of the Count of Orgaz*, one of his most famous paintings. The **museum** housed in the former hospital of La Santa Cruz, has a collection of his work, including the notable *Assumption of Our Lady*. Other valuable works of art may also be seen here; more fine paintings can be seen in the Museum of the Foundation (**Duquesa de Lerma**). Enthusiasts will want to visit the **Casa y Museo del Greco** (El Greco's House and Museum), which stands very close to the place where he lived from 1585 until his death in 1614. The famous *View of Toledo* features among the superb collection of his work to be seen in the museum.

The **Alcázar** (Citadel) stands in a prominent position on the highest point of the town. The old fortress was destroyed and rebuilt many times during the course of its history. In the 16th century Charles V had the fortress converted into a royal residence. It received damage during the wars of the 18th and 19th centuries, but was devastated by the siege that took place here in 1936 during the Civil War. The garrison, then a cadet school, was besieged by forces of the Republican side. The inmates of the garrison, which included many women and children, held out heroically for some eight weeks until relief came. The building has since been reconstructed and is now a national monument.

i Puerta de la Bisagra

*Leave by the **N401/N400**, turn right on to the **N401**, then left on to the **C400** to Consuegra, 63km (39 miles).*

Consuegra, Toledo

3 This part of the itinerary takes you south to the flat desolate heartlands of La Mancha, immortalised by the pen of Miguel Cervantes in his classic about the adventures of Don Quixote and his faithful servant Sancho Panza. The very essence of La Mancha is conjured up here by the silhouette of an old ruined **castle** and 13 white **windmills**, many of which have been rebuilt and some of which are

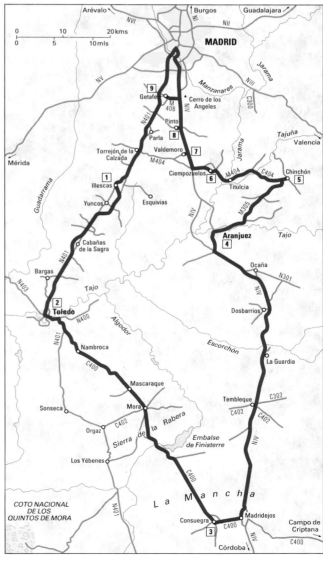

SCENIC ROUTES

3 *Consuegra, Toledo* This route travels south to La Mancha through vast flat expanses of fields that stretch away to invisible horizons. Occasional trees, hills and hamlets relieve the landscape. Its very remoteness and the subtle colours have a definite appeal, a sentiment shared by Cervantes, who chose this setting for the travels of Don Quixote. No visit to La Mancha is complete without a glimpse of the famous windmills in the southern part of the region. You will see them around Consuegra, but for a good 'windmill run' take the **C400** southeast from Consuegra to Campo de Criptana (southeast on the **C400**, then left on to the **N420**).

museums for pottery and wine. The village of Consuegra has a charming main square overlooked by a large tower. It was here that Don Diego died, only son of Spain's great hero, El Cid.

*Take the **C400** east to Madridejos and join the **NIV** north and continue for 78km (48 miles) to Aranjuez, which lies 5km (3 miles) off this road.*

Aranjuez, Madrid

4 The town is dominated by the famous **Palacio Real** (Royal Palace). Grand entrance gates lead to a large courtyard where you can admire the palace's lovely façade. It was built in the classical style, showing harmony and symmetry in its proportions. The grand central staircase is Italian in design, and the walls on either side are hung with tapestries from Belgium. The elegant salons include the **Sala de la China** (Porcelain Salon), the **Salon del Trono** (Throne Room) and **el Arabe** (the Arab), which was built under the instruction of Queen

Isabella II and whose sumptuous decorations bear a resemblance to those of the Alhambra at Granada.

Close by is the **Casa del Principe** (Prince's House). This small palace was built in the neoclassical style by Charles IV for his son and is noted for the Pompeiian Gallery, which is filled with magnificent marbles and statues. Another important building is the **Casa del Labrador** (Labourer's House), which resembles the Petit Trianon at Versailles. Also built in the neoclassical style, it has a richly ornate interior decorated with beautiful silk hangings. Its collection of treasures include Roman mosaics, porcelain clocks and a magnificent gallery of Greek statues.

Several gardens surround the palace. These are beautifully laid out with trees, shrubs and flowers. You will come across waterfalls and pools, with graceful statues and attractive little pavilions. The gardens bear different names, including the **Jardín del Rey** (King's Garden), **Jardín de la Reina** (Queen's Garden), **Jardín de la Isla** (Island Garden), situated on a

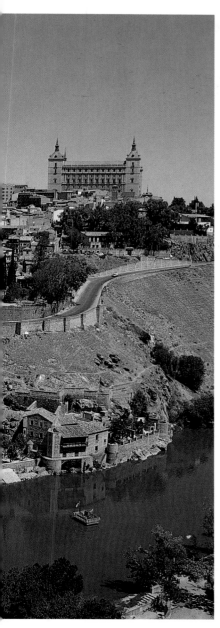

The spectacular setting of Toledo, overlooking the River Tajo. The tower of the cathedral punctuates the centre of the skyline

Ciempozuelos, Madrid

6 A brief stop here is suggested for those with a special interest in art and architecture. Two monuments are of particular note. The Sanatorium is a magnificent example of the neo-Mudejar style of architecture, and the small **parish church** contains the fine painting, *The Heath of Mary Magdalena*, by Claudio Coello.

*Carry on along this road, then turn right on meeting the **NIV**. Drive for a short distance north and turn left to Valdemoro, 7km (4 miles).*

Valdemoro, Madrid

7 More works by the artist Claudio Coello can be seen in the little 16th-century **parish church**, along with paintings by Goya and by his brother-in-law, Francisco Bayeu. Look out for the splendid retables and tabernacle.

*Rejoin the **NIV** and continue north. Turn left to Pinto after a short distance of about 6km (4 miles).*

Pinto, Madrid

8 The major attraction of Pinto is the **Castillo de los Duques de Frías** (Castle of the Dukes of Frias), an imposing structure dating back to the 15th century, where the Princess of Eboli, notorious for her intrigues at the court of Philip II, was confined from 1578 to 1581. The **parish church** was built in the Gothic-Plateresque style and has some finely carved decorations, especially on the pulpits.

*Take the **NIV** again and proceed north. Turn left on to the **M406** to Getafe, 10km (6 miles).*

Getafe, Madrid

9 The town's most distinguishing feature is the Renaissance-style **Iglesia de la Magdalena**, noted for its huge columns and splendid retable. Inside you can see paintings by two fine baroque artists, Claudio Coello and Alonso Cano.

Just beyond the junction of the M406 and the NIV, a turning to the right takes you along to the **Cerro de los Angeles** (Hill of Angels). This conical-shaped hill is considered the geographical centre of Spain and is marked by the imposing 'Corazón de Jesús' (Heart of Jesus) monument, which is topped by a tall figure of Christ and a church. There are sweeping views from here over the vast plains of Castile, the Guadarrama mountains and Madrid.

*Take the road east to the **NIV** and return to Madrid, 18km (11 miles).*

tiny man-made island between two sections of the river, with its avenue of plane-trees, and the **Jardín del Principe** (Prince's Garden), which contains many exotic species of trees.

*Take the regional road (**M305**) northeast for 22km (14 miles) to Chinchón.*

Chinchón, Madrid

5 One of the most attractive features of this charming little village is the **Plaza Mayor**. The square is surrounded by three- and four-storey houses with wooden balconies, which used to accommodate the spectators who watched the famous bullfights here in the old days. The **parish church** overlooking the square contains a painting of the Assumption, which hangs over the high altar and has been attributed to Goya (whose brother was once the town's parish priest).

*Take the **M404/C404** west to Ciempozuelos, a distance of 19km (12 miles).*

RECOMMENDED WALKS

4 *Aranjuez, Madrid* As a contrast to the dry plains of La Mancha, whose baking summer temperatures may not be conducive to much walking about, the fresh green gardens of the **Palace of Aranjuez** offer a most agreeable setting for a quiet stroll. Among the several gardens in the palace grounds, the **Jardín del Principe** (Prince's Garden) has been an inspiration for many artists. Its shady trees and graceful monuments exude a feeling of romance tinged with an air of melancholy that will make you want to linger in the cool shade of the trees and gaze over the river.

FOR HISTORY BUFFS

1 *Illescas, Toledo* Eight kilometres (5 miles) east of Illescas is the small town of **Esquivias**, where Cervantes set up home after his marriage in 1548 to Catalina de Salazar y Palacios, said to have been the inspiration behind his poem *Galatea*. The records of his marriage can be seen in the registry of the church of Santa María.

5 *Chinchón, Madrid* The Valley of Jarama, north of Chinchón where the **C300** joins the **NIII**, was the scene of a tough battle during the Spanish Civil War (1936–9). A great number of American volunteers took part in support of the Republican side, and traces of the old trenches can still be seen.

BACK TO NATURE

Situated in the wooded **Montes de Toledo** (Toledo mountains), in the southern part of the region, is the **Coto Nacional de los Quintos de Mora** (Quintos de Mora game reserve), which is the natural habitat of a wide variety of animals. Here you may spot any number of different animals, such as red deer, roe deer, boars, rabbits and hares. Birdlife includes partridges, wood pigeons, turtle doves, bee-eaters and quail. Also look for eyed and wall lizards among the rocks.

3 days – 668km (416 miles)

TRACES OF DON QUIXOTE

Madrid ● Alcalá de Henares ● Guadalajara ● Sigüenza
Cifuentes ● Cuenca ● La Ciudad Encantada ● Belmonte
Mota del Cuervo ● Ruinas de Segóbriga ● Uclés
Tarancón ● Arganda ● Madrid

In the 16th and 17th centuries, Madrid was ruled by the Habsburgs, then the Bourbons. The *Plaza Mayor* is the outstanding representative of the Habsburg period, a magnificent square, formerly the scene for tournaments, royal proclamations, bullfights and the burning of heretics. An equestrian statue of Philip III stands in the centre. Other legacies of this time are the *Casa del Ayuntamiento*, the *Casa de los Cisneros* (Swans), the *Palacio de los Vargas* and the *Capillo del Obispo* (with a fine retable).

The Churriguera family and their pupils instigated some fine baroque buildings, such as the churches of *Montserrat, Sacramento* and *San Andrés*, the *Bridge of Toledo* and the façade of *Cuartél del Conde Duque* (the old barracks). From the Bourbon period, the *Palacio Real* (Royal Palace) is considered one of the finest examples of neoclassical architecture. It is filled with treasures and works of art.

A white stork attends to its nest, perched precariously on top of a building, in the Alcalá de Henares, birthplace of Cervantes

ⓘ Plaza Mayor 3

From Madrid take the A2 which becomes the NII northeast for 33km (21 miles) to Alcalá de Henares.

Alcalá de Henares, Madrid

1 Alcalá is known as the birthplace of Miguel Cervantes, author of *Don Quixote de La Mancha*, and for the founding of the famous Ildefonso University in 1508. The university developed into one of the most famous centres of culture and science in western Europe. When it was transferred to Madrid in 1837 the town lost its status and subsequently went into a decline.

The old headquarters of the university were rebuilt between 1543 and 1583 by the great Rodrigo Gil de Hontañón and is the present **Colegio Mayor de San Ildefonso** (College of St Ildefonso). This is an elegant Renaissance building with an impressive Plateresque façade, decorated with the founder's coat of arms. It was badly damaged during the Spanish Civil War, but has been well restored. Inside are three graceful patios decorated in different styles. In the Central Hall is the seating area for the public. The walls are decorated with tablets bearing the names of the intellectuals who were here in the 16th and 17th centuries.

The town's main square is called **Plaza de Cervantes**, after the author. The **Calle Mayor**, where Cervantes was born in 1547, leads off the square. The **Casa de Cervantes** (House of Cervantes) was built very

FOR CHILDREN

1 *Alcalá de Henares, Madrid* Alcalá de Henares is renowned for its wide variety of sweets and cakes. It is especially known for its *almendras garrapinadas* (caramelised almonds), which are produced by the nuns of the Convento de San Diego and can be bought from the revolving hatchway in the door of the convent. Many different types of cakes, special to Alcalá, can also be found here, such as *rosquillas de Alcalá* (cakes in the form of a ring), *pestiños* (honey cakes) and *canutillos rellenos* (filled cakes in a tubular shape).

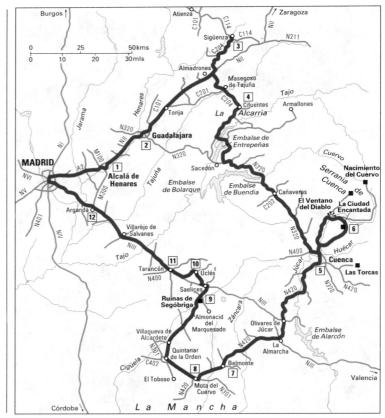

near his birthplace and houses a small museum with interesting items and relics relating to his life.

Cervantes had already written a number of works before he received instant acclaim with the publishing of the first part of *Don Quixote de la Mancha* in 1605. The second part was completed 1615.

ⓘ Callejón de Santa María

*Continue on the **NII** for a distance of 23km (14 miles) to Guadalajara.*

Guadalajara, Guadalajara

2 The finest feature of Guadalajara is the **Palacio del Infantado** (Palace of the Infant). Built between 1461 and 1492 by Mendoza, second Duke of Infantado, the palace was severely damaged by bombs in 1936 during the Spanish Civil War, but has been restored. Its main attraction is the pale façade, with diamond stonework decorations and an intricately carved gallery on top. Inside is a lovely two-storey patio with notable Isabelline arching (a type of ornate decoration used in the 15th century during the reign of Queen Isabella the Catholic). A small **fine arts museum** is housed here.

Among the churches in the town, the 15th-century **Iglesia de María** features a fine Mudejar tower and the 16th-century **Iglesia de San Ginés**

The isolated Cuenca region consists of craggy, boulder-strewn country

contains the tombs of various important personalities. Take a look, also, at the old **Roman bridge** over the River Henares.

ⓘ Travesia de Beladíez 1

*Take the **NII** northeast and take a left turn on the **C204** to Sigüenza, 75km (47 miles).*

Sigüenza, Guadalajara

3 The Castle was founded by the Romans and rebuilt between the 12th and 15th centuries, to become the residence of the bishops until the middle of the 19th century. The castle has a somewhat formidable fortress-like appearance and is a recognisable landmark in the vicinity. It has now been converted into a parador, with magnificent views of the surrounding landscapes.

The **Plaza Mayor** is overlooked by the **cathedral**, a solid structure of great towers and buttresses, built between the 12th and 14th centuries. It has an impressive interior, with several fine chapels. In the **Capilla de Santa Librada** is the tomb of the town's patron saint.

Adjoining the cathedral is the **Museo Episcopal**, where you can see some fine paintings by El Greco and Zurbarán and other works of art.

ⓘ Cardenal Mendoza 2

*Return to the **NII**, turn right for about 1.5km (1 mile), then left to take the **C204** southeast to Cifuentes, 50km (31 miles).*

SCENIC ROUTES

The most spectacular part of the journey is between Cuenca and La Ciudad Encantada. The route follows a winding road through firs and pines up to the Serranía de Cuenca, with superb views of the surrounding mountains, gorges and plains. A look-out point called **El Ventano del Diablo** (Devil's Window) offers an outstanding view extending for miles over the mountains and plains. The route continues through great eroded landcapes of canyons and gorges to La Ciudad Encantada.

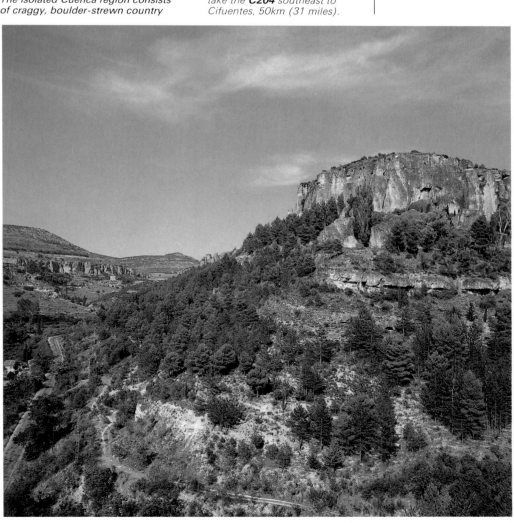

RECOMMENDED WALKS

4 *Cifuentes, Guadalajara* From Cifuentes you can walk in several directions, such as Villanueva or Armallones. South of Cifuentes are the three large reservoirs of Entrepeñas, Bolarque and Buendia.

6 *La Ciudad Encantada, Cuenca* Serious walkers will be in their element among the wild rocky landscapes of the Serrania de Cuenca. Northeast of La Ciudad Encantada is a lovely area of rich vegetation and pine forests, offering some gentle walks. A major attraction here is the sight of the source of the River Cuervo (Nacimiento del Cuervo), which emerges from tall rocks and partly out of a cave in a series of rippling cascades.

Cifuentes, Guadalajara

4 The name of Cifuentes means 'a hundred fountains', and indeed there are springs all over the area. Around La Provincia square is the 12th- to 13th-century **Iglesia de El Salvador**, with a late Romanesque portal and a Gothic rose window, and the **Convento de Santo Domingo**, which features an impressive 16th-century coat of arms on its façade. The ruins of a large 14th-century **castle** can be seen on top of the hill.

*Continue south on the **C204** and just east of Sacedon turn left on to the **N320**, travelling southeast to Cuenca, 142km (88 miles).*

Cuenca, Cuenca

5 The little main square is dominated by the **cathedral**, an imposing structure with an attractive pale-coloured façade. Built between the 12th and 13th centuries, it shows a mixture of Gothic and Renaissance styles. The high arches bear influences of Anglo-Norman architecture. Features of special note are the 18th-century high altar and elaborate 16th-century grille before the choir. The Knight's Chapel contains a number of tombs and panels by the celebrated artist Yañez de la Almedina. Around the corner is the **Museo Episcopal**, which contains two fine El Greco paintings, some

beautiful tapestries and a collection of rich gold religious crosses.

A road from the main square leads to the **Museum of Sacred Art**, which displays some beautiful treasures, principally from the 13th and 15th centuries. The **Iglesia de San Miguel**, situated high above a gorge, has a fine Mudejar ceiling and is renowned for its Holy Week concerts.

A path along the southern wall of the cathedral leads down to the spectacular 'Casas Colgadas', or Hanging Houses, for which Cuenca is famous. The buildings cling to the side of the cliff with balconies that protrude over the precipice. Originally built in the 14th century as a palace, they were later used as a town hall. By the 19th century they had fallen into decay but were restored in the early part of this century. One of the houses has been converted into a **Museum of Modern Art** and shows large, mainly abstract canvases against pure white walls.

Take the regional road north. Soon after El Ventana del Diablo lookout point, turn right on to the minor road to La Ciudad Encantada (the Enchanted City), which is 6km (4 miles) further on.

La Ciudad Encantada, Cuenca

6 By the car park is the entrance to this extraordinary fantasy world of gigantic rock formations, the result of thousands of years of erosion. Nature really has had a go here, and the imagination runs riot with the sheer size and incredible shapes of the rocks, which resemble a Roman bridge, a giant mushroom, a human profile and even the 'lovers of Teruel'. A route is indicated by arrows marked high up on the stones (if you notice them) and leads through a labyrinth of lost worlds.

*Return to Cuenca by the alternative route, taking the regional road south, through Valdecabras. At Cuenca, take the **N420** south to Belmonte (via La Almarcha), 123km (76 miles).*

Belmonte, Cuenca

7 Make a brief stop here to take a look at the old **castle** that stands on top of the hill. It has circular towers and was built by Juan Fernández Pacheco, Marquis of Villena, in the 15th century as a means of defending his extensive territories. It was later abandoned, and was restored in the 19th century. The main features of interest are the splendid Mudejar ceilings, especially in the audience chamber. There is a good view of the typical landscape of La Mancha. If possible, take a look inside the old **Colegiata** (Collegiate Church), which has an impressive collection of altarpieces from the 15th to 17th centuries and fine choir-stalls carved with religious scenes.

*Continue for 16km (10 miles) on the **N420** southwest to Mota del Cuervo.*

The Ciudad Encantada, or enchanted city, where erosion of the limestone rock by the elements has carved out boulders in weird and fantastic shapes

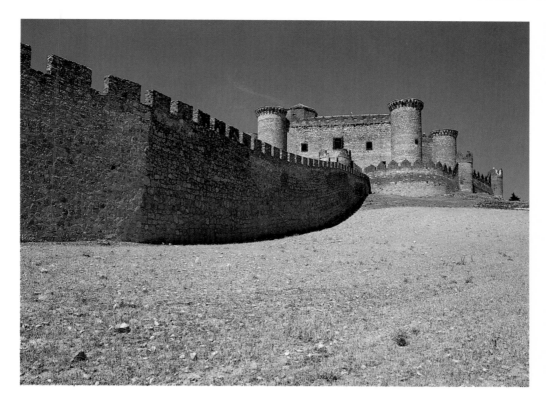

The castle on top of the hill above Belmonte, with its 15th-century round towers, gives good views of La Mancha

Mota del Cuervo, Cuenca

8 Right in the heartland of La Mancha country is the little village of Mota del Cuervo, which offers the familiar sight of white windmills silhouetted against deep blue skies, with the parched plains of La Mancha stretching away into the far distance. Now you are well and truly on the **Route of Don Quixote**, and a look at the windmills, some of which have been restored to working order, explains why the gallant old knight saw them as huge giants and attacked them.

Take the **N301** *to Quintanar de la Orden. Turn right on to the regional road northeast to the Ruinas de Segóbriga (Segóbriga ruins), just before the* **NIII**, *on the right, 60km (37 miles).*

Ruinas de Segóbriga, Cuenca

9 These ruins were once part of an important Roman town and the capital of Celtic Iberia. Here you can see the remains of an old **Roman amphitheatre** and **thermal baths**. Traces can also be seen of an old wall and of the Hispano-Visigothic **basilica**. A **museum** on the site provides a good insight into the history of the area.

Continue on the regional road to join the **NIII**. *Turn left and after 2km (1 mile) branch off right to Uclés.*

Uclés, Cuenca

10 The main attraction here is the massive **monastery**, whose warlike appearance indicates a certain past importance . It once belonged to the knightly Order of Santiago (St James), who were lords of the village

from the 12th century, and is sometimes referred to as the 'Escorial of La Mancha'. It has a magnificent Plateresque façade and an elegant 16th-century cloister. The two towers are also impressive and some remains are left of the old fortification walls.

Return to the **NIII** *and continue northwest to Tarancón.*

Tarancón, Cuenca

11 Make a short break here to look at the **church**, which has a fine Gothic façade and a notable retable inside, and the attractive **Palacio del Duque de Riansares**. Another building of interest is the handsome **mansion** built by Queen María Christina after she married a guardsman, on whom she bestowed the title of Duque de Riansares (Duke).

Continue on the **NIII** *northwest to Arganda.*

Arganda, Madrid

12 The splendid Renaissance church, the **Iglesia de San Juan Bautista**, was built in 1525 and has notable altars in the Churrigueresque style. The **Casa del Rey**, a former country house in gardens, was once the property of the Spanish royal family, and there is an old **castle**, dating from 1400.

Return to Madrid on the **NIII**.

2/3 days – 585km (364 miles)

MONUMENTS
& MOUNTAINS

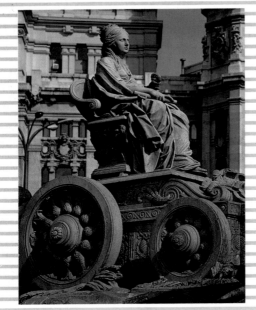

Madrid ● Valle de los Caídos ● El Escorial ● Ávila
Piedrahita ● El Barco de Ávila ● Béjar ● Plasencia
Monasterio de Yuste ● Talavera de la Reina
Navalcarnero ● Madrid

M adrid possesses one of the world's great art galleries in the *Museo del Prado*, housed in a splendid classical building on the Paseo del Prado. Spanish artists represented include El Greco, Velázquez, Goya, Murillo and Ribera. There are also notable works from the Italian, Flemish, Dutch, German, French and English schools of painting, as well as classical sculptures, silver objects and collections of coins.

Picasso's *Guernica*, together with sketches and engravings relating to the painting, are in the *Casón del Buen Retiro*, an annexe of the Prado. The Thyssen-Bornemisza art collection is housed in another annexe, the *Palacio Villahermosa*. Other galleries and museums include the *Museo Arqueológico*, with important collections, the *Palacio Real* (Royal Palace), the *Armería Real* (Royal Arsenal), the *Lazaro Galdiano Museum* and the *Museo Español de Arte Contemporane* (Spanish Museum of Contemporary Art).

> i Plaza Mayor 3
>
> *From Madrid take the NVI then the A6. At exit 2 turn off to the southwest on the M600, then almost immediately turn right to the Valle de los Caídos (Valley of the Fallen), 52km (32 miles).*

The Cibeles fountain in Madrid. Cibeles was the Greek goddess of fertility, here riding in a chariot. Behind is the main post office building

Valle de los Caídos, Madrid

1 A tall cross rising in the distance from a rock mass marks the monument of the Valle de los Caídos, dedicated to all who were killed during the Civil War. At the base of the cross is the entrance to the **basilica**, a vast crypt cut out from the hard granite rock of the mountain. A flight of steps off a large esplanade leads to the **church**, which has a sculpture of a black *piedad* over the entrance door. Fine Flemish tapestries hang between small chapels lining one side of the church. More steps lead to the crypt, which is assigned for worship. A figure of Christ, by the sculptor Zumaya, crowns the altar. Overhead is the vast underground dome, made up of several million mosaic pieces depicting saints, personalities and symbols of the Civil War. Near the altar are the tombs of General Franco, who died in 1975 and José Antonio Primo de Rivera, who died in 1936. Behind the altar is the choir, with stalls for the Benedictine monks from the adjoining monastery.

You can also take a funicular up to the Cross, which bears four huge figures representing the four Evangelists. A flight of steps continues up to the starting point of the Cross, which rises to a height of some 150m (495 feet). You will have a magnificent view from here of the surrounding landscape and other buildings, including the Benedictine monastery. A walk down the hill leads you past the 'Stations of the Cross'.

> *Rejoin the M600, turn right and continue southwest for 14km (9 miles) to El Escorial.*

El Escorial, Madrid

2 The **Monasterio del Escorial** is one of the wonders of Spain. This great granite building, whose full title in Spanish is the Monasterio de San Lorenzo del Escorial, stands as a testimony to King Philip II. He had it built to commemorate his defeat of the French at the battle of San Quentin on 10 August (St Lawrence's Day), 1557, and also as a burial place for his father, the great Carlos V. It was started in 1567 by Juan Bautista de

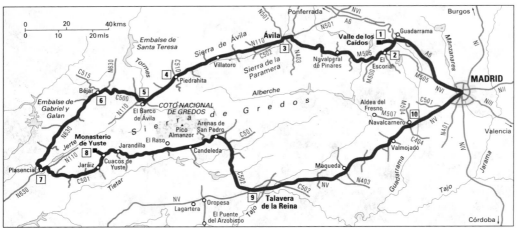

Toledo, who had trained in Italy, and was completed by his assistant, Juan de Herrera, in 1584.

The building centres around the church, which has two tall towers and a dome. The main entrance is through a large courtyard known as **La Lonja**. This leads to the vestibule and follows through to the **Patio de los Reyes** (Courtyard of the Kings). A few steps take you to the entrance to the church, which marks the building's geometric centre. Through the atrium is the **Basílica**, with an impressive dome that stands on four great arches resting on massive pillars. This was once the scene of great religious ceremonies.

The **Panteón de los Reyes** (Royal Pantheon) contains the sarcophagi of most of the Spanish kings since Carlos I. A few still remain unoccupied. The richly decorated **Palacio Real** (Royal Palace) was resided in by King Philip and subsequent Habsburg rulers, and is noted for its magnificent tapestries. The **Biblioteca de Impresos** (library) is sumptuously decorated with tapestries and frescos by many painters. It contains some 40,000 volumes and hundreds of ancient manuscripts, codices and bibles. Two priceless items are the illuminated *Codex Aureus* made for the German Emperor Conrad II (completed in 1039) and the diary of St Theresa of Ávila.

Fine works of art can be seen in the two museums located on the ground floor. The **Arts Museum** has a superb collection of paintings by famous masters. One of these is the *Martyrdom of St Maurice and The*

The Monastery of El Escorial in the foothills of the Sierra de Guadarrama. Originally built as a royal residence and monastery, it houses many treasures

Theban Legionary by El Greco. The **Architectural Museum** has a fascinating display of documents and plans relating to the construction of the monastery.

Of great interest, too, is the **Habitación de Felipe II** (Philip II's cell), where he spent the last years of his life in spartan conditions and troubled by pain. He died in an adjoining alcove in 1598. The **Casita del Príncipe** (Prince's Cottage) lies in lovely gardens to the east of the monastery. It was built by Carlos II in 1772 for his son, the future Carlos IV, and contains elegant furniture and many fine paintings.

☐ Floridablanca 10

*Take the **M505** northwest for 63km (39 miles) to Ávila.*

Ávila, Ávila

3 The medieval walls of Ávila are a familiar landmark in the area and can be seen for miles around. With 88 round towers and nine gates, they extend for 2,526m (2,763 yards), encircling the town. The **Catedral de San Salvador** forms part of the wall and has a rather fortress-like appearance. It was built between the 11th and 13th centuries and combines the Romanesque and baroque styles. Of special note inside are the 16th-century stained glass windows, the

FOR HISTORY BUFFS

2 *El Escorial, Madrid* A short drive south of El Escorial brings you to a spot known as the Silla de Felipe II (Philip II's seat). On the summit of a small hill among some boulders you will see what appear to be four seats carved from the rock. It is said that the king used to come here and meditate, while keeping a watchful eye on the progress of the construction of the monastery. There is a magnificent view from here of the monastery and the whole panorama.

SCENIC ROUTES

West of Madrid the impressive mountain panoramas of the Sierra de Guadarrama give way to the brown windswept plateau and strange boulders to be found around Ávila. Beyond Ávila the route enters the Sierra de Gredos, an area of dramatic mountain ranges and high peaks. The stretch between El Barco de Ávila and Plasencia on the **N110** passes through some spectacular scenery of mountains, valleys and pine forests. The drive from Plasencia to the Monasterio de Yuste and beyond Arenas de San Pedro (**C501**) also offers some outstanding scenery of heavily forested mountains.

Colourful posters advertise the delights of a flamenco festival in Madrid

BACK TO NATURE

The great mountain range of the **Sierra de Gredos**, which dominates the region to the west of Madrid, is an important habitat for birds of prey, and among the many species that can be seen here are short-toed and booted eagles, red kites, the goshawk and the occasional black stork. Among the many flowers and plants, you can find lupins, peonies and lilies-of-the-valley. The Spanish argus butterfly is special to the area. In the centre of this mountainous region is the protected national park of **Coto Nacional de Gredos**, where ibex live high up among the crags.

RECOMMENDED WALKS

The region of Gredos offers countless walks, and there are a few marked paths. There is a very pleasant walk from the Club Alpino to the lake (Laguna de Gredos) at the foot of the Almanzor peak. Other walks include a route along the Gargantas de Gredos del Pinar and the Garganta de Chilla, from El Raso.

painted altarpiece and the alabaster tomb of Cardinal Alonso de Madrigal, who was Bishop of Ávila and died in 1455. The **Basílica de San Vicente** is noted for its 14th-century façade and portal. The Romanesque **Iglesia de San Pedro** (12th–13th century) has a lovely rose window and fine high altar. The 15th-century **Convento de Santo Tomás** (Convent of St Thomas) features beautifully carved choir-stalls and a fine retable by Pedro Berruguete. In the mausoleum is the tomb of Prince Juan, only son of the Catholic monarchs Ferdinand and Isabella, who died in 1497 when only 19.

When you leave the cathedral by the other door you will find yourself within the walls of the old town. On this square stands the former **Convento de Santa Teresa** (Convent of St Theresa), which contains a chapel built in 1638 on the site of her birthplace. Inside you can see writings of the saint and relics – including her well-preserved ring finger. Facing the convent is the old palace of the former Viceroy of Peru. For more insight into St Theresa's life, look out for the **Convento de la Encarnación**, where she first took orders and spent some 30 years of her life, latterly as prioress. St Theresa was an exceptional person, remembered for her mystical writing and autobiography. Founder of a number of convents, she was canonised in 1622.

*Take the **N110** southwest to Piedrahita.*

Piedrahita, Ávila

4 The summer resort of Piedrahita was the birthplace of the Grand Duke of Alba, general of the army of King Philip II. Goya spent some time at the duke's palace here and it is said that there was a love affair between

the painter and the Duchess of Alba, who was the model for his well known painting *La Maja Desnuda*.

*Continue on the **N110** to El Barco de Ávila.*

El Barco de Ávila, Ávila

5 A drive through magnificent mountain scenery brings you to the small town of El Barco de Ávila, where a brief stop will enable you to visit the 14th-century **Castillo de Valdecorneja**, which is in need of repair, and the Gothic **parish church**, which contains some fine paintings. Spare a glance, too, for the old bridge over the River Tormes.

*Take the **C500** west to Béjar.*

Béjar, Salamanca

6 The **Palacio Ducal** (Palace of the Duke), an elegant 16th-century palace with a Renaissance courtyard, houses the **Museo Municipal**. The **Ayuntamiento** (town hall) is noted for its attractive arcades. In the **Iglesia de San Gil** is a museum housing the works of the great sculptor Mateo Hernández, renowned for his animal figures sculpted from hard stone.

i Paseo de Cervantes 6

*Take the **N630** to Plasencia.*

Plasencia, Cáceres

7 The **cathedral**, started in the 13th century and never completely finished, is a splendid structure with an attractive Plateresque north doorway. Inside, the altarpiece is worth a special look for its finely sculpted statues by Gregorio Hernández (17th-century). It also features a fine **Capilla Mayor** (Main Chapel), a 15th-century retable by Hernández and a graceful 15th-century cloister. The old quarters around the cathedral

contain narrow streets, fine façades and many houses with attractive wrought-iron balconies. Stepped streets lead up to the old ramparts, where you can walk and enjoy the fine views.

Take the C501 east for some 45km (27 miles). Turn off to the Monasterio de Yuste 2km (1 mile) north.

Monasterio de Yuste, Cáceres

8 Set deep in the woods is the old Monasterio de Yuste. It was founded by Hieronymite monks in 1404 and severely damaged by the French in 1809 during the Peninsular War. It fell into decay for a long period until its restoration in recent times. The monastery is the place to which Emperor Carlos V retired in 1556 after his abdication, leaving the throne to his son Philip II. You can see the royal chambers where Carlos stayed until he died in 1558, including his bedroom from where he could hear mass. A pathway leads up to a covered terrace from which there are good views of the surrounding plains.

i Trujillo 1

Return to and continue east on the C501. Join the C502 after Arenas de San Pedro and continue south to Talavera de la Reina, 124km (77 miles).

Talavera de la Reina, Toledo

9 Talavera de la Reina is famous for its attractive blue-and-yellow tiles, or *azulejos*, which have been produced since the 15th century. The tiles have been used over the centuries to adorn

Stout walls encircle the old part of Ávila, which has many fine medieval buildings

palaces, mansions, churches and other buildings. Craftsmen took their skills to Mexico after the Conquest in 1521 and the tradition continued. The Museo Ruiz de Luna displays potteryware from the 15th to 19th centuries. Monuments of interest in the town include the 13th-century Romanesque Iglesia de San Salvador, the Gothic Colegiata de Santa María la Mayor (13th–15th centuries), the Mudejar-style parish church of Santiago and the Capilla de Nuestra Señora del Prado, which is adorned with beautiful glazed tiles dating back to the 16th and 18th centuries.

i Ayuntamiento, General Primo de Rivera

Join and take the NV eastwards. Branch off left for a short distance to Navalcarnero, a total of 86km (53 miles).

Navalcarnero, Madrid

10 Make a brief stop here to take a look at the delightful little porticoed square and the fine parish church, which houses a notable retable and a fine work depicting the Apostles. Philip IV was married to Anne of Austria here in 1649.

Rejoin the NV and return to Madrid, 33km (21 miles).

Madrid – Valle de los Caídos 52 (32)
Valle de los Caídos – El Escorial 14 (9)
El Escorial – Ávila 63 (39)
Ávila – Piedrahita 56 (35)
Piedrahita – El Barco de Ávila 21 (13)
El Barco de Ávila – Béjar 30 (19)
Béjar – Plasencia 59 (37)
Plasencia – Monasterio de Yuste 47 (29)
Monasterio de Yuste – Talavera de la Reina 124 (77)
Talavera de la Reina – Navalcarnero 86 (53)
Navalcarnero – Madrid 33 (21)

SPECIAL TO...

9 *Talavera de la Reina, Toledo* El Puente del Arzobispo, located southwest of Talavera de la Reina, is another important pottery centre and produces a great variety of attractively decorated ceramics. Embroidery is a very popular craft in Spain and tends to be practised by families in rural areas.

FOR CHILDREN

10 *Navalcarnero, Madrid* A few miles northwest of Navalcarnero is the small town of Aldea del Fresno, where you will find an excellent Safari Park. A swimming-pool, lively fairground, mini golf and horseback riding feature among the attractions it offers.

2/3 days – 364km (226 miles)

THE ROUTE OF THE ROYAL PALACES

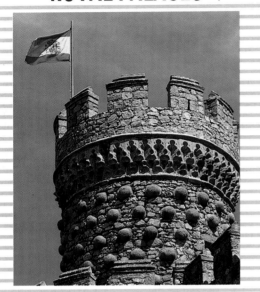

Madrid ● El Pardo ● Colmenar Viejo ● Manzanares el Real
Miraflores de la Sierra ● El Paular ● La Granja
Segovia ● Pedraza ● Sepúlveda ● Riaza
Buitrago del Lozoya ● Torrelaguna ● Madrid

Madrid is a very easy place to enjoy. The *Puerta del Sol* is the nerve-centre of the city, an area for shopping enthusiasts with two large department stores. Other major centres are the elegant section to the northwest of town, around Serrano, Goya and Conde de Peñalver, and an attractive shopping mall under the Palace Hotel in Paseo del Prado. On Sunday, visit *El Rastro* (the flea market), south of Calle Mayor with its colourful stalls, lively crowds and stirring gypsy music. Bullfights take place on Sunday afternoons.

One of Madrid's special delights is to sit in the Plaza Mayor over a drink on a warm evening. There are many bars and old restaurants in this area, including the famous *Mesones*. Madrid also has several beautiful parks. The *Parque del Buen Retiro* is one of the finest. Others include the *Parque de la Casa de Campo*, the *Botanical Garden* and the estate and park of *La Fuente del Berro*.

i Plaza Mayor 3

From Madrid take the NVI northwest. At Puerte de Hierro take the C601 north to El Pardo.

El Pardo, Madrid

1 The way to El Pardo is through the Bosque del Pardo, delightful wooded parklands where you might glimpse deer, wild boar or an eagle soaring above. These were old hunting grounds of the kings dating back to the 14th century. In the middle of this lush greenery lies the little town of El Pardo and the **Palacio de El Pardo**. The palace was built by Philip III over an earlier palace (built by Philip II and subsequently destroyed by fire), and was enlarged in the 18th century by the Italian, Sabatini, who was commissioned by Carlos III. General Franco resided here for 35 years until his death in 1975.

Elegant reception rooms and private apartments are lavishly furnished with ornate clocks, mirrors, lamps and candelabra. You can also see beautiful porcelain from Sevres and an impressive collection of some 360 tapestries. Also on show are General Franco's Great Dining-Room,

RECOMMENDED WALKS

You can do a lot of walking in the region of the Sierra de Guadarrama. The **Valle de la Acebeda** offers a number of attractive walks.

3 *Manzanares el Real, Madrid* South of the castle at Manzanares el Real is the man-made lake, **Embalse de Santillana**, where you can take a pleasant stroll along the shores.

6 *La Granja, Segovia* The old hunting grounds of the **Riofrio Palace** – some 11km (7 miles) south of La Granja – abound in deer that roam freely and tend to be on the tame side. This is another lovely area for a quiet walk.

The intricate decorations on the towers of the castle at Manzanares el Real suggest that it was built as a residence, not for defensive purposes

where cabinet meetings took place, and his private office, which contains a notable portrait of Queen Isabella.

The **Casita del Príncipe** (Prince's Pavilion)' was built in 1772 for the future Carlos IV in the neoclassical style. The **Sala de Mármol** (Marble Room), **Sala Pompeyana** (Pompeiian Room) and **Sala de Valencia** (Valencia Room) are among the most attractively furnished rooms.

In the town across the river is the **Convento de Capuchinos** (Capuchin Convent), which contains a remarkable sculpture, the *Christ of El Pardo*, by Gregorio Fernández.

Head east to join the M607/C607. Turn left and continue north to Colmenar Viejo.

Colmenar Viejo, Madrid

2 A drive past the old royal deer-park takes you to the pleasant little town of Colmenar Viejo, where the main attraction is the Gothic **parish church**. It was built in the 14th century and has an impressive entrance door. Inside is a fine 16th-century Plateresque retable. The house of the parish priest contains some religious objects worked in precious metals.

Continue north to rejoin the M607/C607. Go straight across this road, however, and continue north on the M611. Take a left turn, then left again on to the M608 which leads to Manzanares el Real.

Manzanares el Real, Madrid

3 The 15th-century **castle** was once the property of the Marquis of Santillana, a famous poet at the court of King Juan II in the Middle Ages. It now belongs to the Dukes of El Infantado and has been passed to the state for restoration. The interior is richly decorated. Of special note is the fine gallery, which bears a similarity to the palace of the Duke of El Infantada at Guadalajara. The fact that the barbicans bear decorations suggests the castle was a residence for nobility rather than as a defensive fortress.

Turn northeast on the M608. Turn left at Soto de Real on to the M611 and continue north to Miraflores de la Sierra.

Miraflores de la Sierra, Madrid

4 A look-out point on the outskirts of this picturesque town offers a magnificent view of the mighty mountains of the Sierra de Guadarrama. You can also see the source of the River Manzanares and a number of waterways.

Continue northwest on the same road. Turn left on joining the M604 to El Paular.

El Paular, Madrid

5 The old Carthusian **Monasterio del Paular** lies in the valley of the River Lozoya. It dates back to 1390 and was the first Carthusian monastery in Castile. The monastery was

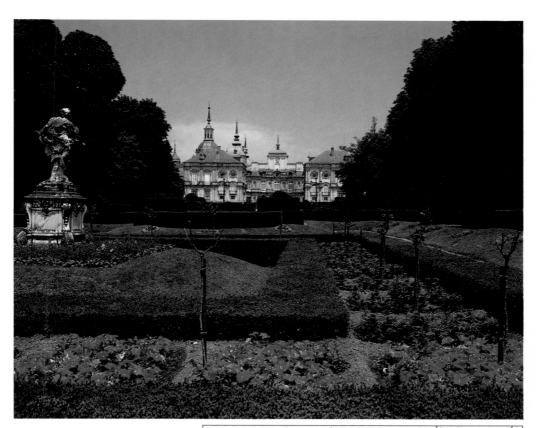

The French-style palace of La
Granja de San Ildefonso and its
gardens were modelled on Versailles

abandoned in the 19th century and
fell into decay. However, it is under
restoration and inhabited by
Benedictine monks. An impressive
Gothic door leads to the interior of the
church. Its main features are a fine
screen and a retable, considered an
outstanding work, with rich sculptures and exquisite filigree work.
Behind the altar is a baroque chapel
with rich decorations in the
Churrigueresque style, including
some fine paintings and marble sculptures. Do not miss the splendid Gothic
cloister with its four sets of vaults.

> Take the **M604** southwest and
> join the **N601** north to La Granja.

La Granja, Segovia

6 La Granja de San Ildefonso, to give
it its full name, is famous for its
magnificent French-style **palace**. The
present palace was commissioned by
Philip V (grandson of Louis XIV) and
was completed in 1723. A few years
later it was remodelled and turned
into a mini-Versailles.

The main façade of the palace faces
the gardens. Inside are a series of
elegant rooms and galleries decorated
in the rococo style with painted ceilings and gilded mouldings. Look out
for the statue of Faith, exquisitely
sculpted to represent a blind person
covered by a veil, to symbolise 'faith is
blind'. On the first floor are the sumptuous Throne Room and the Royal
Bedroom. Outstanding, however, is
the magnificent collection of Spanish
and Flemish tapestries, including the
notable *Life of St Jerome*.

The gardens cover an area of 145
hectares (358 acres). The lower

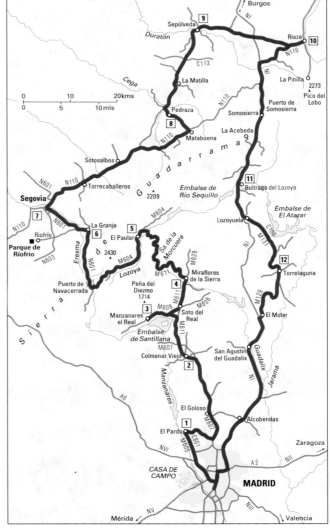

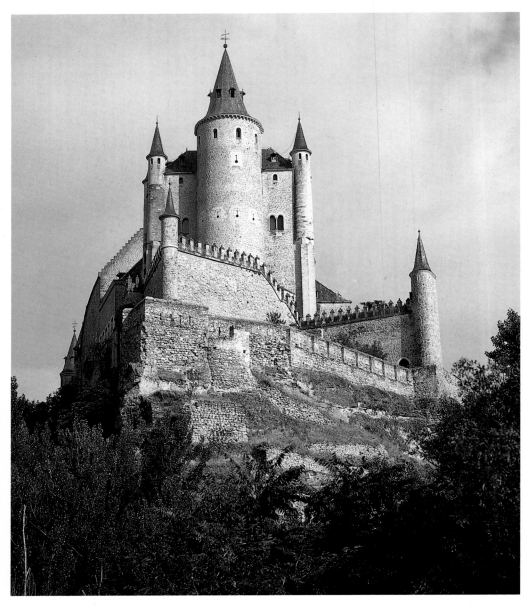

6 *La Granja, Segovia* Children will enjoy a visit to the **Parque de Ríofrío**. Situated in the foothills of the Sierra de Guadarrama, 11km (7 miles) southwest of La Granja, these were old hunting grounds surrounding the Ríofrío Palace, which stands in the middle of the park. Fallow deer and stags roam freely in this beautiful expanse of grasslands and evergreen oak forests. The animals are very tame and can easily be approached, even sometimes eating out of your hand.

7 *Segovia, Segovia* A speciality of Segovia is suckling pig (known here as *toston*). Although this dish can be enjoyed all over the country, there is nothing quite like sampling it right here in the beautiful environment of its home town.

Silhouetted against the sky, Segovia's Alcázar looks like a fairy-tale castle

section is famed for its beautiful fountains. The upper gardens have been left natural and are a habitat of deer.

*Continue on the **N601** northwest to Segovia, 11km (7 miles).*

Segovia, Segovia

7 The **aqueduct** was built by the Romans in the 1st century AD, and is still used for conveying water from the neighbouring sierras to the town. It is considered one of the most impressive monuments of its kind and is a prominent landmark of Segovia. It consists of huge granite blocks held together by butterfly ties formed by molten lead, and 118 arches, 43 of which are double-tiered.

Segovia is also famous for the view of its magnificent **Alcázar**. This was first built in the 12th century and remodelled later. Of interest inside are displays of medieval armour, paintings of former monarchs and some impressive tapestries. It also has some fine Mudejar ceilings.

A pathway leading down to the aqueduct offers wonderful views of the Alcázar silhouetted against the sky, and further views over the surrounding countryside. Within the **Roman walls** are the old quarters, with a small main square, picturesque streets and elegant façades. On the highest point of the town is the **cathedral**, an elegant structure built in the same mellow-coloured stone, with a tall square tower and pinnacles. It was built between 1525 and 1593 and is a fine example of late-Gothic art. Its large interior is noted for its brilliant stained glass windows, impressive sculptures and finely decorated altars. The 15th-century cloister was part of the original cathedral, which was destroyed in the 16th century and reconstructed in the present cathedral. A notable collection of 17th-century Flemish tapestries is housed in the chapter-house. Other buildings of interest include the 13th-century **Capilla de Vera Cruz**, the **Monasterio El Parral** and the 12th-century Romanesque **Iglesia de San Martín**, which overlooks the charming little square, Plaza San Martín.

ℹ️ Plaza Mayor 10

*Take the **N110** northeast. At Matabuena take the unclassified road left to Pedraza.*

Pedraza, Segovia

8 Entry to this old walled village is through the **Puerta de la Villa** (town gate), which leads straight to the delightful **Plaza Major**. A stroll through its quaint narrow streets and hidden corners will take you past many fine buildings bearing coats of arms from bygone days. The huge **castle** standing atop a massive rock was once a prison for François I, King of France, and his son.

Leave Pedraza to the northwest. At La Velilla turn right and take the regional road northeast to Sepúlveda.

Sepúlveda, Segovia

9 This attractive old town still has the remains of old Roman fortifications. The focal point is the pleasant **Plaza Mayor**, which is overlooked by the old **Ayuntamiento** (town hall). Behind are the ruins of an old **castle**. A walk around town reveals some interesting buildings, featuring a style known as the Sepúlveda-Romanesque style of architecture. Up the hill is the ancient **Iglesia del Salvador**. Dating back to the 11th century, it features a galleried portico and separate belfry.

*Take the regional road east across the **NI** to join the **N110**. Turn left on this road to Riaza, 24km (15 miles).*

Riaza, Segovia

10 Riaza is a picturesque little summer resort with ancient walls, old streets, arcades and elegant mansions, which centre around its attractive main square. In the **parish church** is a notable pietà, although in need of repair.

Large fields of sunflowers, faces all turned to the sun, are a typical sight stretching away into the distance around Segovia

*Take the **N110** southwest to join the **NI**. Turn left and continue south on the **NI** to Buitrago.*

Buitrago del Lozoya, Madrid

11 The small medieval town of Buitrago was once the domain of the noble Mendoza family, which wielded much power in Spain in former times. Access to the old town is through a gate in the ancient walls that surround it. Its narrow streets and old houses of brick and wood show strong traces of the Middle Ages. To one side of the town is the **castle**.

*Continue south on the **NI**. At Lozoyuela take a left turn on to the **M131** to Torrelaguna.*

Torrelaguna, Madrid

12 Torrelaguna was the birthplace of the wife of San Isidro Labrador, patron saint of Madrid, and also of Cardinal Cisneros, founder of the famous University of Alcalá de Henares, which was later moved to Madrid. The great medieval poet Juan de Mena died and was buried here. Around the arcaded **Plaza Mayor** are the elegant **Ayuntamiento** and some fine palaces and mansions. An outstanding monument is the beautiful Gothic **Iglesia de Santa María Magdalena**, which was built by Cardinal Cisneros. Inside are the baroque retable, and two Renaissance pulpits.

*Continue south on the **M131**. Turn right on to the **M129**, then rejoin the **NI** and return south to Madrid, 55km (34 miles).*

Madrid – El Pardo **13 (8)**
El Pardo – Colmenar Viejo **29 (18)**
Colmenar Viejo – Manzanares el Real **16 (10)**
Manzanares el Real – Miraflores de la Sierra **16 (10)**
Miraflores de la Sierra – El Paular **27 (17)**
El Paular – La Granja **38 (24)**
La Granja – Segovia **11 (7)**
Segovia – Pedraza **44 (27)**
Pedraza – Sepúlveda **25 (16)**
Sepúlveda – Riaza **24 (15)**
Riaza – Buitrago **41 (25)**
Buitrago – Torrelaguna **25 (15)**
Torrelaguna – Madrid **55 (34)**

BACK TO NATURE

The **Sierra de Guadarrama** forms the northern part of the great Central Cordillera, which sweeps across the Castilean plains west of Madrid. This is a beautiful area of wooded mountains, valleys and rivers, with several tributaries of the Tajo and the Duero rising in the northeastern peaks. The area serves as nesting grounds for a number of birds of prey, including imperial eagles, griffon and black vultures, goshawks, red kites and buzzards. Much of the region is covered with pine forests, among which there is an abundance of plant life, such as Pyrenean broom, bluebells, woodrushes and many wild herbs.

SCENIC ROUTES

The most scenic parts of this route are to be found in the Sierra de Guadarrama, with its typical landscapes of forested mountains and valleys, presenting a sort of oasis in close proximity to Madrid. The road continues through hills and pine forest, and the land becomes lush and green as you approach La Granja. La Granja to Segovia passes through rolling hills and plains, which gradually become an ochre colour around Segovia. On the return journey there are winding roads and sweeping views of the Sierras as you travel from Pedraza through Sepúlveda and Riaza to Buitrago.

FOR HISTORY BUFFS

On the way from Riaza to Buitrago the road climbs up to **Puerto de Somosierra**. Here in 1808, Spaniards defending the pass were attacked and dispersed by a force of Polish lancers under Napoleon, thus clearing the way for his troops, who were able to advance to Madrid, which they entered five days later.

2/3 days – 516km (321 miles)

REMOTE LANDS OF THE WEST

Cáceres ● Trujillo ● Guadalupe ● Mérida ● Badajoz
Alburquerque ● Valencia de Alcántara ● Arroyo de la luz
Cáceres

Cáceres is one of Spain's hidden secrets. It is relatively little known to the average tourist, and yet it has much to offer the visitor. The capital of its own province, it is a busy agricultural centre. Traces can be seen of many past civilisations. The Celts, Romans and Visigoths have all been here and left their mark.

A wealth of treasures is to be found in the old quarters. The *Plaza Santa María* is a lovely square, lined with the golden façades of many fine buildings. Among these are the *Iglesia de Santa María*, the 16th-century *Palacio Episcopal* (Bishop's Palace) and the *Palacio de Mayoralgo* (Mayoralgo Palace).The *Palacio de los Golfines de Abajo* (Lower Palace) near by has an impressive Plateresque façade. The 15th-century Gothic *Iglesia de San Matéo* (St Matthew) towers over the old town. Its main features are its Plateresque façade and a notable retable inside. The Palaces of *Godoy*, *La Isla* and *Los Galarza* are all worth a visit, as is the *Iglesia de San Francisco*.

> ⓘ Plaza del General Mola 33
>
> *Take the **N521** east to Trujillo.*

Trujillo, Cáceres

1 The old town of Trujillo is of great historical interest and has strong associations with the discoveries and conquests of the New World. It is sometimes referred to as the 'Cradle of the Conquistadores' (Conquerors),

A statue of Pizarro, the conqueror of Peru, in the main square of Trujillo, home of many explorers

as a number of leading explorers and conquistadores were born here. The most famous was Francisco Pizarro (1475–1541), who overthrew the mighty empire of the Incas and conquered Peru (1531–34), bringing untold wealth to Spain. He went on to marry an Inca princess, and ended up being killed in his own palace by compatriots. Other natives of Trujillo who have their place in history include Alonso de Monroy, known for his exploits in Chile; Francisco de Orellana (who departed in 1542 to explore the jungles of the Amazon); Diego de Paredes (nicknamed the 'Samson of Extremadura' for his physique), whose involvement was with Venezuela; and Hernando de Alarcón, who explored California.

The discovery of the Americas in 1492 and subsequent explorations put Trujillo on the map, so to say, and the town flourished during the Golden Age of Spain. The main square, **Plaza Mayor**, is one of Trujillo's most attractive features. A splendid equestrian statue of Pizarro in the middle of the square pays tribute to the conqueror of Peru. The monument in bronze is the work of the American sculptors Charles Runse and Mary Harriman (erected in 1927). The square is built on different levels, connected by broad steps and lined with beautiful portals and façades. Of special interest is the **Palacio de los Marqueses de la Conquista** (Palace of the Marqueses de La Conquista). This was built by Hernando Pizarro, brother of the Conquistador, who also went to seek his fortune in Peru, and later returned to his native lands. It is a magnificent palace built in the Plateresque style and noted for its elaborate window grilles and beautiful corner balcony.

Other fine buildings include the **Palacio de los Duques de San Carlos** (see the two-storeyed patio linked by a projecting staircase), the 16th-century **Palacio del Marquis de Piedras Albas** with a Renaissance logia, the former 16th-century **Ayuntamiento** and the **Palace of**

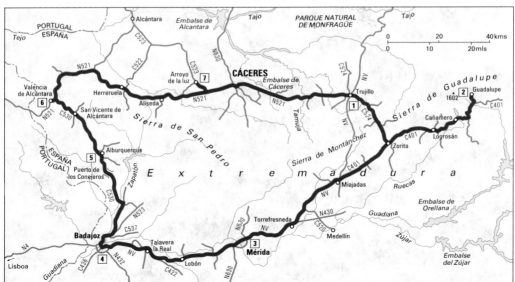

Justice. The old part of town is a fascinating jumble of streets and alleyways, lined with many elegant mansions bearing coats of arms. A walk up narrow cobblestone streets leads to the lovely 15th-century Gothic **Iglesia de Santa María la Mayor**, which stands on the square of the same name. It features a Romanesque bell tower and has an attractive interior, which contains the tomb of Diego García de Paredes, born here in 1466. A Romanesque figure of the Virgin of La Coronada may be seen in the 13th-century **Iglesia de Santiago**.

At the top of the town is the old **castle**, which was built by the Moors on Roman foundations. A wall shrine with the figure of the patron saint, Nuestra Señora de las Victorias, lies above the main gate, known as **El Triunfo** (The Triumph). There are good panoramic views from here of the interesting landscapes of Extremadura.

*Take the **C524** southeast. At Zorita take the **C401** east, then turn left to Guadalupe.*

Guadalupe, Cáceres

2 The main attraction of Guadalupe is the **monastery**, an imposing fortress-like structure of battlements and turrets in mellow stone. It lies high up

The Plaza de San Jorge, Cáceres, a town full of beautiful, unspoilt Gothic and Renaissance buildings

above the little village of Guadalupe.

The monastery was built by Alfonso XI for the Hieronymites, who lived here between the 14th and 19th centuries. Since 1928 it has been occupied by monks of the Franciscan order. The church contains the statue of the much venerated Black Virgin, known as La Virgen Morena, whose headdress is richly encrusted with gems. The sanctuary has long been an important pilgrimage centre, and religious festivals take place here on 8 and 30 September and 12 October, day of La Hispanidad (Day of the Discovery of the Americas).

i Ayuntamiento, Plaza del Generalísimo

*Rejoin the **C401** and take the **NV** from Miajadas south to Mérida.*

Mérida, Badajoz

3 Important Roman remains are a major attraction of Mérida. The original town of Augusta Emerita dates back to the 2nd century AD and was named after its founder, the governor of Augustus. It flourished under the Romans, who built many monuments here, and was then under Moorish domination between 713 and 1229, when it was taken by the Catholic King Alfonso IX.

The **Teatro Romano** (Roman Theatre) is most impressive. The original theatre was built by Agrippa,

SPECIAL TO...

3 *Mérida, Badajoz* Mérida is the scene of an important cultural festival which takes place in the summer during June, July and August. Plays are staged in the open in the elegant Roman theatre and amphitheatre. There are also ballet performances, exhibitions and other events.

FOR HISTORY BUFFS

3 *Mérida, Badajoz* A drive along the **N430** east of Mérida, followed by a right turn on to the **C520**, leads to Medellín, where Hernán Cortés, conqueror of Mexico, was born in 1485. Cortés landed in Mexico in 1519 with a small band of men and advanced to Tenochtitlan, capital of the Aztec Empire, where he was received by the Emperor Moctezuma. By 1521 he had overthrown the Aztec Empire, and he built a new capital. Later Cortés fell from favour and returned to Spain, where he died in 1547, disillusioned and forgotten. A statue of the conqueror stands on the 17th-century bridge over the River Guadiana. The old medieval **castle** stands in a commanding position over the town.

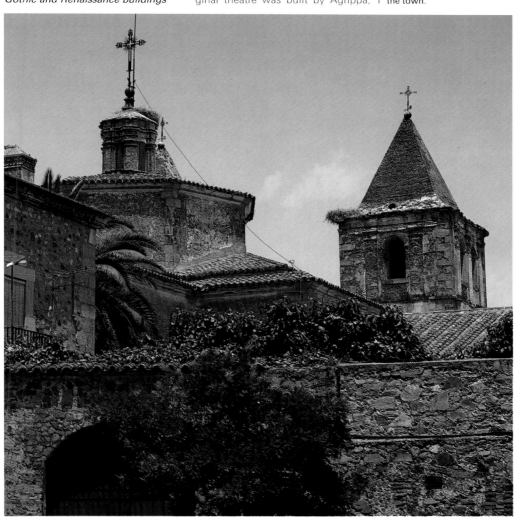

FOR CHILDREN

Cáceres, Cáceres Children can enjoy boating on the lakes in the region. A good choice would be the Embalse de Alcántara, which is northeast of Cáceres and provides facilities for various water sports.

During the festivities of **Carnival** at Shrovetide, Villanueva de la Vera (Cáceres) celebrates the 'Pero Palo', during which a large rag caricature is carried on top of a long pole. The figure represents the devil, and is later decapitated and buried, with music and dancing and great celebrations.

BACK TO NATURE

Cáceres, Cáceres The **Parque Natural de Monfragüe** lies to the northeast of Cáceres, and is a vast area of great rugged peaks, deep gorges and forests, watered by the River Tagus, which cuts right through it. The area is rich in flora and fauna and is a breeding ground for a great variety of birds. Among the many birds of prey that make their home here are the imperial eagle, black vulture, peregrine and several species of owl. Many animals, including deer, wild boar, moufflon (wild sheep), and even the elusive Spanish lynx, live in the area.

son-in-law of Augustus, and rebuilt in the 2nd century BC after it had been destroyed by fire, with a seating capacity for some 6,000 spectators. The theatre provides a magnificent setting, and plays are staged here in the summer. The **arena** dates back to the 1st century BC and it is believed the chariot races that took place here were watched by up to 14,000 people. Below the arena are traces of the **Casa Romana del Anfiteatro** (Patrician Villa), with faintly visible signs of the old pavements and parts of the walls, showing mosaic decorations.

The **Museum of Roman Art** houses a fine collection of Roman, Gothic and Moorish objects, along with Roman sculptures, mosaics, coins, pottery and many items of interest. Other segments of Roman remains are scattered about the area. The **Alcazába** was built by the Moors in the 9th century AD on to an original Visigoth building, and later it was converted into a monastery.

Spanning the River Guadiana is the **Puente Romano** (Roman bridge), an impressive structure extending for 792m (866 yards) with 64 arches. The bridge is an important feature of Mérida, along with the **Acueducto Romano** (Roman aqueduct), which is another outstanding structure. The bridge over the small River Albarregas is also Roman.

The little town of Mérida has a pretty main square, the Plaza de España, which is lined with arcades and overlooked by the **Iglesia de Santa María** (13th–15th century). To the northwest is the **Arco de Trajano**, a Roman triumphal arch. This imposing monument reaches a height of almost 13m (43 feet) and was once the north gate.

ℹ️ Calle el Puente 9

Continue on the **NV** *west for 62km (39 miles) to Badajoz.*

Badajoz, Badajoz

4 The town of Badajoz is situated on the banks of the River Guadiana, not far from the Portuguese border. It is the capital of the province of Badajoz and the seat of a bishop. The town was called *Colonia Pacensis* by the Romans and received its present name from the Moors. A small Moorish kingdom was established here for a time, until it fell to the Catholic King Alfonso IX of Leon in 1229. Over the years its strategic position, so close to Portugal, caused the town to be involved in many bitter battles during the various European wars.

The town is overlooked by the old Moorish **Alcazába**, from which there are good views of the surrounding countryside.

The focal point of the town is the Plaza de España, which is overlooked by the 13th-century Gothic **Catedral de San Juan** (St John). It has a fortress-like tower and a fine 17th-century Renaissance façade and doorway. There are some fine old tapestries in the sacristy and a small Diocesan museum in the chapter-house. The **Palacio de la Diputación** houses the **Museo Provincial** (provincial museum), which features paintings by artists from the region. The **Puente de Palmas** is an impressive 16th-century granite bridge over the River Guadiana that has 32 arches.

ℹ️ Pasaje de San Juan 1

Take the **N523** *north. Branch off on to the* **C530** *and continue north to Alburquerque.*

Alburquerque, Badajoz

5 A drive over the mountain pass of Los Conejeros will bring you to this picturesque little village. Alburquerque, which is dominated by the remains of a massive 13th-century castle, was once the scene of fierce fighting between the Portuguese and the Moors. A climb up to the castle offers fine views of the surroundings.

The Plaza de Toros, Mérida, echoes the style of the town's ancient Roman amphitheatre, with Moorish-style decoration

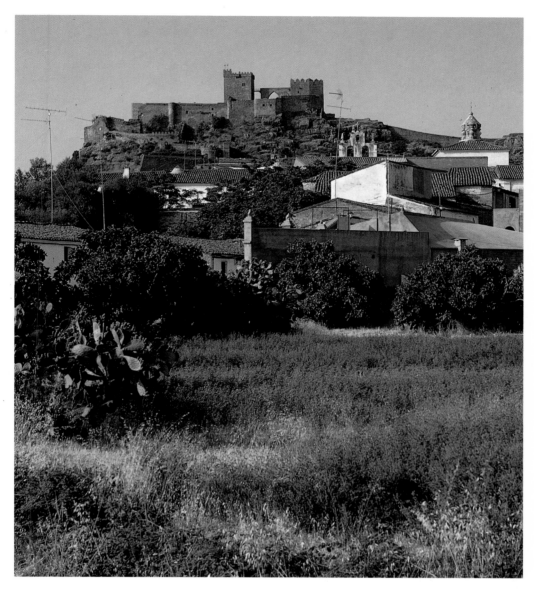

The unspoilt old village of Alburquerque is dominated by the extensive remains of a fine 13th-century castle

The village down below is surrounded by old walls and well worth strolling around. The two most interesting monuments are the large, 13th-century Gothic **Iglesia de Santa María del Mercado** and the parish church of **San Mateo**, built in the Gothic-Renaissance style.

*Continue on the **C530** and take a left turn to Valencia de Alcántara.*

Valencia de Alcántara, Cáceres

6 The little frontier town of Valencia de Alcántara serves as a customs post for travellers to Portugal, 14km (8½ miles) away. It is very pleasant, with old walls and the ruins of a 13th-century Moorish castle. Churches of special interest are the 13th-century **Iglesia de la Encarnación**, noted for its fine Gothic façade, and the 16th-century **Iglesia de Nuestra Señora del Rocamador**, whose Christ figure is ascribed to the artist, Berruguete.

A number of dolmens have been discovered in the area, signifying the presence of prehistoric man.

*Take the **N521** east and turn left on the **C523** to Arroyo de la luz.*

Arroyo de la luz, Cáceres

7 On the way here you might care to make a detour to the town of Alcántara, which features a famous **Roman bridge** over the gorge of the River Tajo. The bridge dates back to AD106 and is an impressive structure of huge dimensions.

The charming little town of Arroyo de la luz is an important pottery centre for the region. Its main building of interest is the **Iglesia de la Asunción**, which features an impressive Gothic portal and contains a notable carved retable inside, a work of the artist Luis Morales, a native of Badajoz.

*Rejoin the **N521** and return to Cáceres.*

Cáceres – Trujillo **47 (29)**
Trujillo – Guadalupe **83 (52)**
Guadalupe – Mérida **132 (82)**
Mérida – Badajoz **62 (39)**
Badajoz – Alburquerque **45 (28)**
Alburquerque – Valencia de Alcántara **35 (22)**
Valencia de Alcántara – Arroyo de la luz **92 (57)**
Arroyo de la luz – Cáceres **20 (12)**

SCENIC ROUTES

This region is an area of dry, brown-coloured lands, with bare, rugged mountains and dry valleys, combined with fertile lands. One of the most scenically attractive areas is along the **C530** from Alburquerque to Valencia de Alcántara.

RECOMMENDED WALKS

Cáceres, Cáceres The north of Cáceres and Trujillo offers interesting scenery, although much of the area is somewhat isolated. There are pleasant areas for walking along the shores of the reservoirs to be found in the area, and by the banks of the River Tagus. The reservoir Embalse de Cáceres is located quite near Cáceres, to the northeast.

2/3 days – 586km (365 miles)

HISTORICAL CITIES & CATHEDRALS

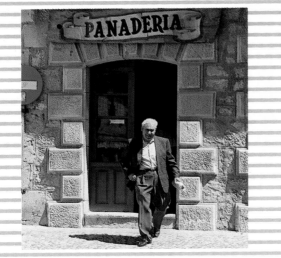

Salamanca ● Villanueva de Cañedo ● Zamora ● Valladolid
Palencia ● Burgos ● Lerma ● Aranda de Duero
Peñafiel ● Tordesillas ● Salamanca

From the left bank of the River Tormes there is a splendid view across the old *Roman bridge* to Salamanca on the other side of the river. The *Plaza Mayor* is regarded as one of the most attractive squares in Spain. On the north side is the 17th- to 18th-century *Ayuntamiento* (town hall), which features an impressive Churrigueresque façade and a belfry from the following century.

The 15th-century *Casa de la Conchas* (House of Shells) is famous for its façade covered with carved scallop-shaped shells. The old *Catedral de Santa María de la Sede* was built in the 12th century and is a fine example of the Spanish Romanesque style. The *Museo Episcopal* (diocesan museum) has a splendid collection of works by the great 15th-century Spanish painter, Fernando Gallego, and many other relics of interest. Adjoining it is the *Catedral Nueva* (new cathedral), 16th- to 18th-century, which shows a combination of the Gothic, Churrigueresque and baroque styles. The *University of Salamanca* is the oldest in Spain and has a magnificent entrance door decorated in the Plateresque style.

i Espana 39

From Salamanca take the N630 north towards Zamora. After Huelmos de Canedo, take a right turn to Villanueva de Cañedo, 28km (17 miles).

Villanueva de Cañedo, Salamanca

1 The main attraction here is the 13th-century **Castillo del Buen Amor**, an old fortified palace with large circular towers. It has an impressive interior with a fine Mudejar coffered ceiling and an inner patio.

Rejoin the N630 and continue north for 42km (26 miles) to Zamora.

Zamora, Zamora

2 Zamora was long under Moorish domination, and was the scene of many battles between the Moors and the Christians, during which 'El Cid', conqueror of the Moors, played a role. The **cathedral** stands near the right bank of the River Duero. It was built between 1151 and 1174 and is largely Romanesque, with a square tower and an impressive Byzantine-style cupola. Some splendid sculptures adorn the **Puerta del Obispo** (Bishop's Door).

The daily ritual of buying bread in the local shop in Lerma, an old medieval town with narrow cobbled streets and several elegant mansions

Inside, the aisles are Romanesque-Gothic. In the **Capilla Mayor** (Main Chapel) is a notable 15th-century altarpiece and several impressive tombs. The cloister houses a museum that contains a collection of 15th- to 17th-century Flemish tapestries.

The little 12th-century **Iglesia de Santa Magdalena** is a particularly fine example of the Romanesque style of architecture that was most evident in Zamora in the 12th century. Other churches built in a similar style are those of **Santo Tomás, Santiago de Burgos** and **Santa María de la Horta**. The 12th-century **Iglesia de San Cipriano** is noted for its finely decorated façade. Standing on the **Plaza Mayor** (main square) are the 17th-century **Ayuntamiento** and the Gothic **Iglesia de San Juan**, which has attractive paintings around the altar. There is a good view of the town from the **Puente Viejo** (old bridge).

i Santa Clara 20

Take the N122 east. Join the N620 at Tordesillas and continue northeast to Valladolid, 96km (60 miles).

Valladolid, Valladolid

3 The busy industrial town of Valladolid lies in the heart of the 'Meseta Central' plateau, in an area of flat landscapes. The **cathedral** is located near the Plaza Mayor. This was started in 1580 on a grand scale by the renowned architect Juan de Herrera, and continued in the 18th century by Alberto Churriguera, but was never completed. Of special note is an impressive 16th-century high altar by the sculptor Juan de Juni. Adjoining the cathedral is the **Museo Episcopal** (Diocesan Museum), which contains religious relics, jewellery and a magnificent silver monstrance in the shape of a temple, made by the great Toledo craftsman, Juan de Arfe.

The former **Colegio de San Gregorio** (St Gregory's College) was built between 1488 and 1496. It has an Isabelline-Gothic façade carved with elaborate decorations of coats of arms and strange forms. The **Museo Nacional de Escultura** (National Museum of Sculpture) on the first floor has an impressive collection of Spanish sculptures, including works of several of Spain's prominent artists of the 16th and 17th centuries.

The town's **Museo Arqueológico** (Archaeological Museum) is housed in the old Renaissance **Palacio de Fabio Nelli** and displays Roman sculptures, 13th- and 15th-century frescos and tapestries. The 12th- to 14th-century **Iglesia de Santa María la Antigua** is the oldest church in Valladolid and features a fine Romanesque tower. The 13th-century **Iglesia de San Pablo** has a superbly decorated façade, flanked by two simple towers. The **university** dates back to the 14th century and features a magnificent 18th-century baroque façade.

i Plaza de Zorilla 3

There is no mistaking what is sold in this shop in Palencia

*Continue on the **N620**. Branch off left on to the **N611** to Palencia.*

Palencia, Palencia

4 The Gothic **cathedral** stands on the small square called Plaza Santa, just off the Plaza Mayor. It was built between 1321 and 1516 on the ruins of a Romanesque chapel erected by Sancho the Great. The interior is decorated in a mixture of Gothic, Isabelline, Plateresque and Renaissance styles. Some fine sculptures include works by Gil de Siloé and Simon of Cologne. The **Capilla Mayor** (main chapel) contains a magnificent main altarpiece with paintings by Juan of Flanders. The **Chapel of the**

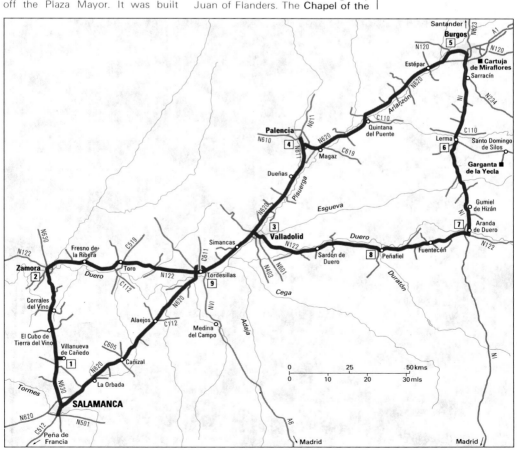

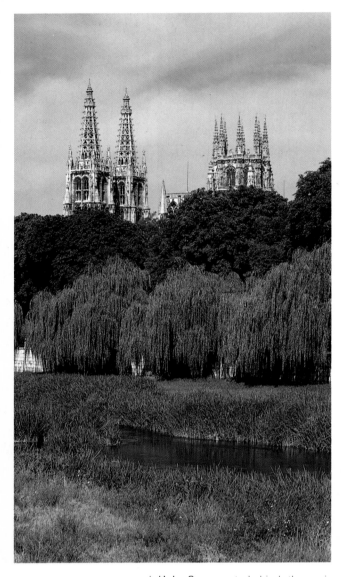

The wonderfully intricate towers of Burgos Cathedral are just visible above the trees

as 'El Cid Campeador' (El Cid the champion). His body found a final resting place in the cathedral here in 1929.

The cathedral was founded by Ferdinand III in 1221, with a second phase of building in the 15th century, when its two tall pinnacles were added by John of Cologne. This imposing limestone structure has a richly decorated Gothic façade. In the transept is the tomb of El Cid. His wife Ximena lies beside him. There is a fine 16th-century altarpiece in the **Capilla Mayor** (main chapel) and the finely carved choirstalls also date from the 16th century. The **Capilla del Condestable** (Constable Chapel) was designed by Simon de Cologne in 1482 in the Isabelline style. In the centre is an elaborately carved tomb of the constable and his wife.

A number of beautifully designed chapels are placed around the interior of the cathedral. Of particular note are those of Santa Ana, whose magnificent retable includes the impressive *Vine of Jesse*, and the **Capilla del Santo Christo**, which contains a much venerated image of Christ. The 14th-century cloister contains an impressive figure of *Christ at the Column* by Diego de Siloé (16th-century). In the Chapter-house are some beautiful 15th- and 16th-century Flemish tapestries. Of special interest is the **Capilla de Santa Caterinas** (St Catherine's), which has some interesting historical documents, including the marriage contract of El Cid.

There are numerous monuments to visit in the city. The **Santa María Arch**, built in the 14th century, is an entrance gate and defence. The 14th-century **Iglesia de San Gil** is noted for its pietà sculpture and magnificent 13th- to 14th-century altarpiece. The Gothic **Iglesia de San Estéban** has an impressive doorway and the 15th-century **Iglesia de San Nicolás** features a notable high altar and lovely vaulting. In the **Plaza del General de Primo de Rivera** stands an equestrian statue of El Cid, brandishing a mighty sword.

The 15th-century **Casa del Cordón** is the place where Christopher Columbus was received in 1496 by the Catholic monarchs Ferdinand and Isabella after returning from his second voyage across the Atlantic. King Philip I died here in 1506.

About 4km (2½ miles) southeast is the **Cartuja de Miraflores** (Charterhouse of Miraflores). This lovely Carthusian house was founded by King John II and rebuilt in the 15th century. In the Gothic **church** are the resplendent tombs of King John, his second wife Isabella of Portugal and the Infante Alfonso, whose early death in 1468 resulted in the succession to the throne of his sister, Queen Isabella the Catholic. Above the tombs of King John and Isabella rises a magnificent altarpiece by Gil de Siloé and Diego de la Cruz.

[i] Paseo del Espolon 1

*Take the **NI** south for 37km (23 miles) to Lerma.*

Holy Sacrament, behind the main chapel, features a notable retable by Valmaseda. Among many valuable objects in the **Treasury** is a beautiful 16th-century silver *custodia* by Juan de Benavente. A museum in the cloister contains an El Greco painting, together with other fine works of art and some 15th-century sculptures.

The 13th-century **Iglesia de San Francisco** (St Francis) has a sacristy with fine Mudejar vaulting. The **parish church of San Miguel** (13th–14th century) is noted for its Romanesque portal and impressive tower. In the 16th-century **Convento de Santa Clara** (Convent of St Clare) is a reclining figure of Christ. Of special interest is the **Capilla de San Bernardo** (Chapel of St Bernard), where El Cid's marriage took place.

[i] Calle Mayor 105

*Leave southeast by the **N610**. Rejoin the **N620** and continue northeast for 85km (53 miles) to Burgos.*

Burgos, Burgos

5 Burgos is famed for its **cathedral** which is one of the largest and most impressive in Spain. The city was closely associated with the great Rodrigo Díaz de Vivar, better known

FOR CHILDREN

5 *Burgos, Burgos* Obvious attractions for children are a little lacking on this tour. One particular aspect of **Corpus Christi** processions in Burgos, however, has a great appeal for children, judging by the reaction of the local ones at least! During the processions a huge silver monstrance is carried on a richly ornate cart that is manoeuvred by a man concealed underneath, giving the impression that the cart is moving mysteriously on its own.

Lerma, Burgos

6 The 17th-century **Palacio del Duque de Lerma** (Ducal Palace) is one of several elegant mansions built during this period. Of special interest is the tomb of Archbishop Cristóbal de Rojas of Sevilla which lies in the 17th-century **Colegiata** (Collegiate Church).

Continue on the NI south for 43km (27 miles) to Aranda de Duero.

Aranda de Duero, Burgos

7 The main attraction here is the late-Gothic **Iglesia de Santa María la Real**. Founded in the 15th century by Ferdinand and Isabella, its chief splendour is the magnificent Isabelline doorway with rich gilded decorations. Take a look, too, at the attractive little 13th-century **Iglesia de San Juan** and the **Capilla de le Virgen de las Vinas**, which is a popular pilgrimage centre.

ⓘ Ayuntamiento, Plaza Mayor 1

Take the N122 west to Peñafiel.

Peñafiel, Valladolid

8 The splendid silhouette of the **Castillo de Peñafiel** rises high above the little village of the same name. Built in the 14th century, the castle has 12 round towers and an impressive keep. Main attractions in the village are the **Plaza del Coso**, where the bullfights were watched from the balconies of the surrounding houses, and the 14th-century **Iglesia de San Pablo** (St Paul), which features some fine Mudejar architecture and Renaissance vaulting over the **Capilla Infante** (16th-century).

Continue west on the N122. At Valladolid take the N620 southwest to Tordesillas, 85km (53 miles).

Tordesillas, Valladolid

9 In the **monastery** here, Juana la Loca (the mad one), daughter of Ferdinand and Isabella and mother of Emperor Carlos V, locked herself away for the rest of her life after the death in 1506 of her husband Philip the Fair. She died here in 1555. The monastery, built between the 14th and 18th centuries, has some patios with Mudejar decorations and a Gothic **church** with a 15th-century altar.

ⓘ Ayuntamiento, Plaza Mayor 1

Return to Salamanca on the N620.

Salamanca – Villanueva de Cañedo 28 (17)
Villanueva de Cañedo – Zamora 42 (26)
Zamora – Valladolid 96 (60)
Valladolid – Palencia 46 (29)
Palencia – Burgos 85 (53)
Burgos – Lerma 37 (23)
Lerma – Aranda de Duero 43 (27)
Aranda de Duero – Peñafiel 38 (24)
Peñafiel – Tordesillas 85 (53)
Tordesillas – Salamanca 86 (53)

Children in Salamanca in the beautifully decorated local costumes, worn for festivals and other special occasions

SCENIC ROUTES

Much of this itinerary offers interesting rather than spectacular scenery. One of the most attractive sections of the drive is between Zamora and Toro on the **N122**, which follows the course of the River Duero, offering pleasant views.

BACK TO NATURE

6 *Lerma, Burgos* A regional road just after Lerma leads southeast to the ancient **Monasterio de Santo Domingo de Silos**, which offers an interesting visit. A few miles further on are the **Garganta de la Yecla** (Yecla Gorges), a fascinating wonder of nature, consisting of a deep gash in the rocks, very narrow in places, with a little stream flowing between. You can follow the course of the gorges.

RECOMMENDED WALKS

Salamanca, Salamanca There are some beautiful areas for walking around the **Peña de Francia**, to the south of Salamanca. It offers superb mountain scenery, together with woods, lush green valleys and picturesque little villages dotted about the countryside.

Much of the route follows the course of the River Duero, where you can take some time off and stroll along the banks of the river. Around Tordesillas there are pleasant pathways along the river shaded by poplars and other trees.

GREEN SPAIN

This region in the north of Spain consists of the Basque country, Cantabria, Asturias and Galicia. Although there are historical, cultural and administrative divisions, the area shares some common geographical factors. It borders Spain's Atlantic seaboard and has a wetter climate than any other part of Spain, resulting in fresh green landscapes that cover most of the region, apart from the arid plains of the southern Basque country.

The top end of the region runs along the Bay of Biscay, or 'Mar Cantábrico', and has a magnificent coastline of rugged cliffs, inlets and fine sandy beaches. The Basque mountains start where the western Pyrenees end and give way to the Cordillera Cantábrica, which sweeps across the north. They include the Picos de Europa, and rise to more than 2,500 m (8,000 feet). Galicia juts out into the Bay of Biscay to the north, and into the Atlantic to the west, and has a distinctive coastline of rugged cliffs and fiord-like inlets known as the 'Rías Altas' in the north and the 'Rías Bajas' down the west, while the south borders Portugal.

The four areas have very different histories. The early inhabitants of the Basque were a strong, independent race, with a long history of seeking self-determination. Cantábria, further west, played an important part in the history of Spain; the discovery of a number of caves in the region containing wall paintings prove the presence of Palaeolithic man. Asturias was once a separate kingdom, playing an essential part at the beginning of the Reconquest in the forming of Castile and the unification of Spain.

Galicia was occupied by the Celts from the 6th century BC. The area developed around Santiago de Compostela, where the tomb of St James the Apostle (Santiago) became the goal of pilgrimages from all over Europe from the 9th century onwards. Galicians have their own language, Gallego, which bears some resemblance to Portuguese.

The northern regions of the Basque country consist of fresh green pastures. There are maize-growing areas and plantations of fruit and walnut trees. Further south are vast plains with vineyards and fields of corn. Cantábria is known for its dairy products, and Asturias is a cider-producing area. Fishing plays an important role in Galicia's economy, and the region is famous for its seafood. Inland, the way of life is still very rural. Small farms are dotted about the countryside, with the familiar sights of the *horreos* (storage barns on supports) and ox-drawn carts with solid wheels. A variety of crops are grown, and the area is known for its wines.

In the Basque country many names are written first in Basque and then in Castilian. Galicia has a similar situation with its own language, you will find the use of the word *rua* for street, as opposed to *calle* in Castilian.

Tour 22

Tucked away in the northwestern corner of Spain is Galicia, a little world of its own. Its jagged coastline of high cliffs and estuaries is reminiscent of the Norwegian fiords, and its country-side, climate and culture are far removed from the popular images of Spain.

A tour around Galicia is full of surprises, combining green hills, rivers and valleys, Roman towns and a spectacular coast interrupted by picturesque little fishing villages. The highlight of the journey is a visit to Spain's most important shrine, which has been the centre of pilgrimages for centuries. The town and its cathedral are among the most important and attractive monuments in the country.

Tour 23

This tour will be a delight for anyone who enjoys spectacular mountain scenery. The route travels south from Oviedo into the Picos de Europa, making a stop in one of the major towns in the area, whose cathedral is known for the beauty of its stained glass windows. Following this there are a number of charming little mountain towns to visit. One of the most attractive parts of the tour is a trip to an important sanctuary in a secluded setting, surrounded by a magnificent panorama of green forested mountains. This is thought of as the birthplace of Christian Spain, as the first steps towards resistance to the Moorish occupation took root here. The tour rounds off with a drive along the northern coast and takes a look at the region's most important port.

The carved apostles in Oviedo Cathedral are among the best examples of 12th-century sculpture in Spain

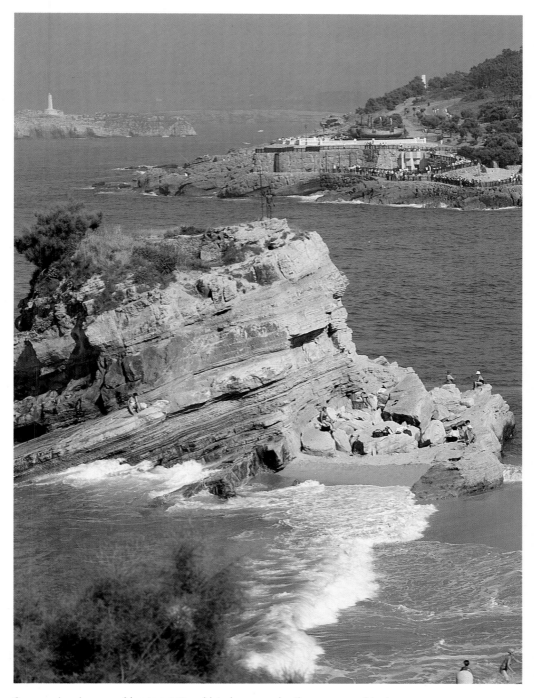

Sun, sand and sea combine to create a stunning coastline around Santander

Tour 24

Green hills, valleys and rural villages form the background of this tour, which will appeal to those who look for peace and quiet in beautiful surroundings.

Exploration of the hinterland will take you through some solitary countryside. Delightfully unspoilt mountain villages dotted about the slopes will give you an insight into a way of life that has seen little change with the passage of time. The coastline here is softer than that of the neighbouring regions, and some of the seaside resorts are very picturesque, with attractive harbours, promenades and splendid sandy beaches. Famous pre-historic caves in the area provide cultural interest.

Tour 25

The Basque country is characterised by green landscapes of wooded hills and lush valleys. Dotted about are little stone farmhouses called *caserios*. It has a rugged coastline with magnificent sandy beaches.

This itinerary takes you on an exploratory tour of the region, which includes some beautiful drives along the coast and stops in picturesque little resorts. A visit to Spain's busiest northern port provides a contrast to some of the typical little Basque mountain villages you will encounter in the interior of the country. The people and customs of the Basque country give the region an unmistakable character, which you will no doubt discover on your travels.

3 days – 702km (435 miles)

THE WORLD OF GALICIA

La Coruña ● Betanzos ● Lugo ● Monforte de Lemos
Orense ● Vigo ● Pontevedra ● Isla de la Toja
Cambados ● Padrón ● Santiago de Compostela ● Noia
Cabo Fisterra ● La Coruña

The capital of Galicia, La Coruña (Corunna) was the starting point for King Philip II's doomed 'invincible' Armada sent against England in 1588. The following year, the port was the scene of a fierce battle with Sir Francis Drake's forces and suffered severe damage.

The *Paseo de los Cantones* is a pleasant promenade that skirts the bay. On the Plaza Mayor is the *Palacio Municipal* with a good collection of contemporary paintings. Near by is the 18th-century *Iglesia de San Nicolás*. The *Iglesia de les Capuchinas* has a fine painting of St Francis by Zurbarán. The old town, the *Ciudad*, is an area of narrow cobbled streets and little squares. Look out here for the Romanesque *Iglesia de Santiago*, the *Colegiata de Santa María del Campo* and the *Iglesia de Santo Domingo*. The *Torre de Hércules* (Hercules' Tower), a lighthouse of Celtic origin but mainly Roman, offers splendid views.

i Darsena de la Marina

From La Coruña take the **NVI** *for 23km (14 miles) to Betanzos.*

Betanzos, La Coruña

1 Betanzos is a small town of great charm, with medieval walls and steep narrow streets, lined with attractive houses and balconies. It has several notable churches. The **Iglesia de Santa María del Azogue** (of the market), 14th to 15th century, has an elegant façade and a fine Flemish altarpiece. The **Monasterio de San Francisco** (St Francis) was built in the 14th century, in the shape of a cross, by the Conde de Andrade (Count Andrade), lord of Betanzos. In the church is his tomb, a vast sepulchre resting on a boar and a bear. Another notable church is the parish **church of Santiago** (St James), rebuilt in the 15th century by the tailors' guild. Note the fine carving of St James, known as the Slayer of the Moors, over the doorway. Inside are several chapels, one of which contains an impressive retable in a typical Isabelline style.

i Ayuntamiento (town hall), Plaza del Generalisimo 1

RECOMMENDED WALKS

You can follow in the footsteps of the old pilgrims along a section of the Way to Santiago. **Cebreiro, Portomarín** or **Vilar de Donas** could be suitable starting points. However, you can seek guidance from the local tourist office.

2 *Lugo, Lugo* You can also follow in the footsteps of the old Roman sentries, who once trod the path along the top of the 3rd-century walls of Lugo. A walk along the ramparts offers magnificent views of the surrounding countryside.

Away from the crowds in Santiago de Compostela, the streets are quiet and picturesque. This famous city has attracted pilgrims to St James' shrine from all over Europe since the Middle Ages

Continue on the **NVI** *for 73km (45 miles) to Lugo.*

Lugo, Lugo

2 Massive great slate walls surround the old Roman city of Lugo. Originally a Celtic settlement, it became a city of some importance under the Romans, who called it *Lucus Augusti*. Much of the old town was destroyed by fire, first under the Moors and then the Visigoths, and it was the scene of fierce battles during the Napoleonic Wars. The *murallas* (town walls) have a perimeter of over 2km (1¼ miles). They date back to the 2nd century AD and were reinforced in the 14th century.

The **Plaza de España** is the town's attractive main square. It is lined with elegant buildings and is graced by a fountain in the centre, with an image of *Hispaña*. The **Ayuntamiento** (town hall) on the east side of the square has an impressive rococo façade. On the western side is the **cathedral**. It was first erected in the 12th century, with alterations and additions continuing in the 15th and 18th centuries. Parts of the building show the Romanesque style, with traces of French influences due to the fact that Lugo was on the route of the French pilgrims going to Santiago. Much of the cathedral is Gothic. It has twin towers and an impressive 18th-century façade. Notable features inside are the rococo altarpiece in the **Capilla Mayor** (main chapel), decorated choir-stalls and lovely 18th-century Gothic cloister. In the south ambulatory is the wooden statue of the 'English' Virgin, which was transported here from St Paul's Cathedral, London, during the 16th century.

The **Museum** has a collection of paintings and religious relics. Worth a visit is the 13th-century **Iglesia de Santo Domingo**, which features some fine Romanesque doorways and an impressive Churrigueresque retable. An interesting display of ceramics, coins and regional handicrafts can be seen in the **Museo Provincial** (Provincial Museum).

i Plaza de España 27

Take the **NVI** *southeast and after about 6km (4 miles) turn right on to the* **C546** *south to Monforte de Lemos, 65km (40 miles).*

Monforte de Lemos, Lugo

3 The picturesque little village of Monforte de Lemos is partly encircled by old ramparts and overlooked by an old **castle** with a huge tower, which once belonged to the Counts of Lemos. Of major interest in the village is the **Colegio de la Compañía** (Jesuit College), whose church contains a beautiful 17th-century retable by Francisco Moure and three paintings by El Greco. Note, too, the fine 16th-century Renaissance doorways of the former Benedictine **Monasterio de San Vicente del Pino**.

La Coruña's shell-shaped harbour to the south of the town, where modern office blocks rub shoulders with traditional buildings with their characteristic glazed balconies on each floor

Take the **C546** southwest for 48km (30 miles) to Orense (Ourense).

Orense, Orense

4 Orense was discovered by the Romans for its thermal springs, around which the ancient town developed and from which it got its name, *Aquae Urentes*. In the 6th and 7th centuries it was the seat of Suevian kings. The town suffered damage during the Moorish invasion in 716, but was built up again in the 10th century. Modern Orense is a busy commercial centre, but the old section of the town is delightful. The **Palacio del Obispo** (Bishop's Palace) stands on the corner of the Plaza Mayor and is noted for its attractive courtyard. This is now the **Museo Arqueológico** (Archaeological and Fine Arts Museum), where you can view items from prehistoric and Roman times and religious relics.

The **Catedral de San Martín** was first built between the 12th and 13th centuries and renovated in the 16th and 17th centuries after damage caused by wars and earthquakes. It is noted for its triple-arched portal, **Pórtico del Paraíso** (Paradise), which is richly decorated and preserves some of its original colouring. Note the large 16th-century Gothic retable and the carved choirstalls. An interesting item is the crucifix in the **Capilla**

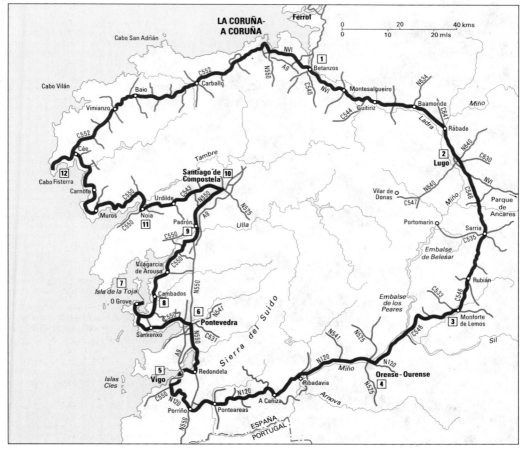

FOR HISTORY BUFFS

La Coruña, La Coruña
Northeast of La Coruña is the town of **Ferrol**, birthplace of General Francisco Franco, who ruled Spain for 39 years until his death in 1975. The town is one of Spain's major naval bases and is built around a beautiful bay, overlooked by the castles of **San Felipe** and **La Palma**.

BACK TO NATURE

2 *Lugo, Lugo* Near Lugo, in the Sierra de Ancares, is the **Parque de Ancares** (Ancares Park), which is rich in wildlife. Deer and wild boar are some of the animals you can see here.

5 *Vigo, Pontevedra* The archipelago called the **Islas Cies** is a paradise for birdwatchers. The islands are reached by ferry from Vigo and have been declared a Natural Park. They are important breeding grounds for marine birds, and here you can see colonies of herring gulls and guillemots. Great numbers of ducks also converge here in the winter.

del Cristo Crucificado (Chapel of the Crucified Christ), said to have been found on the coast of western Galicia and brought here in 1330. The **Museo Episcopal** (Episcopal Museum) located in the Chapter-house, has an interesting display of 13th-century enamels, statues and altars.

The 13th-century Romanesque **Iglesia de la Trinidad**, located in the southern section of the town, features two large round towers and a fine Gothic doorway. The **Puento Viejo** (old bridge), which spans the River Miño, is quite an impressive structure, dating back to the 13th century. The little chapel in the nearby **Campo de los Remedios** contains a statue of the Virgen de los Remedios, to whom pilgrimages are made.

ℹ️ Curros Enriquez 1

*Take the **N120** west for 104km (65 miles) to Vigo.*

Vigo, Pontevedra

5 Vigo is a major naval and fishing port, and one of Galicia's largest towns. It has Roman origins. However, its real growth began in the 16th century, when trading links were established with America. During the 15th and 16th centuries it was constantly under threat of attack by English ships, which sought to divest the Spanish fleets of their precious cargoes from overseas. In 1702 a returning Spanish fleet was virtually destroyed by English and Dutch seamen. Treasures of immense value were seized and the Spanish fleet never recovered from the attack.

Fishing is Vigo's main industry, commemorated in this memorial overlooking Vigo Bay

Vigo is a pleasant town with old and new sections. The old part, the fishermen's quarters, called the *Berbes*, can be fun and there is plenty of lively action in the **Pescadería** (fish market) when business is on. A stroll along the Paseo de Alfonso XIII promenade offers a good view of the harbour. In the new town there are some attractive buildings around the **Plaza de Compostela**. There is a sweeping view of the town and bay from the **Castro** (castle) on top of the hill.

ℹ️ Jardines de las Avenidas

*Head northeast toward Redondela. Turn left on meeting the **N550** and travel north to Pontevedra, 34km (21 miles).*

Pontevedra, Pontevedra

6 This small provincial capital lies on the wide curve of the banks of the River Pontevedra. It has a bustling new town, and an old section that has changed little with time. The old port was known as *Pontis Veteris* (the old bridge) and parts of the old encirclement walls can still be seen.

The 18th-century **Iglesia de la Peregrina** (Pilgrimage), in the old quarter, is built in an unusual Italian-inspired baroque style. The Gothic **Iglesia de Santa María la Mayor** (St Mary Major) is set in lovely gardens and is noted for its impressive baroque façade. The ruins of the 14th-century **Iglesia de Domingo** houses the **Museo Arqueológico** (Archaeological Museum), which has items from Roman times and the Middle Ages. In the **Museo Provincial** (Provincial Museum) you can see Celtiberian exhibits and paintings.

ℹ️ General Mola 2

*Take the **C550** west for 35km (22 miles) to Isla de la Toja.*

Isla de la Toja, Pontevedra

7 This has long had a reputation as Galicia's most exclusive summer resort. It is linked to the mainland by a bridge. **O Grove**, back on the mainland, is an attractive little fishing harbour, known for its excellent shellfish.

*Retrace the route for 5km (3 miles) from O Grove, then continue on the **C550** west then north to Cambados.*

Cambados, Pontevedra

8 Cambados is a pleasant little village by the sea. The manor house of **El Pazo de Fefinanes**, which stands on the grandiose square of the Plaza de Fefinanes, is a typical example of the Pazo style of architecture, a style unique to Galicia and popular with the nobility in the 17th and 18th centuries.

*Continue on the **C550** toward Padrón. Turn left on to the **N550** just south of the town, a distance of 35km (22 miles).*

Padrón, La Coruña

9 Padrón is the spot where the legendary vessel carrying the Apostle St James landed. He is said to have preached Christianity in Spain for seven years before returning to Judaea. In the **parish church** by the

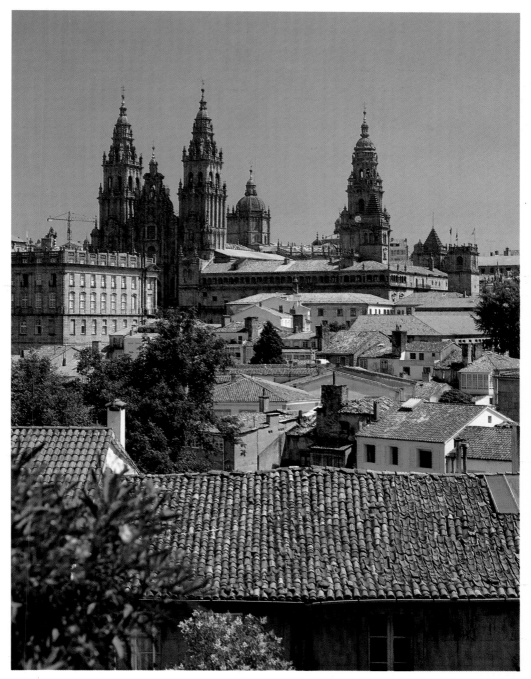

The ornate baroque façade and towers of the Cathedral of Santiago de Compostela rise over the city's rooftops

bridge is the mooring stone of the boat. The 11th-century **Colegiata de Santa María** (Collegiate Church of St Mary) contains some rather impressive tombs of bishops.

*Take the **N550** north for 20km (12 miles) to Santiago de Compostela.*

Santiago de Compostela, La Coruña

10 Santiago de Compostela is Spain's most famous pilgrimage centre, and the **cathedral** is one of its most glorious monuments.

According to legend, the remains of the Apostle, St James, were found in 813 on the site of the present cathe-dral by the bishop of Iria Flavia, who was guided by a star. The name of Compostela is derived from *Campus Stellae* (field of the star). St James was made patron saint of Spain and by the middle of the 10th century great masses of pilgrims were travel-ling from all over Europe, through France and along the north of Spain, to visit his shrine. The route they took became known as the **Camino de Santiago** (The Way to Santiago). The cathedral, which stands on the **Plaza del Obradoiro** (or Plaza de España), dominates the whole town. It was built between 1060 and 1211, and is considered to be one of the finest achievements of Romanesque archi-tecture. It is combined with a magnifi-cent baroque façade from the 16th and 17th centuries. The richly carved decorations that adorn the west entrance are the work of the sculptor, Fernando Casas y Novoa.

SPECIAL TO . . .

During your travels in Galicia you will notice many stone buildings constructed on tall granite supports, with a saddle roof and a cross on top. These *horreos* are mainly used to store maize and were built in this way to protect the crops from humidity and vermin.

Between May and July the wild horses are rounded up in the mountains and brought to special corrals (*curros*) to be branded and have their manes and tails cut. This forms part of a rodeo-type festival known as **La Rapa das Bestas** (the marking of wild horses), held in various towns in the region.

FOR CHILDREN

10 *Santiago de Compostela, La Coruña* Children can enjoy a visit to the **Paseo de la Herradura** park in Santiago de Compostela, which has swings and roundabouts and various amusements laid on. The park also offers wonderful views over the town.

There are a number of colourful fiestas in the region, which would appeal to children. They would probably particularly enjoy **Fiestas de los Maios**, which features mostly children and young people. This is celebrated all over Spain on 1 May, but is very attractive in Betanzos, which is also the scene of a popular pilgrimage on Easter Monday.

SCENIC ROUTES

Galicia offers very attractive landscapes of soft green hills and valleys, with striking coastal scenery. Among the most beautiful parts of the journey are the coastal drives from Pontevedra to La Toja, and from Santiago de Compostela to Cabo Fisterra on the **C550**, where this typical coastline of the Rías Bajas offers magnificent views of rugged cliffs and inlets, wooded hills and sandy beaches.

A statue of St James stands high on the front gable between two imposing towers. Within the west front entrance is the magnificent **Pórtico de la Gloria** (Door of Glory), a masterpiece of 12th-century Romanesque work by Mateo. The interior is simple, the main focus being the **Capilla Mayor** (main chapel). Above the high altar is a silver shrine with a richly decorated statue of St James, and below is the crypt, which contains the tombs of the Apostle and his two disciples, St Theodore and St Athanasius.

Other notable features are the beautiful wrought-iron grilles, the large Plateresque cloister and the finely carved **Puerta de las Platerías** (Goldsmith's Door). The museum and treasury contain some interesting religious items. When in the cathedral be sure to ask about the **Botafumeiro**. This is a gigantic incense-burner that is normally kept in the library and brought out on feast days and special occasions. It is then hung from the transept dome and swings madly from side to side, climbing higher and higher, with eight men attached to it by ropes and clinging on for dear life. This goes back to the time when large numbers of pilgrims descended on the cathedral to worship at the shrine of St James and some form of fumigation was necessary.

On the cathedral square, which is very impressive, are the handsome **Palacio del Obispo** (Bishop's Palace) and the 18th-century **Ayuntamiento** (town hall). Other monuments of interest in Santiago include the **seminary of San Martín Pinario** (16th–17th century), which features an elegant doorway and lovely courtyard, the twin-towered **Convento de San Francisco** and the Romanesque **Iglesia de Santa María Salomé**. The 18th-century university is noted for its handsome classical façade.

ℹ️ Plaza del Obradoiro

*Take the **C543** west for 37km (23 miles) to Noia (Noya).*

Noia, La Coruña

11 Noia is a pleasant little village situated in a large bay, with a few churches and handsome mansions. A notable building is the **Casa de los Churrachaos**, formerly the home of the local feudal lords.

*Take the **C550** northwest to Cée. Turn left on to the road to Cabo Fisterra (Cape Finisterre), 93km (58 miles).*

Cabo Fisterra, La Coruña

12 A most fitting end to this tour is a stop at Cabo Fisterra – 'end of the world' – to enjoy the dramatic setting of the lighthouse, poised on top of a great rock jutting out to sea. This is the most westerly point of Spain and was once the 'edge of the unknown'.

*Return to La Coruña northeast on the **C552**, 115km (71 miles).*

La Coruña – Betanzos **23 (14)**
Betanzos – Lugo **73 (45)**
Lugo – Monforte de Lemos **65 (40)**
Monforte de Lemos – Orense **48 (30)**
Orense – Vigo **104 (65)**
Vigo – Pontevedra **34 (21)**
Pontevedra – Isla de la Toja **35 (22)**
Isla de la Toja – Cambados **20 (12)**
Cambados – Padrón **35 (22)**
Padrón – Santiago de Compostela **20 (12)**
Santiago de Compostela – Noia **37 (23)**
Noia – Cabo Fisterra **93 (58)**
Cabo Fisterra – La Coruña **115 (71)**

The lighthouse on the tip of Cabo Fisterra marks the most westerly point in Spain

A traditional way of decorating the old wooden granaries in the area around the town of Oviedo is to hang up long strings of ripe, golden corncobs

THE GREEN BELT OF ASTURIAS

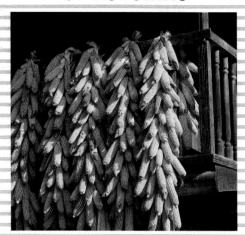

Oviedo ● León ● Mansilla de las Mulas ● Potes ● Lebeña
Covadonga ● Cangas de Onís ● Gijón ● Oviedo

ℹ Plaza de Alfonso, 11 El Casto 6

From Oviedo take the N630 south to León, 121km (75 miles).

León, León

1 León is known for its beautiful cathedral of Santa María de la Regla. As the centre of a thriving mineral industry the town presents a sharp contrast between the new and the old. It lies at the confluence of two rivers, the Torío and Bernesga, and is the capital of the province of León. It was the capital of the kingdom of León for a period between the 10th and 13th centuries, and fortification walls were built around the city by the Asturian kings. The year 1230 saw the unification of the kingdoms of León and Castile and a loss of status for León. In the Middle Ages it was one of the main staging points for pilgrims travelling to Santiago de Compostela.

The old quarters lead off from the main square, or Plaza Mayor, which is surrounded by attractive portals. The cathedral lies to the north of the square. It was built between the 13th and 14th centuries and is a remarkable work of Gothic architecture. The west façade is outstanding, with two great steeples and a central turreted gable, with a large rose window and three ornately carved doorways. The cathedral is renowned for its superb stained glass windows, the earliest of which date back to the 13th century and are to be seen in the central choir chapel and the rose windows in the west and north fronts.

Oviedo is capital of the province of the same name and the major town of Asturias. It is a thriving industrial centre with a university, and is the seat of a bishop. The town developed in the 8th century around the former site of *Ovetum*.

A number of interesting monuments can be seen in the old part. The *Basílica del Salvador* (the Cathedral) is located to the north of the Plaza Mayor. Built in Gothic style, it features a remarkable south tower, which rises to a height of some 82m (270 feet) and offers a splendid view over the surroundings. The *Capilla del Rey Casto* (Chaste King's Chapel) is the pantheon of the kings of Asturias. The entrance to the *Cámara Santa* is adorned by six columns and has an impressive collection of religious works of art. Other buildings of interest are the 16th- to 18th-century *Palacio del Obispo* (Bishop's Palace) and the churches of *San Tirso* (9th century), *Pelayo*, also dating from the 9th century, but rebuilt in the 18th century, and *Santa María la Real*, which contains some notable tombs.

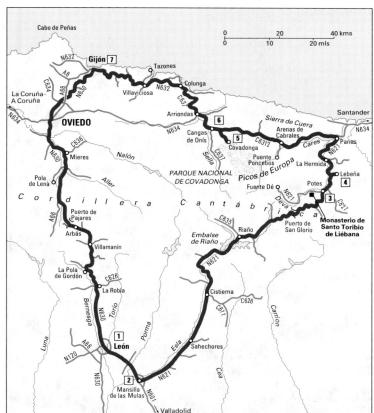

SCENIC ROUTES

This itinerary takes in the famous Picos de Europa, and most of the route passes through magnificent scenery. Between Oviedo and León (**N630**) the route becomes very attractive after Mieres, with some superb views over the beautiful Cordillera Cantábrica (Cantábrian mountains). The drive from Cistierna to Riaño on the **N621** offers magnificent views and continues to Gijón through some of the most spectacular scenery of Asturias, with an outstanding stretch, known as the Cares Route, between Panes and Cangas de Onís.

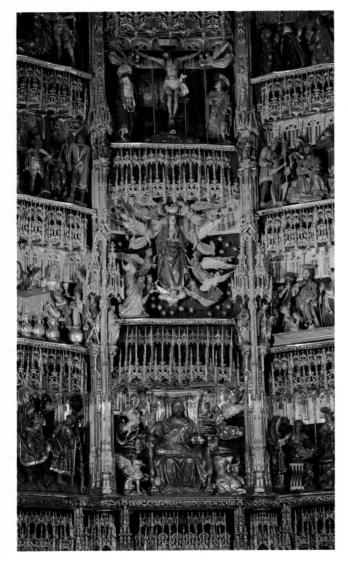

The richly decorated altarpiece in Oviedo Cathedral illustrates scenes from the life of Christ

ded by walls and has an attractive main square lined with arcades.

*Take the **N621** northeast through Riaño to Potes, for 127km (79 miles).*

Potes, Asturias

3 Potes lies in a valley below the sharp peaks of the Picos de Europa. This little mountain village has great charm, with old wooden houses and a large 15th century tower, which is now the town hall. It is an excellent centre for excursions into the mountains.

A trip is recommended to the **Monasterio de Santo Toribio de Liébana**, 3km (2 miles) west. The monastery was founded in the 7th century by Franciscans, and became important in the following century when a piece of the True Cross was brought here from Jerusalem. This can be seen in a small chamber beyond the cloister. There is a fine view of Potes and the surrounding mountains from the end of the road.

Another excursion from Potes that should not be missed is to **Fuente Dé**, situated 21km (13 miles) to the west. A road along the River Deva leads through forests and mountains to the Fuente Dé Parador. Near by is the terminal of a cable car that takes you up some 800m (2,625 feet) through magnificent scenery to the top of the rock. There are superb panoramic views from the look-out point here, called the **Mirador del Cable**, extending over the valley of the River Deva, the town of Potes and the central range of the Picos de Europa.

*Continue on the **N621** north to Lebeña, which is reached by bearing right off this road, 10km (16 miles).*

Lebeña, Asturias

4 The small Mozarab **Iglesia de Santa María de Lebeña** lies at the foot of steep cliffs, among elegant poplars. It was built in the 10th century and has been well preserved. Note the fine vaulting and horseshoe-shaped arches, which bear finely carved Corinthian capitals.

*Rejoin and continue north on the **N621**. At Panes take the **C6312** west and at Soto de Cangas branch left to Covadonga, 77km (48 miles).*

Covadonga, Asturias

5 The **sanctuary** of Covadonga is tucked away in a remote valley. The setting is superb and the place exudes a certain aura of mysticism, which is strongly felt in Asturias. The kingdom of Asturias was founded in this region after the defeat of Muslim forces in 722 by a Gothic nobleman called Pelayo, who led the Asturians to a resounding victory against the Moorish occupiers.

The sanctuary is dedicated to the patron saint of Asturias, **la Virgen de las Batallas** (Virgin of the Battles). Pilgrimages are made here on 8 September to venerate her image, which stands over the altar in the

FOR CHILDREN

1 *León, León* Situated along the banks of the River Bernesga in León you will find a playground with all sorts of entertainment for the children.

BACK TO NATURE

5 *Covadonga, Asturias* The **Parque Nacional de Covadonga** (Covadonga National Park) is a vast region of great natural beauty, known for its magnificent forests of beech, oak and other trees. It is watered by the rivers Cares and Deje and contains the two glacier lakes, Enol and Ercina. It is home to the wild cat, polecat, fox, wolf, badgers and chamois, which inhabit the higher slopes. Among the many different types of birds, you can see various species of eagles, owls and magpies, while the rivers are full of fish including salmon and trout, which are preyed upon by secretive otters.

The **Capilla Mayor** (main chapel) has an impressive 15th-century Gothic altarpiece with a magnificent painting of the Entombment. Some fine sculpted monuments can be seen in the chapels. The cloister is in the Plateresque style and has some notable frescos. The museum contains some interesting relics of religious interest.

The **Colegiata de San Isidoro** (Collegiate Church of St Isidore) dates back to the 12th century and forms part of the ancient ramparts. It features a huge Romanesque tower and two impressive doorways. In the Capilla Mayor is a fine 16th-century altarpiece and the remains of St Isidore, to whom the church was dedicated. The adjoining pantheon has some Romanesque paintings on the ceiling.

A number of handsome buildings are located around the central Plazuela de San Marcelo, which include the **Ayuntamiento**, a splendid building with twin towers.

ⓘ Plaza de Regla 3

*Take the **N601** south to Mansilla de las Mulas, 17km (11 miles).*

Mansilla de las Mulas, León

2 Make a brief stop to look around this little village, which is surroun-

Santa Cueva (Holy Cave). Behind are the tombs of Pelayo, who died in 737, his wife Gaudiosa, and King Alfonso I. The **Basílica** was erected at the end of the 19th century in neo-Romanesque style and features two tall spires. Beneath the Cross of Victory is a bronze statue of Pelayo. The **Tesoro de la Virgen** (Virgin's Treasury) contains some fine treasures, including a brilliant diamond-studded crown.

Rejoin the C6312 and turn west to Cangas de Onís, for 4km (2 miles).

Cangas de Onís, Asturias

6 Once the Reconquest of Spain was initiated by the Christians at the Battle of Covadonga in 722, the seat of court was set up at Cangas de Onís and Asturias became known as a

An old bridge in Cangas de Onís, which was the starting point of the Reconquest of Spain

symbol of the Christian resistance against the Moors. Some elegant old mansions can still be seen from those glorious times. Of major interest is the 8th-century **Capilla de Santa Cruz** (Chapel of the Holy Cross), which stands on a Celtic burial mound. Look out for the old **Puente Romano** (Roman bridge), which spans the gorge of the River Sella.

Take the C637 northwest. On reaching the N632 turn left (west) to Gijón, 78km (48 miles).

Gijón, Asturias

7 Before arriving at Gijón you might like to branch off at Villaviciosa and take a short detour along a lovely route to the charming little fishing harbour of Tazones.

Gijón is one of the most important towns in Asturias, with a busy port and large harbour. It is situated between two wide bays. The old town

FOR HISTORY BUFFS

7 *Gijón, Asturias* About 30km (18½ miles) southeast of Gijón is the town of **Villaviciosa**, which is marked by one very historic event – the result of a mistake. In 1517 the Habsburg Emperor Carlos V sailed to Spain to claim his kingdom and should have landed in Santander. Instead the grand flotilla arrived at Tazones and sailed up the estuary to Villaviciosa, to the surprise and delight of the local people, who set about laying on some festivities to celebrate the occasion. The future King of Spain stayed here overnight. However, he did not take kindly to the sailing error, it seems, and so did not react to the welcome from the villagers.

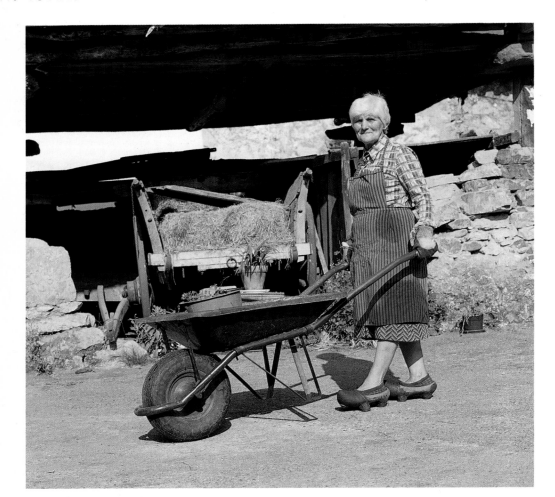

A granary worker near Oviedo wearing special clogs

SPECIAL TO...

Those who have a weakness for extremely strong-tasting cheese will enjoy *picón*, a blue cheese variety produced in Arenas de Cabrales by a slow fermentation process, which takes place in caves. This can go down very well with a glass of cider, which is a speciality of Asturias and a popular drink here. The area to the east of Gijón is an apple-growing region that produces the cider (*sidra* in Spanish). In the middle of July there is a cider festival in Nava. It follows the tradition of raising the pitcher of cider above the head and pouring it down into the glass from a great height.

RECOMMENDED WALKS

The Picos de Europa provide countless hikes and walks in beautiful surroundings. A drive south of Arenas de Cabrales brings you to **Puente Poncebos**, from which you can take a magnificent walk along the Cares Gorge. A pathway cut out from the rock takes you along the gorge, offering fantastic scenery and dizzy views of the swirling waters of the River Cares far below. You need a good head.

There are also some fine areas for walking in the beautiful oak forest, **Bosque de Muniellos**, or around the **Lagos de Somiedo**.

was built on an isthmus, while the harbour stretches away to the west.

The original town appears to have been under Roman and Visigoth occupation, and was known as *Gigia* during that time. It was then under Moorish domination for a period in the 8th century, after which it was for a time residence of the kings of Asturias. King Carlos V founded the harbour in 1522, and it provided shelter for the remaining ships of the Spanish Armada after the disastrous outcome of their planned attack on England in 1588. The harbour was rebuilt in 1766 and has since been enlarged several times.

The town was severely damaged during fighting in the Spanish Civil War. Much of it was then rebuilt and has been enlarged more recently, with the result that Gijón is essentially a modern town, with few reminders of the past.

Gijón was the birthplace of Gaspar Melchor de Jovellanos (1744–1811), renowned in Spain as a writer, statesman and economist. Jovellanos was advanced in his thinking. He put forward his own ideas on agrarian reform and in 1794 he founded the Instituto Jovellanos as an institution for education in the natural sciences. This is located to the northeast of the town and now serves as the Provincial College of Industry and Nautical Science.

He is honoured by a statue that stands on the square in the centre of the town, Plaza del 6 de Agosto. The house of his birthplace, **Casa de Jovellanos** (located in the old part of

town), has been restored and is now a museum with paintings by Asturian artists. Buildings of major interest are the large baroque **Palacio del Conde de Revillagigedo** (15th- to 16th-century), with two imposing towers, and the 16th-century **Colegiata de San Juan** (Collegiate Church of St John).

The port is very busy and has large docks that handle commercial business and passenger lines. The harbour has been considerably enlarged in recent times and extends to the west for several kilometres. Gijón is also a popular seaside resort. Its long sandy beach, **Playa de San Lorenzo**, is usually packed in summer.

The old fishermen's quarter, known as the **Cimadevilla**, is built up the slopes of the Santa Catalina hill. Here you will find an area of tiny, narrow streets, old houses, bars and lots of activity. There are fine views of the harbour and the mountains of the Picos de Europa from the top of the hill.

*Return to Oviedo southwest on the **N630**, a distance of 29km (18 miles).*

Oviedo – León **121 (75)**
León – Mansilla de las Mulas **17 (11)**
Mansilla de las Mulas – Potes **127 (79)**
Potes – Lebeña **10 (6)**
Lebeña – Covadonga **77 (48)**
Covadonga – Cangas de Onís **11 (7)**
Cangas de Onís – Gijón **78 (48)**
Gijón – Oviedo **29 (18)**

2/3 days – 390km (244 miles)

A colourful selection of pottery on display outside one of Santillana del Mar's old, half-timbered houses, typical of this lovely town

LANDSCAPES OF CANTABRIA

ⓘ Plaza de Velarde 1

From Santander take the N611 southwest. Turn right on to the C6316 to Santillana del Mar, 27km (17 miles).

Santillana del Mar, Santander

1 Santillana del Mar, an architectural delight, with beautiful mansions and churches, together with picturesque balconied houses and typical red-tiled roofs. Its little squares and old façades appear like stage settings from the past. Many buildings are from the Renaissance, medieval and baroque periods. Coats of arms on many façades relate to seamen of former times who returned from important voyages of discovery.

A focal point is the **Plaza de Ramón Pelayo**, which is lined with elegant civil buildings of the 14th- to 16th-centuries. The **Colegiata** (Collegiate Church), one of the loveliest buildings, dates back to the 12th century and is a notable example of Romanesque art, with fine sculptures in the nave and aisle. The cloister contains an impressive Renaissance altarpiece. The **Museo Diocesano** (Diocesan Museum) in the Regina Coeli Convent has a small collection of religious art from the area.

From Santillana take the road for 2km (1 mile) to the car park of the Cuevas de Altamira (Caves of Altamira).

Cuevas de Altamira, Santander

2 The Altamira Caves are among the most significant in the world for the prehistoric wall paintings discovered there in the latter part of the 19th-century. Excessive tourism harms the paintings, and the numbers of visitors are restricted. You should apply well

Santander ● Santillana del Mar ● Cuevas de Altamira
Comillas ● Cabuérniga ● Carmona ● Reinosa ● Retortillo
Cervatos ● Castro Urdiales ● Laredo ● Santoña
Santander

Santander's history goes back to the Romans, but much of the city was rebuilt after being devastated by a tornado in 1941. The Gothic *cathedral* is located just off the wide Avenida de Alfonso XIII. First erected in the 13th century it has been rebuilt three times. The remains of the martyred saint, Celedonio, are in the large crypt. Museums include the *Museo de Bellas Artes* (Fine Arts Museum) and the interesting *Museo Provincial de Prehistoria y Arqueológia* (Prehistoric Museum), with some items from the Altamira caves. The majestic royal *palace of La Magdalena* was presented to Alfonso XII at the beginning of the 20th century, when Santander was a favourite summer resort of the Spanish kings. It is now the International University.

Santander's annual *International Music and Dance Festival* is held in August and lasts for a month.

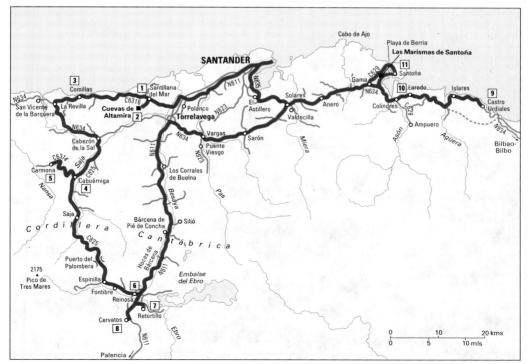

SCENIC ROUTES

The road from Cabuérniga down to Reinosa travels through the beautiful Cordillera Cantábrica mountains on the **C625**, over the passes of Puerto de Tajahierro and Palombera with magnificent views to Reinosa. The **N611** from Cervatos up to Torrelavega offers lovely scenery all the way. The first part of the journey follows a winding mountain road with many bends before passing through the dramatic Hoces de Bárcena gorge. The drive from Torrelavega on the **N634** becomes very attractive again after Solares.

FOR CHILDREN

There are some very pleasant resorts along the coast that boast superb beaches and are most suitable for children. Castro Urdiales is one of the most attractive spots, and Laredo also offers a splendid sandy beach around a wide curving bay.

in advance to: Centro de Investigacion de Altamira, Santillana del Mar, Cantábria.

The caves have a depth of 270m (885 feet) and are most impressive, containing paintings of animals that were hunted by palaeolithic man some 14,000 to 9,000 years BC. The paintings still retain their colours and reveal the unmistakable shapes of bison, deer and wild boar, among others. There is a small museum by the caves, and another cave nearby has stalactite and stalagmite formations.

More prehistoric animal paintings can be seen in the caves of **El Castillo** and **La Pasiega** in Puente Viesgo, just south of Torrelavega on the N623.

Rejoin the C6316 and continue west for 17km (11 miles) to Comillas.

Comillas, Santander

3 The little town of Comillas rises up the slopes of a hill overlooking the sea. The resort has some elegant buildings and a pleasant beach. Of special note is the neoclassical **Palacio del Marqués de Comillas** (Palace of the Marquis of Comillas), which stands in attractive gardens. In the grounds is a building known as 'El Capricho' (meaning 'the whim'), which was built by Antonio Gaudí,

architect of the Sagrada Familia and other curious buildings in Barcelona, as a wedding gift for his daughter. Near the sea is the impressive **Pontifical Seminary**, where priests receive their training. The cemetery has an abundance of flowers.

Continue west on the C6316 to join the N634 and head southeast. Then turn south at Cabezón de la Sal on to the C625 to Cabuérniga, 33km (21 miles).

Cabuérniga, Santander

4 A stop is suggested here to take a quick look round this little mountain town, capital of the valley, with its quaint old houses and large wooden balconies. The town has some historical significance as the birthplace of several prominent archbishops of the past.

Take the C6314 northwest for 11km (7 miles), to Carmona.

Carmona, Santander

5 Carmona is another small unspoilt village, typical of the area, where clogs are still worn a lot and the pattern of life has seen little change from the old days. The detour is worthwhile, not only for a glimpse of

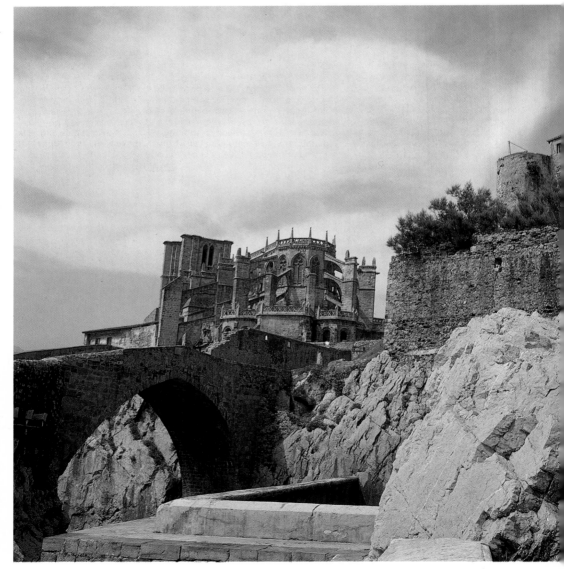

this picturesque little place, but also for its beautiful surroundings.

Return to the C625 at Cabuérniga and continue south for 52km (32 miles) to Reinosa.

Reinosa, Santander

6 Set high up in the valley of the River Ebro is the pleasant little mountain town of Reinosa. Now a popular summer resort, it merits a short visit to look around its picturesque streets.

Continue south on the N611. After a short distance turn left to Bolmir. Just east of Bolmir turn right to Retortillo, 6km (4 miles).

Retortillo, Santander

7 The main point of this stop is to see the Roman ruins of Juliobriga, just outside the village. These appear to have formed part of an old fortified village, and you can get a good idea of its layout from the bell tower of the old ruined Romanesque church.

Return by the same route to the N611. Turn left and drive south to nearby Cervatos, just off the road, 7km (4 miles).

The old harbour bridge and lighthouse at Castro Urdiales

Cervatos, Santander

8 The major feature of interest in this small village is the 12th-century Romanesque **Colegiata** (Collegiate Church), which is noted for the unusual carvings that adorn the frieze above the portal. In particular, note the figures of the three monkeys, shown covering their ears, eyes and mouth, signifying prudence and wisdom in the beliefs of eastern cultures.

Take the N611 north. At Torrelavega take the N634 east to Castro Urdiales, 141km (88 miles).

Castro Urdiales, Santander

9 This is one of the most attractive little fishing ports along the coast and has long been a popular summer resort. It was once a Roman port of some significance. The 13th- to 15th-century Gothic **Iglesia de Nuestra Señora de la Asunción** (Our Lady of the Assumption) features an impressive **Puerta del Perdón** (Door of Pardon) and a fine display of antiquities in the treasury. Other buildings of note are the Gothic **Iglesia de Santa María**, the **Castillo** of Santa Ana (now a lighthouse), the old medieval fortress and the ancient Roman bridge. The resort is very agreeable, with a picturesque harbour and several pleasant promenades.

Take the coastal road N634 west to Laredo, some 25km (16 miles).

Laredo, Santander

10 The little town of Laredo lies to the east of the wide bay of Santoña. With its pleasant villas and splendid beach it has developed into a popular seaside resort, attracting great numbers of holidaymakers in the summer season. The old part of town is picturesque, with some handsome old buildings and the ruins of two former monasteries.

Continue west on the coastal road and turn right at Cicero for 5km (3 miles) to Santoña.

Santoña, Santander

11 To the west of the bay is the port of Santoña, which sits on a small peninsula beneath a steep rock. The town was fortified in earlier times and attracted the attention of Napoleon, who is said to have had plans to take it over. The Romanesque **Colegiata** was built between the 12th and 13th centuries.

About 2km (1¼ miles) away is the splendid beach of **Berria**.

Take the C629 southwest to Gama and rejoin the N634, continue west and turn right at Solares back to Santander.

RECOMMENDED WALKS

6 *Reinosa, Santander* There are plenty of places for walking in the Cordillera Cantábrica. The village of Fontibre (northwest of Reinosa) is a good base for a number of walks, with marked trails that you can take in various directions. The Valle de Campo is a beautiful area of poplar trees and lush vegetation, where you will come across the source of the Ebro, one of Spain's most important rivers. You can also follow some of the streams in the area, which pass through fresh green forests.

SPECIAL TO ...

Many colourful festivals are celebrated throughout the year in this region.

3 *Comillas, Santander* **La Folia** takes place at San Vicente de la Barquera (west of Comillas) on the Sunday after Easter and is a striking spectacle at sea, with decorated boats, music and joyful celebrations.

10 *Laredo, Santander* The **Battle of the Flowers** is another very colourful festival, celebrated on the last Sunday of August, with processions and floats in the shape of huge flowers. The 'encierros', which take place in different parts of Spain, focus around the running of bulls into pens. A traditional fiesta based on this takes place in Ampuero, south of Laredo, on 8 September.

FOR HISTORY BUFFS

11 *Santoña, Santander* Santoña has historical interest as the birthplace of Juan de la Cosa, mariner and cartographer, famed as the producer of the world map that Christopher Columbus used on his first voyage across the Atlantic. Some say his ship, the *Santa María*, was named after the church of Santa María in the town.

BACK TO NATURE

11 *Santoña, Santander* **Las Marismas de Santoña**, located around Santoña, is an area of wetlands. It is home to a variety of migratory birds, and has a rich marine life. Among the many species of birds to be found here are spoonbills, shelduck and grey plovers. There is a wonderful view of the whole area and the Bay of Santoña from the top of Monte Buciero.

EXPLORING THE BASQUE COUNTRY

San Sebastián ● Zarautz ● Guetaria ● Zumaia ● Ondárroa
Lequeitio ● Guernika-Lumo ● Bilbao ● Vitoria
Salvatierra ● Tolosa ● Fuenterrabía ● San Sebastián

San Sebastián (Donostia in Basque), is the capital of the Basque province of Guipúzcoa. The elegant buildings that line the seafront promenade are a reminder of the 19th century, when San Sebastián became Spain's most fashionable resort. The *Alameda del Boulevard* is a lively area of cafés, restaurants and shops. To the west is the busy fishing harbour. The grand *Casa Consistorial* (town hall), formerly the Gran Casino, overlooks the bay. The lovely *Paseo de la Concha* promenade skirts the bay, lined with handsome buildings.

The old town sprawls up the slopes of Monte Urgull. Its focal point is the *Plaza de la Constitución*. A stepped pathway leads up to the Monte Urgull. On top of the hill is the old fortress, *Castillo de la Mota*. Here you will find a military museum, and an imposing figure of Christ on top of a small chapel. The view over the bay is magnificent by day and spectacular at sunset.

On the west side of the harbour is the *Museo Oceanográfico*, an oceanographic museum with some fascinating exhibits, including models of ships and the skeleton of a whale.

The clear, vibrant colours of these stained glass windows contrast with the mellow stone of the buildings

🄸 Miromar/Calle Andria

*From San Sebastián take the **NI** south. Turn right on to the **N634** to Zarautz, 26km (16 miles).*

Zarautz, Guipúzcoa

1 You may like to make a quick stop en route in the picturesque little fishing port of **Orio**, which lies along the bank of an estuary.

The summer resort of Zarautz (Zarauz in Basque) is situated in an old harbour backed by the tall Monte de Santa Barbara. It has a splendid beach and is a popular summer resort. Monuments of major interest are the Gothic/baroque **Iglesia de Santa María**, the **Iglesia de San Francisco** and the hermitages of **San Pelayo** and **San Pedro**. The **Torre Lucea** (Lucea Tower) and the **Palacio del Marqués de Narros** (Narros Palace) from the 15th century, are also impressive. The place was once an important shipyard. It was here, between 1519 and 1522, that the *Victoria*, which carried Juan Sebastián Elcano, companion of Magellan, around the world, was built.

*Continue on the **N634** for 4km (2 miles) to Guetaria.*

Guetaria, Guipúzcoa

2 There is some magnificent scenery as you approach Guetaria and a fine view down over the pretty little fishing village which stands on a promontory. The Gothic **parish church of San Salvador** overlooks the harbour, and has underground tunnels linking it to the harbour. Over the breakwater is the little fortified **Isla San Anton** (island of San Antonio – known as the 'Ratón de Guetaria', mouse of Guetaria, for reasons unknown), which rises up steeply to a lighthouse.

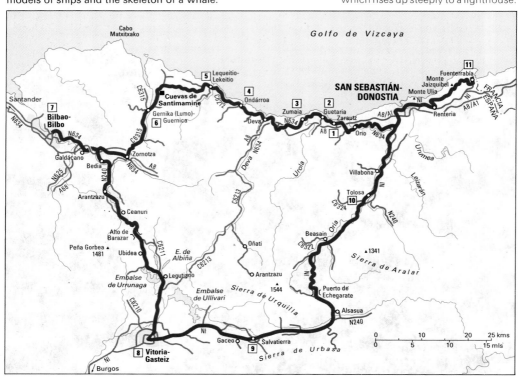

A drive or walk up here offers a rewarding view of the area. The **Ayuntamiento** (town hall) contains some interesting frescos describing the voyage around the world of the famous navigator, Juan Sebastián Elcano, who was born here.

Continue west for 6km (4 miles) to Zumaia (Zumaya).

Zumaia, Guipuzcoa

3 Nestling at the foot of the Monte Santa Clara hill is Zumaia, another delightful little resort with a charming harbour and attractive houses. The **Villa Zuloaga**, formerly an old monastery, is now a museum founded by the great painter Ignacio Zuloaga, and has a fine collection of paintings by Zuloaga, El Greco, Goya and many of Spain's most famous painters. The **Iglesia de San Pedro** is an attractive little Gothic church.

Follow the coast road, the N634, west. At Deva, turn right on to the C6212 for 23km (14 miles) to Ondárroa.

Ondárroa, Vizcaya

4 You are now in the neighbouring province of Vizcaya. The resort of Ondárroa is set in a bay protected by low hills. The town is a combination of attractive old cottages and more modern blocks. It has a sandy beach and a pleasant harbour with lively fisherman's quarters. An old Roman bridge, the **Puente Romano**, spans the river.

Continue on the coast road C6212, northwest for 12km (7 miles) to Lequeitio (Lekeitio).

The Gothic church of Santa María, surrounded by elegant traditional houses, overlooks Lequeitio's busy harbour

Lequeitio, Vizcaya

5 Lequeitio is another popular seaside resort of attractive houses and a good beach, which separates the resort area from the fishing port. The 16th-century **Iglesia de Santa María** is a fine example of Vizcaya Gothic architecture. Narrow cobbled streets lead down to the old part of town. The palaces of Abaróa and Uribarren are particularly elegant buildings.

Take the C6212 west for 23km (14 miles) to Guernika-Lumo.

Guernika-Lumo, Vizcaya

6 The famous painting, *Guernica*, by Pablo Picasso serves as a reminder of the terrible event that took place here in 1937 during the Spanish Civil War, when German aircraft bombed the town, killing a large number of the population. The town was devastated, and has been rebuilt in the traditional style. Originally displayed in the Museum of Modern Art in New York, Picasso's painting now hangs in the Casón del Buen Retiro, an annexe of the Prado Museum, in Madrid, together with all the preliminary sketches.

The **Casa de Juntas** (Assembly Hall) contains an interesting library and archives. The Sala de Juntas (council chamber) is the venue of the General Assembly of officials of the provinces of Biscay. It also serves as a chapel, which is known by the rather

SPECIAL TO ...

The national sport of the Basque country is **pelota** (also known as *jai-alai*). There are variations, but it is a type of handball played between four men in a court called a *frontón*, using scoop rackets and a small, hard ball that travels at tremendous speed. The sport is supposed to be the fastest in the world. Each town and village has a court and a team.

The Basque has its own folklore, including the unusual *aurresku*, a war-like dance, and the *ezpata dantza*, a sword dance, accompanied by flutes and a drum.

FOR HISTORY BUFFS

6 *Guernika-Lumo, Vizcaya* Guernika was once the capital of the small kingdom of Vizcaya. When the unification of Spain was under way, representatives of the different communities met in the shade of an old oak tree, in order to try to obtain certain rights for the people of the Basque country. The stump of the old **Tree of Guernica** can be seen in the small round temple in the Casa de Junta (Council Hall). It serves as a symbol of the deep-rooted desire of the Basques for self-determination. Seeds from the old tree have produced a new Tree of Guernica, in the courtyard of the Council Hall.

grand title of 'la Iglesia Juradera de Santa María de la Antigua'. Near by is a monument commemorating the 1937 attack on the town.

Some 5km (3 miles) north are the **Cuevas de Santimamine**, where wall paintings were discovered in 1917. Mainly of bison, horses and some other animals, they are believed to date back some 13,000 years.

i Ayuntamiento (town hall), Plaza Fuero 3

> Take the **C6315** south and join the **N634** west to Bilbao (Bilbo).

Bilbao, Vizcaya

7 Bilbao is the capital of the Basque province of Vizcaya and its largest port. It is essentially a busy industrial town, which may be off-putting to the visitor at first glance, but does have its attractions and is well worth a visit.

Along the right bank of the river is the Paseo del Arenal, a pleasant esplanade that leads to the old quarters, known as **Las Siete Calles** (Seven Streets). The Plaza Nueva is a charming square built in the neoclassic style and the Gothic **Catedral de Santiago** (14th–16th century) nearby is noted for its modern west front, large bell tower and Gothic cloister. The Ayuntamiento (late 19th-century) has an imposing tower and a Moorish-style ceremonial hall. The **Museo Arqueológico, Etnografico e Historico Vasco** (Basque Archaeological, Ethnographical and Historical Museum) has a collection of tombs, arms and carvings.

In the new town, the **Palacio de la Diputación del Señorío de Vizcaya** (Palace of the Regional Government) has a modest picture gallery and museum of provincial history. Near by is the **Museo de Bellas Artes** (fine arts museum) with works by famous Dutch and Spanish painters of the 15th and 16th centuries. The **Museo Moderno** contains works by contemporary Spanish painters.

i Delegado de Cultura y Turismo en Vizcaya, Gran Vía 17

> Return east along the **N634** and take the **N240** southeast for 66km (41 miles) to Vitoria.

Vitoria, Alava

8 Vitoria is the capital of Alava, the largest of the Basque provinces, and the seat of a bishop. A focal point of the old town is the **Plaza de la Virgen Blanca**, which is surrounded by houses and balconies typical of Vitoria. In the centre is an imposing monument commemorating Wellington's victory over the French at the battle of Vitoria in 1813. Overlooking the square is the 14th-century **Iglesia de San Miguel**. A stone image of the Virgen Blanca (white Virgin), patron saint of the city, can be seen in a niche on the outside portal. Inside is a fine 17th-century altarpiece by Juan de Velázquez and Gregorio Hernández. The **Catedral de Santa María** was built between the 14th and 15th centuries in the shape of a Latin cross and is noted for its richly decorated triple-arched tympanums. An impressive *Assumption* can be seen in the Capilla Mayor (main chapel), and paintings by famous artists can be seen in the side

chapels. Look out also for a bullfighting scene carved on one of the pillar's capitals.

Near by in the Plaza Santo Domingo, is the **Museo de Arqueológia** (Archaeological Museum), which displays objects from the Celtiberian and Roman times, among other items. The 14th-century **parish church of San Pedro** features a fine doorway and impressive sculpted tombs of the Alava family. Vitoria was a centre for craftsmen since the middle of the 15th century who worked predominantly in the wool and iron trades. The **Portalon**, built in wood and brick, is a remaining example of one of the many trading houses of the medieval and Renaissance times. Other attractive areas are the Plaza del Machete and the Cuchillería (street of cutlery), where you will find the 16th-century **Casa del Cordón** (House of Cordons), noted for a fine Gothic ceiling, and the Bedaña Palace, a fine 16th-century mansion with a magnificent façade. The new **cathedral of María Inmaculada**, which was consecrated only in 1969, shows a rather unusual neo-Gothic style.

i Oficina de Información de Turismo, Paseo de Ribes Roges

> Take the **NI** for 25km (16 miles) to Salvatierra.

Salvatierra, Alava

9 The picturesque little town of Salvatierra was founded by Alfonso X in 1256. It still preserves its medieval streets and parts of the old defensive walls. Its two main churches, those of **San Juan** and **Santa María**, have a somewhat fortress-like appearance.

Follow the NI east and then north for 61km (38 miles) to Tolosa.

Tolosa, Guipúzcoa

10 Tolosa was capital of the province of Guipúzcoa for a period in the middle of the 19th century and is now a thriving industrial town (known for the *boinas*, or Basque beret). There are Roman antiquities and ancient buildings of the Templars. The **Iglesia de Santa María** has the appearance of a cathedral.

i Centro de Iniciativas Turísticas, Calle San Juan

Continue on the NI north, by-passing the centre of San Sebastián, and then east. Turn off north for Fuenterrabía.

Fuenterrabía, Guipúzcoa

11 The little town of Fuenterrabía was a stronghold over a long period of time and the scene of many battles. It is now a popular seaside resort. The remains of its ancient walls are preserved as a national monument and the 12th-century **Palacio del Rey Carlos V** (now a parador) was built as a defence against pirate raids. There are good views from here. Other buildings worth a look are the 16th-century **Iglesia de Santa María** (mainly Gothic with Renaissance influences), and the 17th-century **Ayuntamiento**. A short drive up to the ridge of Jaizquíbel leads to the **Santuario de Nuestra Señora de Guadalupe** and offers fine views.

Rejoin the NI back to San Sebastián, 25km (16 miles).

San Sebastián – Zarautz **26 (16)**
Zarautz – Guetaria **4 (2)**
Guetaria – Zumaia **6 (4)**
Zumaia – Ondárroa **23 (14)**
Ondárroa – Lequeitio **12 (7)**
Lequeitio – Guernika-Lumo **23 (14)**
Guernika-Lumo – Bilbao **36 (22)**
Bilbao – Vitoria **66 (41)**
Vitoria – Salvatierra **25 (16)**
Salvatierra – Tolosa **61 (38)**
Tolosa – Fuenterrabía **52 (32)**
Fuenterrabía – San Sebastián **25 (16)**

The spectacular setting of Ondárroa, a popular resort with a pretty fishing harbour

SCENIC ROUTES

The Cornisa Cantábrica (Cantabrian Corniche) is a magnificent stretch between Zarautz, Guetaria and Zumaia on the **N634**. A zigzagging road follows the coast, offering magnificent views. From Zumaia the drive continues along the coast, on the **C6212**, with beautiful views, to Lequeitio. The **NI** offers some scenic parts after Alsasua, with excellent views over the Puerto de Echegarate, and again passes through beautiful scenery between Tolosa and San Sebastián.

RECOMMENDED WALKS

Many areas all over the region offer splendid walks, and information is available from the local tourist offices.

7 *Bilbao, Vizcaya* A short walk is a climb up the hill from behind the church of San Nicolás de Bari, which brings you to the Gothic-style **Begoña Basilica**. It was built in 1588 and is the place of worship of Begoña, the patron saint of Bilbao. A colourful *romería* is held on 15 August.

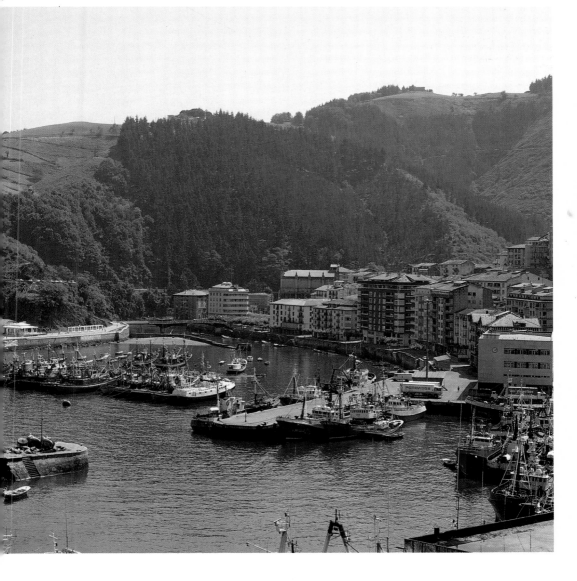

INDEX

References to captions are in *italic*.

ACKNOWLEDGEMENTS

The Automobile Association would like to thank the following photographers, libraries and associations for their help in the preparation of this book.

J EDMANSON & P ENTICKNAP were commissioned to take all pictures not mentioned below in this book (AA PHOTO LIBRARY).

BILBAO TOURIST BOARD 115 Lequeitio Harbour, 116 Aizcolary, 116/7 Ondárroa

INTERNATIONAL PHOTO BANK Cover Casares, 9 Sóller, 30 Ceramic display, 31 Deià, 32 Puerto de Pollença 33 Palma market.

SPECTRUM COLOUR LIBRARY 19 Sitges, 55 Niebla Church, 114 San Sebastián stained glass

Author's acknowledgements Mona King thanks the following for their help: the Ayuntamiento de Madrid, Madrid; the Secretariá General de Turismo, Madrid; the Spanish Tourist Office, London and the Tourist Authorities in Sevilla.